THE SHAME OF POVERTY

The Shame of Poverty

ROBERT WALKER

With Grace Bantebya-Kyomuhendo, Elaine Chase,
Sohail Choudhry, Erika Gubrium, Ivar Lødemel,
JO Yongmie (Nicola), Leemamol Mathew,
Amon Mwiine, Sony Pellissery, and YAN Ming

OXFORD
UNIVERSITY PRESS

OXFORD

UNIVERSITY PRESS

Great Clarendon Street, Oxford, OX2 6DP,
United Kingdom

Oxford University Press is a department of the University of Oxford.
It furthers the University's objective of excellence in research, scholarship,
and education by publishing worldwide. Oxford is a registered trade mark of
Oxford University Press in the UK and in certain other countries

© Robert Walker 2014

The moral rights of the author have been asserted

First Edition published in 2014

Published in the United States of America by Oxford University Press
198 Madison Avenue, New York, NY 10016, United States of America

British Library Cataloguing in Publication Data

Data available

Library of Congress Control Number: 2014935450

ISBN 978-0-19-968482-3

Contents

List of Figures and Tables   vi
List of Abbreviations   vii
Acknowledgements   viii

1. The Origins of Poverty   1

2. Poverty Research and Measurement   15

3. Constructions of Shame   32

4. Poverty, Shame, and Stigma   49

5. Cultural Conceptions of Poverty and Shame   67

6. Conceiving of Poverty Without Shame   85

7. Shame in the Everyday Experience of Poverty   97

8. Responses to Poverty-Related Shame   120

9. Shaming People in Poverty: Attitudes and Actions   132

10. Shaming People in Poverty: Media and Policy   157

11. Poverty, Shame, and Society   182

References   199
Index   223

List of Figures and Tables

FIGURES

2.1 Absolute poverty (1984–2010)   27

2.2 Absolute and relative poverty (mid-2000s)   27

2.3 Poverty dynamics and chronic poverty   28

2.4 Multidimensional poverty (post-2005)   29

3.1 From Scheff's model of shame and solidarity   41

4.1 Model of the poverty–shame nexus   66

5.1 Depiction of poverty, shame, and shaming   75

7.1 The seven countries compared, 2012   99

9.1 Global perceptions of the causes of poverty: percentage citing 'laziness
and lack of willpower'   134

9.2 Perceptions of the causes of poverty in Britain, 1976 to 2010   136

10.1 Framing and shaming   159

10.2 'Work is a duty towards society' (2005–2007)   161

10.3 'People who don't work turn lazy' (2005–2007)   161

10.4 'Humiliating to receive money without having to work
for it' (2005–2007)   162

10.5 Perceived causes of poverty by recent benefit receipt 2008   173

10.6 Policy and media dynamics   180

11.1 Poverty and shame in Britain, 2012   186

11.2 Poverty and shame as perceived by affluent Kenyans, 2013   187

TABLES

3.1 Shame, guilt and alienation   36

7.1 People in poverty: respondents' characteristics   98

10.1 Perceptions of the causes of poverty by level of relative household income 162

List of Abbreviations

ASBO	an Anti-Social Behaviour Order is a civil order made in the United Kingdom
BISP	Benazir Income Support Programme in Pakistan
BPL	Below the Poverty Line, an administrative criterion used in India
DLA	Disability Living Allowance, a welfare benefit in Great Britain
HDI	Human Development Index
ILO	International Labour Organization
MPI	Multidimensional Poverty Index
MSLS	Chinese Minimum Standard of Living Scheme (Dibao)
NAADS	National Agricultural Advisory Services in Uganda
NAV	Ny Arbeids- og velferdsforvaltning (the Norwegian work and welfare office)
NBLSS	National Basic Living Security System, a social assistance scheme in South Korea
NDP	National Development Plan
NGO	non-governmental organizations
NHS	National Health Service in the United Kingdom
NREGA	National Rural Employment Guarantee Act in India
OPHI	Oxford Poverty and Human Development Initiative
PDS	Public Distribution Service in India
PEAP	Poverty Eradication Action Plan in Uganda
PRWORA	Personal Responsibility and Work Opportunities Reconciliation Act in the United States
QP	Qualification Programme in Norway
SCG	Senior Citizens Grants in Uganda
TN	Tamil Nadu
UDHR	Universal Declaration of Human Rights
UNDP	United Nations Development Programme
UPE	Universal primary education in Uganda
VFG	Vulnerable Family Grants in Uganda

Acknowledgements

All books are collaborations and this one more than most. Much of the evidence presented derives from research funded by the United Kingdom Economic and Social Research Council and the Department for International Development under the ESRC-DFID Joint Fund for Poverty Alleviation Research (grant number RES-167-25-0557). This research was intensely collaborative involving a group of scholars who worked together to secure funding and then to collect and analyse the many kinds of information that make this book possible: Grace Bantebya-Kyomuhendo, Elaine Chase, Sohail Choudhry, Erika Gubrium, Ivar Lødemel, JO Yongmie (Nicola), Leemamol Mathew, Amon Mwiine, Sony Pellissery, and YAN Ming, whose contribution is recognised on the title page. Their detailed work is available in the companion volume, *Poverty and Shame, Global Experiences*, edited by Elaine Chase and Grace Bantebya-Kyomuhendo. Frederick Golooba-Mutebi, Sattwick Dey Biswas, and Monimala Sengupta were also directly involved in the research at various stages, and Alan Hedges provided invaluable methodological guidance.

But many other people have also contributed to the ideas that shape and are reshaped throughout the volume. Vitally important are the people with direct experience of poverty and others living in the same communities who gave up their time to be interviewed, sharing experiences that provide the foundations for this work. Others whose thoughts were influential include members of the project advisory group chaired by Lutz Leisering: Jimi Adesina, Jo Boyden, Charlotte Heath, June Tangney, and Timo Voipio; participants in a seminar held in Oxford in 2012 to reflect on the early findings: David Campbell, Mike Daly, Amelia Gentleman, Joanne Green, Krzysztof Hagemejer, Sophia Ireland, Sian Jones, Dann Kenningham, Kornelia Kozovzka, Helen Longworth, Gareth Matthews, Kate Lloyd Morgan, Maeve Regan, Magdalena Sepulveda, Deborah Shipley, Bedreldin Shutta, Yasmin Sidhwa, Diana Skelton, Nicola Smith, Jane Stephenson, Brian Woods, and Ruslan Yemstov; policy-makers and practitioners who engaged with the study in Oslo (in 2010 and 2011), Anand (in 2011), Beijing (in 2012), and Kampala (in 2012) who are too numerous to mention by name but no less important for that; my students in Oxford who repeatedly offered challenges based on first principles long since forgotten by the older mind: Selcuk Beduk, Zlata Bruckauf, Stephen Danley, Mariann Dosa, Gabrielle Emanuel, Rys Farthing, Luca Ferrini, John Frame, Eleanor James, Sophia Lee, LEE Soohyun, Annie McEwen, Sarah McLoughlin, Thorn Pitidol, Usha Kanagaratnam, Saltanat Temirbekovna Rasulova, Hamsa Rajan, Kei Takahashi, Laura Valadez, Kaushal Vidyarthee, Lana Yoo, and ZHANG

Yao; and friends and colleagues who have encouraged and questioned: Rosemary Akinyi, Nick Bailey, Fabrizio Barca, Ben Baumberg, Christina Behrendt, Fran Bennett, Guillaume Charvon, CHEN Yanyan, Michael Cichon, Brendan Coyne, Mary Daly, Susie Devins, Cristina Diez, Paul Dornan, Eldin Fahmy, Donna Friedman, Declan Gaffney, Xavier Godinot, David Gordon, Chris Goulden, Julia Griggs, HAN Xiao, Kate Legge, David Levy, Ruth Lister, Mattias Lundberg, Carolina Ohls, Carol Matiko, Simon Pembleton, Maria Ogando Portela, Thierry Viard, and YAN Haiying.

The cover design includes a detail taken from a work entitled 'Tell Me a Lie' by Gema Ávala that comprises hundreds of tiny golden shirts shaped as an oval (http://www.gemaalava.com). I find connections to the linen shirt without which, as Adam Smith observed, a 'creditable day-labourer' in eighteenth century Britain would have been 'ashamed to appear in public'; to gross inequality manifest as conspicuous consumption; and to our actions and beliefs that contribute to the shame of poverty. I am most grateful to Gema, therefore, a Cultural Adviser to the World Council of Peoples for the United Nations, for her generosity in allowing us to reproduce her work. While Gema might not agree with my understanding of the work, she is interested in the way that people respond differently to the same situation and explores this in her art by leaving space for interpretation. It is ironic, therefore, that this book should conclude that people respond similarly to the different material manifestations of poverty experienced in various parts of the world; they feel ashamed and report that they are made to feel ashamed by officialdom and by the people around them.

Three people out the many who have helped warrant special mention. Lindsey Richardson, when a Master's degree student at Oxford, read Amartya Sen in preparation for a seminar and drew attention to his reflections on poverty and shame; she is, thereby, midwife to the research that shapes this volume. Elaine Chase is not only largely responsible for the British component of the research but has been an intellectual sparring partner throughout, always coming back for more with new ideas and a great sense of humour. Finally, Jennifer Walker has for 40 years been my most successful critic and sought to check me on each step of the journey, through life as well as during the writing of this book.

Despite all the collaboration and the good advice that I have received, I may well have misunderstood some things and got others wrong in the reading, analysis, and interpretation of the source material. Despite invaluable editorial input from Elaine Chase and Jennifer Walker, I alone can be held responsible for these mistakes.

Robert Walker
Oxford

1

The Origins of Poverty

Few, if any, politicians campaign on a manifesto to increase poverty. Yet, while the very word 'poverty' demands policies to reduce it, taking the United Nation's (UN's) definition of extreme poverty (an income of 1.25 US dollars (USD) per day), over 20 per cent of the world's population remain poor (World Bank, 2013). Another 40 per cent make do with incomes that do not exceed USD 2/day while, even within the European Union, 120 million people are officially recognized to be at risk of poverty or social exclusion (Eurostat, 2013). The challenge is better to understand why poverty has proved to be such an intractable issue.

A small part of the problem is that experts cannot agree on definitions. Global policy, exampled by the Millennium Development Goals, typically uses absolute measures of poverty, while domestic debates in most OECD countries are couched in terms of indicators that define people to be poor relative to other members of their own society. Differences over measurement reflect and fuel confusion over what it means to be poor and the implications that poverty has for wider society. Even more important, there is little agreement as to whether poverty is largely caused by structural factors or by personal failings, leading to disagreement about how best to tackle the problem.

This book and its companion volume, *Poverty and Shame: Global Experiences*, edited by Elaine Chase and Grace Bantebya-Kyomuhendo, seek to inform each of these issues by taking seriously the psychosocial dimensions of poverty and particularly the contention that there is a universal and immutable link between poverty and shame. The understanding that poverty causes shame is not new; the degradation of people forced by poverty to do the unthinkable in order to survive is the subject matter of numerous novels and fables in many cultures (see Chapters 5 and 6). Radical novelists in many countries have also suggested that the rich should feel shamed by the poverty around them. That they sometimes do, and that the shame of poverty extends beyond the people experiencing it, is evidenced every time someone deliberately avoids a person begging or steps around somebody sleeping on the street. Nor has the world of scholarship totally neglected the shame attached to poverty. Adam Smith, writing in 1776 at a time when many people could not afford leather shoes, argued that shoes were nevertheless a necessity of contemporary life and that 'the poorest creditable person of either sex would be ashamed to appear in public without them' (2009, p. 519). In the modern era, Peter Townsend (1979, pp. 241 and 841) drew attention to the 'social shame of those with little money' and, in the context of claiming benefits, the desire of potential applicants 'to avoid the shame of pleading poverty'. Amartya Sen (1983, p. 159) expands on the significance of these observations, asserting that shame lies at the 'irreducible absolutist core' of the idea of poverty. What previous authors have not generally done, however, is to reflect on the implications of this shame for understanding the nature and persistence of poverty and the effectiveness or otherwise of policies introduced to combat it.

Therefore, drawing on empirical research underpinned by psychological and sociological theory, the two volumes break new ground by highlighting shame as a missing consideration in explanations of poverty and in the design of policy. Following the scientific literature, shame is taken to be externally imposed by society, via individuals and through social institutions, but internalized and experienced as a powerful negative emotion that results in social withdrawal and a sense of powerlessness. The resultant lack of agency and social exclusion associated with the shame induced by poverty helps to shape the felt experience of being poor. Moreover, it may well serve to exacerbate the underlying causes of poverty and to lessen the impact of policies designed to tackle the problem. Furthermore, the salience of poverty-related shame is arguably intensifying as social status and personal identity become progressively more determined by individual economic success in societies that are increasingly individualistic and market orientated. This dynamic model of poverty is examined and further developed with reference to original empirical evidence drawn from seven contrasting societies and reported in detail in the companion volume: *Poverty and Shame: Global Experiences*. This new research conducted in China, India, Norway, Pakistan, South Korea, Uganda, and the United Kingdom investigates the cultural determinants of shame, the mechanisms of shaming, and the place of shame in the experience of poverty. The research was jointly funded by the UK Economic and Social Research Council and UK Department for International Development.

Any argument must begin with a clear definition of terms. Unfortunately, the meaning of poverty has changed over time, varies by place and culture, and remains contested—shaped by ideology and politics. However, almost regardless of definition, it is clear that poverty persists on a large scale and blights the lives of millions of people in rich countries as well as in less developed ones. Chapter 2 documents this fact after introducing the reader to some of the complexities inherent in defining and measuring poverty.

If poverty is central to politics, shame is fundamental to the way in which societies work. Indeed, it has been used by some scholars to differentiate between types of society that are deemed to be fundamentally different in kind (Hiebert, 1985; Goetz and Keltner, 2007). However, insights concerning the nature and social functions of shame need to be gleaned from a number of disciplines; this is undertaken in Chapter 3.

In Chapter 4, the concepts of poverty and shame are brought together to elaborate on the heuristic, dynamic model of poverty already sketched out in the present chapter. The model seeks to refine understanding of both the nature and experience of poverty by explaining how it is socially constructed, often in ways that further the interests of those who are not poor to the detriment of those who are. Politics and policy are important elements in this process. By deliberately or inadvertently imposing stigma, they frequently reinforce the dynamics that perpetuate poverty. If policies were explicitly designed to respect the dignity and rights of people confronting hardship, they could suppress the destructive dynamic and be much more effective in the fight against poverty.

While the model purports to be relevant to all societies, modern and traditional, rich and poor, this cannot yet be definitely demonstrated (although see Chapter 11 for steps in this direction). Sufficient evidence is simply not available. However, each of the remaining chapters draws on the research from contrasting cultures in the search for differences that would undermine the universality of the model, and similarities and complementarities that might support the proposition that shame is always associated with poverty and is a factor in its persistence. Chapters 5 and 6 draw on cultural materials, notably literature, film, and oral tradition, better to understand the social construction of poverty and shame and the linkages perceived to exist between them. Chapter 5 reports evidence for the existence of a consistent poverty–shame nexus, while Chapter 6 documents occasions when the relationship between poverty and shame is particularly complex or, rarely, non-existent.

Space is given to the voices and perceptions of people experiencing poverty in Chapters 7 and 8. Chapter 7 reveals that while material circumstances vary enormously across the case-study countries, poverty feels very similar in all settings; people simply cannot afford to live up to their own expectations and those of others. Consequently they feel ashamed, and believe that they are made to feel ashamed, because they cannot be good partners, parents, friends, and citizens. Chapter 8 explores the consequences of the shame that people in poverty encounter and its often debilitating effects.

Chapter 9 largely confirms the view of people experiencing poverty that they are shamed and stigmatized by society; affluent people repeatedly agree that they despise people in poverty and seek to avoid them. It also demonstrates that the structures and implementation of policies are regularly stigmatizing. Chapter 10 explains why this is so, drawing attention to the ways in which poverty is conceptualized and policies are framed. These often reflect the (mis) understandings of politicians and more affluent citizens who, if poverty were to be properly addressed, would respectively need to take political risks or incur financial and other costs. Chapter 11 concludes that while it will be very difficult to build political support—either nationally or globally—to eradicate poverty, it may not be impossible. Being cognizant of the shame associated with poverty and showing how it can be countered are necessary first steps to achieving this goal.

However, reviewing the contents of this volume has led to conclusions being drawn before the hypothesis that there is a poverty–shame nexus has been thoroughly examined. Such an examination must begin by asking what poverty is, a question that is surprisingly difficult to answer.

DETERMINING WHAT POVERTY IS

Everybody knows poverty when they see it, and yet there is endless academic debate about what it is and much popular discourse as to whether it even still exists in the rich countries of the global North. The rhetorical power of the term is not in dispute. The success of Band Aid in the 1980s, with pop concerts and albums raising funds to support antipoverty programmes in Ethiopia, and the Make Poverty History Campaign that briefly united numerous national and international NGOs (non-governmental organizations) around the 31st G8 summit in Gleneagles, Scotland in 2005 illustrate that poverty can be used to mobilize public opinion. The Millennium Development Goals, which included halving extreme poverty by 2015 as their first objective, were agreed by 189 nations and have succeeded in focussing global political debate and generating an unprecedented, if still modest, degree of coordinated action. Likewise, in 2010 the European Union agreed to reduce poverty by twenty million in the decade to 2020, and while progress has proved limited, partly as a consequence of the emphasis on austerity following the financial crisis of 2008, there are few other explicitly social targets around which the twenty-seven member states would be likely to unite.

The Oxford English Dictionary (OED, 2013) defines poverty as 'the condition of having little or no wealth or few material possessions; indigence, destitution' while an expanded interpretation is given to being 'poor' that links conditions to social expectations:

> having few, or no, material possessions; lacking the means to procure the comforts or necessities of life, or to live at a standard considered comfortable or normal in society.

This expansion, the distinction between what is often termed absolute and relative poverty, is crucial but also a sleight of hand. As Ringen (2009, p. 7) observes, the difference between lacking material possessions, what might be termed deprivation, and poverty is a matter of degree: 'Deprivation turns into poverty when there is too much of it'. Poverty, then, is extreme and unacceptable deprivation and the definition of what is extreme and unacceptable is inherently a matter of judgement, a moral rather than a scientific question, 'something each society must decide for itself' (Ringen, 2009, p. 7). The distinction between absolute and relative poverty, therefore, is a false one since the concepts differ only in degree; distinguishing between them rests on the same moral judgement that is both socially constructed and politically imbued since, if poverty is unacceptable, something needs to be done about it.

Citing Stedman Jones (2004), Ringen (2009) associates the commitment to tackling poverty with the vision of Tom Paine in Britain and Condorcet in France, who, 'in the aftermath of the French and American revolutions, invented the idea of societies without poverty—until then poverty had never been envisaged as anything but a normal state of affairs'. Important though the legacy of these writers and their ideas is to the development of the modern welfare state, the reality is that the discussion of poverty and the appropriate responses predate the eighteenth century by at least two millennia. What is true of these much earlier discussions, however, is that, as with Paine and Condorcet, the conceptualization and visibility of poverty was inherently political.

China and Confucius

Confucius writing in the sixth century BCE (551–479 BCE; *Analects*, VII), argued that:

> In a country well governed, poverty is something to be ashamed of. In a country badly governed, wealth is something to be ashamed of.

China at the time was a hierarchical feudal society, overwhelmingly rural and dependent on agricultural production. However, large parts of China were inhospitable and from the earliest times there is evidence of large-scale building of flood barriers and irrigation systems, for example, along the Huang He (Yellow River), that required collective action and defence that was achieved through a central authority. Confucius modelled his philosophy of government on a probably idealized vision of the early rulers of China, notably the Duke of Zhou—co-founder of the Zhou dynasty in the eleventh century BCE, who were seen as benevolent and caring towards their subjects, who responded with love and respect. The well-governed society was one in which rulers established equality of opportunity such that everyone could become rich through hard work and virtuous living rather than needing to engage in impropriety and corruption. Poverty in a well-run society was therefore a product of individual failings and a justifiable cause of shame.

Confucius believed in the inherent goodness of people. Rather than laws to coerce people, he thought that a well-ordered society would encourage and facilitate people to live a virtuous life that would in turn strengthen society through altruism and moral reciprocity:

> If you govern the people legalistically and control them by punishment
> they will avoid crime but have no personal sense of shame.
> If you govern them by means of virtue and control them with propriety
> they will gain their own sense of shame and thus correct themselves.
>
> *The Analects of Confucius*, 2.3

But, while everyone was presumed to be equally virtuous at birth, wisdom was the privilege of the few. In the well-ordered society those with greatest wisdom would justly rule over those with less.

Few, if any, Chinese rulers succeeded in living up to Confucian principles. During his own lifetime Confucius feared that society was on the verge of disintegration due to the disregard of rulers for the well-being of the people, a view echoed by Mecius, perhaps his most celebrated follower, over one-hundred years later. In such circumstances people were forced to behave badly simply in order to survive. Moreover, for more than 700 years the powerful imperial bureaucracy replenished itself through a process of referral that kept positions of influence in the hands of the aristocracy. However, even within this period, notably under Emperor Han Wu-ti (156–87 BCE), examinations were introduced that were eventually to become, in 605 CE, the Imperial Examination System that was to last for over a millennium. Any Chinese male, irrespective of wealth or status, was theoretically able to take the examination and to become a high-ranking government official; by the eleventh century BCE, 400,000 were taking the examination annually (Ebrey, 1999).

This Confucian mechanism for generating equality of opportunity created a meritocracy that reinforced the notion that poverty was of people's own making. Those who did not succeed, including the vast majority who could not succeed, would not only accept their fate, but find peace and happiness in the pursuit of a virtuous life, the 'Tao':

> Riches and honours are what all men desire.
> But if they cannot be attained in accordance with the Tao they should not be kept.
> Poverty and low status are what all men hate.
> But if they cannot be avoided while staying in accordance with the Tao, you
>   should not avoid them.
>
> *The Analects of Confucius*, 4.5

India and Vedic Culture

If Confucian rulers in the first millennium BCE explained poverty in terms of the failure of people to take up opportunities, and Confucian philosophers blamed bad governments that created inadequate opportunity, contemporary Vedic rulers, rather conveniently, explained poverty in terms of sins committed in a previous life. The ancient Vedic civilization in India that began around 1,500 BCE was not blind to poverty. Originally a nomadic people that subsequently developed agriculture and then sizeable urban communities, Vedic culture has left a lasting legacy through the promulgation of Hinduism and the caste structure that survives in modern India. The transition from a nomadic to an agricultural society was accompanied by the development of a class structure comprising: the dominant priestly class (Brahman); the warrior ruling class (Kshatriya); farmers and merchants (Vaishya); and the Shudra, the vast mass of the population including the vanquished, darker skinned, Anarya people, together with the Nishada, forest dwelling peoples on the fringes of Vedic culture. The *Upanishads*, religious scripts written between 800 BCE and 400 BCE, make repeated reference to the great hardship inflicted by poverty and include prayers for respite from 'poverty, this hunger and this social ostracism', from the suffering and sorrow, from the moneylenders 'who calculate interest daily' and from 'the sins committed . . . due to poverty' (Bandyopadhyaya, 2007, pp. 55–7). While references to poverty are generalized in the *Upanishads* there can be little doubt that poverty was disproportionally borne by the Shudra and Nishada.

The class and subsequent caste structure was reflected in, and arguably reinforced by, the content of the *Upanishads* and later religious writings. The *Purusha Sukta* explains the origins of class in the sacrificial body of the divine Purusha with the Brahmans coming from his mouth and the Shudras his feet. In Advaita philosophy, Brahma, the highest divine being, becomes a Shudra 'to live permanently in poverty, suffering and sorrow without desire or attachment to worldly life', thereby justifying the inequality and poverty that characterized Vedic society (Bandyopadhyaya, 2007, p. 88). Elsewhere, in the *Yajurveda* (*c.*600 BCE), the doctrine of *karma* was introduced explaining social position in terms of behaviour in a previous life, such that poverty was interpreted as being a sin caused by evil deeds that was 'the equivalent to death and wealth as equivalent to heaven' (Bandyopadhyaya, 2007, p. 56). The concept of karma was further developed later in the *Mahabharata* (*c.*400 BCE) and the *Bhagavad Gita* (*c.*150 BCE) promoting the virtues of living a good life without desire for immediate reward in this life, thereby perpetuating the status quo. This canonical suppression of the Shudra, and most of those in poverty, was reinforced by civil edicts that prohibited progression from a servile occupation, explicitly denied Shudras education, forbade the accumulation of wealth or the holding of arms and, in the Gupta era (*c.*400 CE), subdivided the Shudra class into a hierarchy of discrete occupations based on a concept of 'cleanliness'.

Within the Vedic culture, therefore, poverty was recognized and accommodated within a socio-philosophical tradition that both explained, and furthermore justified, its existence with reference to the divine. This reinforced the legitimacy of the prevalent social inequalities, removed any moral imperative for structural reform, and was used by the ruling class to justify the imposition of further barriers to social mobility. However, the canonical writings also hint at more practical responses to poverty that addressed subsistence needs while reinforcing the position of the Brahman and Kshatriya. The wealthy were encouraged to pray in gratitude for their wealth and for the forgiveness of sins that might cause them poverty in the next life, and exhorted to give food directly to people begging as an aspect of their karma. Prayers could normally be said only through the services of a priest for which payment was usually required, and food was sought from worshippers as a sacrifice that could be shared in religious celebrations. There is written evidence that sacrificial feasts attracted the hungry, and that religious centres competed in terms of the size of the feasts provided. In this way, resources were transferred from the ruling class, to and via the priests, to at least some of the masses suffering from hunger.

Ancient Rome

The ancient Graeco-Roman world, contemporary with the mid and later Vedic era, was a largely agrarian society where distinctions between rich and poor generally reflected the ownership of land. In the heyday of the Greek city state and early Rome, precious little social distinction was made on economic grounds; distinctions between citizens, free men, and slaves were far more important, a factor that makes the study of poverty based on contemporary accounts very difficult (Osborne, 2006). However, it is clear that by the first century BCE, poverty had become politicized. Prior to that, the beneficence ('*euergesia*') of political leaders and, to the extent that they can be distinguished, that of the financially successful was bestowed on the community as a whole, generally through provision of temples, circuses, and theatres. But, in the first century BCE, the time of the late Roman Republic, such gifts ('*congiaria*') 'were seen as properly directed to the poor' (Osborne, 2006, p. 2). The motors of change were two-fold. First, the growth of Rome, to a population of around one million, made the city, and hence the fate of the entire Republic, precariously dependent on the acquisition and transport of excess food from rural areas. Secondly, the need to recruit a large army led to the property requirement for legionary service being abolished in the second century BCE. This meant that, in times of food shortage and at the end of every military campaign, rulers were confronted by the threat of civil disorder and had, by 58 BCE, responded by introducing the distribution of free grain ('*frumentatio publico*'; the 'corn dole') (Finley, 1973). Augustus, the first emperor, sought to reduce the numbers receiving *frumentatio*, thereby creating a longstanding divide between the entitled (*plebs frumentaria*) and excluded (*plebs sordida*) (Yavetz, 1969; Morley, 2006), while later emperors retained the system recognizing that responding to food crises in this way provided opportunities to display imperial power to good political effect (Osborne, 2006).

While the *frumentatio* was very substantial in scale, variously paid out to between 150,000 to 320,000 recipients (Garnsey, 1989), it was targeted only on citizens and, indeed in some localities (for example in the Romano Egyptian city of Oxyrhynchus) and at certain times, only to selected, well connected groups of citizens (Rea, 1972). The large majority of poor survived through labour, scavenging, begging, theft, and even by selling themselves or their children into slavery (despite debt bondage, *nexus*, being made illegal in 326 BCE). Until the third century CE, the accepted stance among most of the Roman elite was that people begging, who were invariably viewed with disgust and contempt, should be ignored (Parkin, 2006). While the likes of Cicero and Seneca advocated a generous response to the needy, it is clear that the needy were limited to their own kind who might, in time, be able to reciprocate. In any case, the affluent were probably protected from people begging by their retinues; no laws against begging were passed in the early Imperial era, which suggests that the large numbers of people begging in the streets must have been sustained by the alms of non-elites. The latter may have been given for reasons of generosity, pity, solidarity, threat or fear, but what is more clear is that people begging were differentiated with those who were elderly or infirm being most likely to attract financial support; the first known Roman legislation in 382 CE makes the same distinction (Parkin, 2006).

The Christian texts of the fourth and fifth centuries CE reveal a markedly different thinking current in the late Roman era, one that was to shape European development for a millennium or more. Rather than the elites doing all that they could to distance themselves from people in poverty, they were asked to embrace poverty as the lifestyle chosen by their Lord and to give alms as the route to their salvation. Their lives were to be judged by God on the basis of their charitable giving, using not the Roman legal code that punished more those of lowest standing, but one that treated rich and poor alike. Moreover, in promoting this change of perspective, Christian preachers took care not to differentiate between groups of people in poverty (Finn, 2006). Christ did not advocate helping some but not others and, equally, it was important to avoid triggering the latent contempt for certain groups in poverty that could limit people's generosity and constrain how the church used the alms it collected. After Christianity was promoted to being the Imperial religion under Emperor Constantine, the civil authorities actively delegated certain responsibilities for supporting the disadvantaged to the church and, indeed, for acting as intercessors between rich and poor (Corbo, 2006).

While the Roman discourse concerning poverty differed radically in the fourth century CE from that in the fourth century BCE, the fundamental inequalities were not radically different except that urban life, and hence urban poverty, was more prevalent. Outside Rome, 'not even the state showed much concern for the poor' (Finley, 1973, p. 40) and, within the metropolis, their growing political power had not gained them virtue beyond the idealized portrayal taken from the Christian scriptures. Rather, 'writers and politicians continued to treat them as the dregs of society, responsible for their own destitution by their own moral failings' (Osborne, 2006, p. 15).

The Judeo-Christian Tradition and Islam

However, the influence of the Christian church was to outlive the political structures of Imperial Rome and, ironically, 'the poor' were to remain a major source of the church's political power and growing wealth (Grig, 2006). In time, the early Christian encouragement freely to give to those in poverty was accompanied and sometimes superseded by the formal, more or less compulsory, collection of tithes, a tax on agricultural output imposed by the church. The practice was given a legal basis in England in 855 CE with the mission to aid 'the poor' often being subsumed within the need to fund the broader and sometimes secular mission of the church. In 1188 CE, the Saladin tithe was instigated, in effect a royal tax raised to fund the Crusades after the fall of Jerusalem, but one that was collected by the church. Similar mechanisms operated throughout much of Europe during the medieval period, and were later exported as in integral part of colonialism to, for example, Latin America, where the Argentinian and Peruvian governments still collect tithes to support the Catholic church. Austria, Denmark, Germany, Finland, and Norway among other countries retain church taxes, and Sweden only phased them out in the year 2000.

The origin of tithes to support religious foundations can be traced to the ancient civilizations of the Sumerians and to Babylonia (Ringgren, 2003). Within the Judaic tradition, they were sometimes instigated explicitly for the benefit of those experiencing poverty: orphans, widows, strangers (naturalized foreigners prevented from owning land and a source of casual menial labour), and Levites (a landless tribe of Israel, members of which worked in the temple) (Deuteronomy 26:12–14; Exodus 12:45; Leviticus 22:10; 25:6, 40). They reappear within Islam as Zakat, one of the five Pillars of Islam, the obligation on all Muslims of means to donate a proportion of their capital or income from savings to 'the poor and needy'.

While some claim that Zakat was payable by and to Muslims and non-Muslims alike, the modern interpretation is that payments were, as they generally still are, restricted to the Muslim poor. However, the concept of poverty was quite expansive, largely focussing on condition rather than cause and embracing those with inadequate incomes as well as the destitute, debtors, travellers without means, slaves, and converts. Payments could be made to slaves to gain their freedom and to converts who required assistance to settle into an Islamic way of life. A core idea is that Zakat has the merits of purifying the recipient (who avoids both the humiliation of begging and temptation of envy) and the giver (who is kept from greed and selfishness). This in turn leads, according to the Koranic argument, to a more equitable and cohesive society (Robinson, 1999; Zysow, 2009). The obligation of Zakat was interpreted as a prescription by God and seemingly enforced rigorously from the earliest period of Islam leading some to claim, with sincerity if little hard evidence, that 'by the end of the Prophet's period' the 'first universal welfare system in human history' had been established 'throughout the entire Arabian Peninsula' (Parvez-Video, 2013). Zakat may be used to pay those who collect it and, from early in Islamic history, state authorities took responsibility for its collection as still happens in many Islamic countries.

Towards Modernity

With the dissolution of the monasteries between 1536 and 1541, the church in Britain lost much of its wealth and the system of tithes was transferred to the state and secular landowners. With the church now unable to continue to minister to the poor, the state took over the financial responsibility, initially, in 1552, under the oversight of Justices of the Peace. Given that public funds were at stake, the Roman distinctions between the *plebs frumentaria* and *plebs sordida*, between entitled and excluded, and between deserving and undeserving, re-emerged. (The English word 'deserving' dates from this period (1576), and in 2013 was defined in the *Oxford English Dictionary* with reference to the 'deserving poor'; OED, 2013.) These moral distinctions as to the cause of poverty were explicit in the 1601 Poor Law: the 'impotent poor' were those who were too young, too old, or too sick to work and for whom provision had to be made; 'the able-bodied poor' were those who could not find work and were provided with indoor or outdoor relief in cash or kind; and 'rogues and idlers' were those who would not work but were to be made to work, after 1607 in 'Houses of Correction'. Similarly in continental Europe, in cities such as Geneva, Lyon, Strasbourg, and Ypres, church charity was replaced by secular institutions, the 'common chest'; begging was prohibited and benevolence superseded by 'the subjection of the poor to a systematic and disciplinarian programme of education and improvement' (Michielse, 1990, p. 3).

The Tudor Poor Law was retained in Britain until after the first industrial revolution when, in the late 1820s, economic recession and industrial transformation meant that newly urbanized workers, dispossessed of land, had no alternative but to seek public assistance in large numbers. At that point, demands on the Poor Law system precipitated reform that sought even more emphatically to distinguish between the innocently poor and the disreputable pauper. In fact, the 1834 reform, by removing the distinction between 'rogues and idlers' and the 'able-bodied poor', had 'the perverse effect of stigmatising the entire body of the poor', turning the Poor Law into 'a Pauper Law' (Himmelfarb, 1984, p. 24).

This error was arguably avoided by Germany, when fifty years later, after a sustained recession and concerned by the growth of socialism, Chancellor Bismarck introduced legislation that he described as 'practical Christianity' (Busch, 1898). This, in less than a decade, provided workers with health, accident, old-age, and disability insurance, a development that was to become the foundation model for welfare states across much of Europe that, in the post-World War II era, served to foster collective social security. However, the Bismarckian model largely omitted persons who, for whatever reason, failed to secure remunerative employment for extended periods of their lives. Such people, often the majority of those who were by modern standards poor, remained largely reliant on charitable support from the churches until the mid-twentieth century when means-tested, state social assistance began to assume greater importance. The goal of Bismarckian policy was, and remains, social cohesion not the prevention of poverty or its relief. This is also true of the Nordic welfare states, and in many southern European countries the church remains the place of last resort for people experiencing poverty. Moreover, social assistance, designed to support those on the normative fringe of society is often punitive, discretional, conditional on behavioural change, and based on psychological models of individual and/or familial inadequacy that have long been associated with social work (Neubourg et al., 2007; Walker et al., 1984).

In Britain, welfare policies continue to reflect the distinctions of 1834 that have, if anything, become more marked following recent and ongoing reforms. As in North America, poverty relief has almost always been a more important object of policy than social cohesion. Social insurance policies were systematically dismantled from 1979 onwards and remain in name, but not substance, only in the retirement pension and the universal National Health Service. Moreover, in the last twenty years receipt of almost all benefits has been made conditional on participation in work-related activity as well as on lack of income. The rhetoric is that poverty is caused not only by individual failures but by the provision of welfare itself, which is deemed to create a culture in which 'worklessness has become ingrained into everyday life' (Smith, 2012). The current presumption underpinning policy, and reflected in public attitudes, is that all people in poverty claiming benefit are 'paupers', undeserving unless proved otherwise (Walker and Chase, 2013).

POVERTY AS A POLICY PROBLEM

Skipping across 3,000 years of history, it is evident that, once recognized, poverty is invariably construed to be a policy problem. This is because poverty raises humanitarian issues, sometimes of a life and death nature, but also because it has the potential to challenge the status quo (see Chapter 10). Nevertheless, there have been repeated attempts to define and construe poverty in such a way that it does not warrant a policy response. This strategy was perhaps most effective in ancient Vedic society when religion located the causes of poverty in a previous life and aspirations for change were contained through instigation of the karma and caste structure. Only minimally affected later by British colonial thinking, this perspective continues to shape and constrain policies on the Indian subcontinent. Within Confucian philosophy, rulers are obliged to create the conditions for individuals to flourish rather than to support those who do not and, although not wanting to assert rigid cause and effect between Confucianism and modern policy, the developmental and variously authoritarian policies characteristic of China and South East Asia can be interpreted in this light.

In policy terms, the legacy of the monotheistic traditions of Christianity and Islam is more direct. Divine example and instruction, metaphor, parable, and iconography all locate poverty and poverty relief at the doctrinal heart of both religions. In practical terms, appeals to poor and socially excluded groups fuelled a growth in the numbers of adherents that was supported financially by alms collected from the more wealthy faithful who gave to 'the poor' as a means of achieving personal salvation. Perhaps inevitably, the intimate links between religion and state have meant that political considerations linked to wealth and power have often overshadowed concern with poverty. Moreover, with the growth of secularism, notably in traditionally Christian societies, the anxieties evident in the Roman Republics have become increasingly apparent; policies have been shaped by the desire to stem social unrest and social breakdown and now are often informed by a cost–benefit logic that appeals to electorates, limiting expenditure solely to the deserving and conditioning access to benefits on good behaviour.

While not wishing to pre-empt later discussion of the poverty–shame nexus, it is important to note the consistency with which, at least since the beginning of written history, poverty has been associated with personal failings. Within the Vedic and Confucian traditions, personal weakness is a cause and a consequence of poverty, either the result of sins in a previous life or this one, quite possibly the product of the simple need to survive through begging, crime, or prostitution. In ancient Rome, poverty was a source of fear about what the rabble (*vulgus*) might do collectively to challenge privilege, and about what could happen if the fragile supports of individual privilege were to buckle, casting the affluent into the pit of degradation in which 'the poor' were believed to reside. Christianity and Islam, following on the Judaic tradition, turned poverty into a metaphor for simplicity and righteousness, and a contract between the giver and God based on pitying 'the poor' that served to fund the church, synagogue, and mosque:

> He that hath pity upon the poor lendeth unto the LORD; and that which he hath given will he pay him again.
>
> Proverbs 19:17

Christianity suggested that poverty might be a means of salvation in its own terms ('Blessed be ye poor: for yours is the kingdom of God'. Luke 6:20), but coupled this with the edict 'if any would not work, neither should he eat' (Thessalonians II, 3:10). This edict was, of course, later to become a key consideration in secular welfare provision, a litmus test often used to separate the deserving from the undeserving, the poor from the pauper, the innocent from the rogue and idler. It has often come to be assumed, therefore, that even if personal failing is not always the cause of poverty, it sometimes is. This creates the conundrum of determining when it is one and not the other, and the risk that everyone in poverty is presumed guilty until it can be proved otherwise.

Poverty, then, while describing destitution that blights the lives of millions of adults and children, is first and foremost a political construct. Not surprisingly, therefore, as explained in Chapter 2, research on poverty is not independent of political ideas and influence.

2

Poverty Research and Measurement

Poverty is never neutral. As explained in Chapter 1, it is a product of politics and invariably divides opinion. Those wishing to eradicate poverty have to confront the forces of the status quo and the power of entrenched interests. One weapon that is potentially at their disposal is evidence such as that relating to the nature, and especially the volume, of poverty that exists. Hence, much of the research undertaken on the conceptualization and measurement of poverty has been conducted with the express intention of bringing about policy reform and social change. The science of poverty has therefore developed as the active child of the political process and, to play with words, is less pure science than applied politics.

This chapter documents the changing understanding of poverty, charting the shifting emphasis from absolute to relative measures and from unidimensional to multidimensional ones, before briefly reporting the latest statistics on the global extent of poverty. The intention is to set subsequent discussion of poverty in an international context, while drawing attention to the limitations of what is known or thought to be known. It will become evident that shame associated with poverty is scarcely mentioned; it is only when people in poverty are given voice, and when poverty is presented as the denial of the right to human dignity, that shame acquires salience.

ABSOLUTE AND RELATIVE MEASURES

The first studies of poverty in the modern era—Henry Mayhew (1851), Charles Booth (1892), and Seebohm Rowntree (1901) in Britain, and W. E. B. Du Bois (1899) and Robert Hunter (1904) in the United States—were all responses to the social conditions and politics of their time. Mayhew's encyclopaedic study *London Labour and the London Poor* grew out of a journalistic assignment to follow up on a severe outbreak of cholera in Bermondsey in 1849; such was the social and geographic segregation of London at the time that Mayhew appropriately described himself as a 'traveller in the undiscovered country of the poor' bringing back stories about people 'of whom the public has less knowledge than of the most distant tribes of the earth' (Douglas-Fairhurst, 2010). By the time of Booth's study in 1890, the poor were much more visible following violent riots in the 1880s and shrill debate about the effectiveness of the Poor Law system and the role of wilful indolence and alcohol abuse in explaining poverty. A pamphlet by the Congregational Union, *The Bitter Cry of Outcast London: An Inquiry Into the Condition of the Abject Poor*, published in 1883, caused consternation and prompted Booth to check its claims, which he did by systematically collecting accounts from local investigators such as school-board visitors and counting the numbers of households with incomes graded as being 'poor' and 'very poor' (Glennerster, 2004). Booth was possibly the person who invented the concept of a poverty line, or threshold, although he left no details of how the threshold was set (although it seems that he may have made use of local administrative criteria). He was surprised to find that about 7.5 per cent of the population surveyed were 'very poor' and over 30 per cent were 'poor', discoveries that led him subsequently to campaign for the introduction of pensions.

Booth's study prompted Seebohm Rowntree to undertake a further study in York in 1899, which he lived to replicate in 1936 and 1950 (Rowntree, 1901, 1941; Rowntree and Lavers, 1951). Rowntree's lasting contribution was to seek a scientific means of establishing a poverty threshold but, again, this was conceived in the context of a live discussion about both the level and causes of poverty. In effect he was challenging a resistant readership by asking 'Are you seriously suggesting that you can expect families to live on less than this?' (Glennerster, 2004, p. 22).

Rowntree's principal measure was based on judgements about whether families were living in 'obvious want and squalor' made by his assistants who visited each home in York. But he sought also to calculate a minimum needs-based threshold for which he took advice from an American nutritionist who had derived measures of necessary food intake from working with prisoners in controlled settings. He compared these to diets provided in the local poor house, costed them on the basis of local York prices, and added rent and elements for clothing to arrive at his primary 'poverty line'. This indicated that 10 per cent of York residents were experiencing primary poverty compared to 28 per cent who were nevertheless living in obvious want and squalor, termed 'secondary poverty'. The difference in the two figures indicated persons in 'families whose total earnings would be sufficient for the maintenance of merely physical efficiency *were it not that some portion of it is absorbed by other expenditure, either useful or wasteful*' (Rowntree, 1901, p. 115; original emphasis). In differentiating between primary and secondary poverty Rowntree was speaking directly to a then current debate concerning how much poverty could be attributable to wasteful expenditure; it remains a contentious issue that reoccurs throughout this and the companion volume.

It is usual to describe Rowntree's concept of 'primary poverty' as a measure of absolute poverty, although he was well aware of both the scientific limitations of his technique and its political purpose (Veit-Wilson, 1986). His work formed a model for many subsequent 'absolute' measures including the official US poverty standard developed by Mollie Orshansky (1988; ASPE, 2012) and, perhaps most importantly, the $1 a day measure used for the Millennium Development Goals and the revised $1.25 a day measure of extreme poverty employed in UN World Development Reports (Ravallion et al., 2009). These global standards are based on analysis of national poverty lines adopted by governments in the developing world and fixed to equate with those of the poorest countries; the later $1.25 standard is the mean value of the poverty lines used in the fifteen countries with lowest per capita consumption. Some 80 per cent of the national poverty lines in the eighty-eight developing countries analysed are based on derivatives of Rowntree's basic needs approach, including a measure of food requirements to which is added an amount for non-food spending.

Absolute measures were widely used in developed countries until the latter half of the twentieth century, and appeared to demonstrate that a combination of economic growth and the introduction of state welfare had largely resolved the problem of poverty. However, a new generation of academic activists, including Brian Abel-Smith and Peter Townsend (1965) in Britain and Harrington (1962) in the US, pointed out that the basic necessities of life had also changed. They argued that lack of income meant that people could not afford to buy the things or to engage in the activities that were expected of them, causing them to be excluded and stigmatized. This led Abel-Smith and Townsend to propose measures of relative poverty, initially devising a poverty standard fixed at 1.4 times the income threshold used to determine eligibility for receipt of social assistance in the UK. Later analysts chose to set poverty standards as arbitrary percentages of national mean income (which is comparatively easy to measure) or median national income (which has become the preferred indicator because it is less distorted by income inequalities) (Atkinson et al., 2002). Since households vary in size and children are presumed to need and to consume less than adults, it is necessary to adjust measures of income to take account of such differences, a procedure termed equivalization (Banks and Johnson, 1994). Although there have been many attempts to devise relative poverty thresholds grounded in objective research or social consensus (Collins et al., 2012; Pantazis et al., 2006), it is still the norm to set poverty lines as an arbitrarily percentage of equivalized household income, typically income below 40 per cent, 50 per cent, or 60 per cent of the national median.

Measures of relative poverty are intellectually and politically attractive because they reflect local living standards and expectations, and hence take better account of the social exclusion occurring as a result of people being unable to afford to fully participate in society. However, there are some disadvantages compared with absolute measures. Politically, absolute measures are appealing because substantial falls in poverty can be achieved simply through economic growth whereas relative poverty can generally only be reduced by active redistribution of income (and/or other resources, economic or social). Also, counter-intuitively, relative poverty can appear to rise during periods of economic growth and fall in recessions if, as is often the case, the economic cycle is associated with fluctuations in income inequality. Perhaps not surprisingly, therefore, absolute measures of poverty, or, at least, quasi-absolute measures that hold a relative threshold constant in money terms, have enjoyed somewhat of a renaissance among advanced industrial countries. They have recently been reintroduced alongside relative measures in Britain (DWP, 2007), and are included among the Laeken indicators (initially agreed at the European Council of December 2001 held in the Brussels suburb of Laeken) used to monitor the impact of the European social inclusion agenda (Atkinson et al., 2002). However, while absolute measures have often seemed preferable for use in poorer developing countries, justified by the fact that national poverty lines vary little between countries despite different levels of overall consumption, economic development is making this true for fewer and fewer countries (Ravallion et al., 2009). Hence, the OECD has recently made the case for the adoption of a relative measure for developing countries (Garroway and de Laiglesia, 2012).

MULTIDIMENSIONALITY AND SUBJECTIVE POVERTY

From Booth (1892) onwards, all the aforementioned studies have relied on low income as a measure of poverty. Although intuitively reasonable, many scholars have argued that poverty is both much more and somewhat less than limited income. Ringen (1988), for example, suggests that income is an indirect and inadequate measure of poverty and that focussing on it can actually be misleading. For him, poverty equates to consumption that is so low as to exclude poor people from a 'normal way of life'. While income poverty could ostensibly be resolved by ensuring that those in poverty have higher incomes, additional income would not guarantee reduced deprivation. The generic warning is that, while simple measures are generally preferable to complex ones, simplicity can be seductive and introduce bias.

Deprivation

Townsend (1979) sought directly to measure deprivation or participation (as he sometimes called it) by compiling lists of items and activities that people might have to forego because of low income. Having determined who went

without what things, he sought to find a level of income at which disproportionate numbers of people began to be excluded. While his work was criticized
at the time because of the normative basis of the items considered and
Townsend's failure to take account of personal preferences (Piachaud, 1981),
his ideas took hold. Within the international development world, there was a
move by the International Labour Organization (ILO) to define poverty in
terms of access to health, education, and other services rather than just lack of
income (Maxwell, 1999). This was further extended with the work of Robert
Chambers (1994) to embrace powerlessness, isolation, and participation, and
through encouragement by the Brundtland Commission on Sustainability and
the Environment (WCED, 1987) to think about the inclusion of livelihoods
and sustainability. Subsequently, the United Nations Development Programme (UNDP, 1997, p. 5) introduced the Human Development Index
(the HDI, a composite index based on life expectancy at birth, schooling,
and gross national income) and with it the interpretation of poverty as being:
'the denial of opportunities and choices . . . to lead a long, healthy, creative life
and to enjoy a decent standard of living, freedom, dignity, self-esteem and the
respect of others'. Since 2010, a version of the HDI has been available that
takes account of inequality and hence seeks to measure the actual level of
human development rather than the potential human development that could
be achieved if there were no inequality.

A plethora of indicators of deprivation have been developed and employed
in advanced industrial societies (Berthoud et al., 2004; Calandrino, 2003;
Gordon et al., 2000, 2013; Gordon 2006; Nolan and Whelan, 1996, 2010,
2011). The availability of better data mean that, unlike the HDI, these measures have typically been based on individual-level information such that the
cumulative impact of the different dimensions of poverty on people's lives can
be assessed. Some studies, following Townsend, have determined a priori lists
of possessions and activities and recorded the numbers of people who lack
them. Increasingly, though, possessions and activities are selected as indicators
because they are believed by the majority of respondents to be 'social necessities' that 'nobody should have to do without' (Gordon and Pantazis, 1997;
Gordon et al., 2000, 2013). Normally deprivation thresholds are then set in
terms of a prescribed but arbitrary number of possessions or activities that
cannot be afforded. Yet other studies have engaged members of the public in
determining a minimum acceptable standard of living, based on desirable
patterns of consumption (Bradshaw, et al., 2008; Davis et al., 2012). All such
'democratic' or 'consensual' approaches generate measures that are inherently
relative and consistent with the theorizing of the Nobel laureate Amartya Sen
(1999) whose ideas have had a profound influence on global debates about
poverty. He argues that poverty is not (just) a lack of income, but rather the
failure of a person to achieve minimum capabilities (that are universal)

through the acquisition and use of commodities ('functionings') that are context specific and hence relative (Lister, 2004; Robeyns, 2005).

Studies that compare material deprivation and income poverty show them to be only moderately correlated. Calandrino (2003), for example, found that just 32 per cent of British lone parents were both income poor and deprived. Likewise, by taking data for all types of families from twenty-eight European countries, including Iceland and Norway, Whelan and Maître (2012) report moderate correlations between income and six dimensions of disadvantage (basic deprivation, consumption, household facilities, neighbourhood environment, personal health status, and access to public facilities) and only modest correlations between them. These findings appear to lend support to Ringen's contention that the concepts of income poverty and material deprivation should be differentiated. Moreover, the aim in focussing on deprivation is to facilitate better understanding of the manner in which lack of income constrains participation in customary ways of living, which requires 'measures of deprivation that are significantly related to but by no means identical to income' (Whelan and Maître, 2012, p. 19).

Exclusion and Well-being

However, low income and material deprivation are not the only attributes that have been used to measure poverty. As already noted, within a European context, Whelan and Maître (2012) include health and access to services as indices reflecting policy debates in which poverty is often coupled with social exclusion, a concept that is generally taken to refer to the outcomes and processes through which people and groups are systematically denied access to rights, opportunities, and resources (Todman et al., 2009). The origins of the concept date back to French Social Catholicism and to the idea of persons excluded from society's normative framework, but it came into popular usage in the 1980s as a means of continuing political discussions about poverty and disadvantage at a European level when conservative leaders in Germany and the UK refused to countenance the continued existence of poverty (Room, 1995).

This provenance complicates use of the term in a research context, but does not negate evidence of the social isolation that accompanies poverty that can create mutually self-reinforcing processes whereby people lack the support, information, and contacts that might help them to find work and, in other ways, to engage more fully in society (Cattell, 2001; Ferragina et al., 2013; Gallie et al., 2003). Likewise, people in poverty are often excluded from civic participation for a complex range of reasons, including alienation and a sense of powerlessness, and (a theme in later chapters) may themselves be excluded by others. Such exclusion may also result from more prosaic factors including reliance on public transport, limited access to childcare, and the time constraints imposed by the need to make do with limited resources (Pantazis et al., 2006). There is also often a complex interplay between poverty, people, and the places in which they live. In urban areas, constraints imposed by access to jobs and housing mean that people in poverty tend to be geographically concentrated, often in areas with poor amenities and higher rates of crime and antisocial behaviour; in rural areas, differential out migration, limited infrastructure, and geographic isolation arguably help to shape the experience of poverty. There is considerable political controversy and some academic disagreement about the extent to which the experience of personal poverty is compounded by locality, but it is certain that poverty is mediated by place and place by people's poverty (Dorling et al., 2007).

Alongside deprivation and social exclusion, there are other more subjective aspects of poverty that people experiencing hardship report and that, for them, often define the experience of poverty more directly than lack of income (Alkire, 2007). These include the health consequences of poor housing and living environments, and the psychological strain attached to managing competing claims on scarce and irregular resources made by external agents and members of the family (Middleton et al., 1994; Payne, 2006). Variable resources and differently changing circumstances may create different pressures and even unique kinds of poverty characterized by varying degrees of vulnerability. It has been suggested, for example, that short transient spells of poverty differ from the experience of repeated spells, the latter implying much uncertainty, and from chronic poverty characterized by extended spells that may offer a degree of stability but with few accumulated assets and therefore little margin for error (Hulme et al., 2001; Walker with Ashworth, 1994). There is also evidence that people in poverty can feel constrained not only with regard to shaping their own lives, but in influencing the views and behaviour of other people and in successfully challenging the bureaucratic and systemic structures that coerce them (Edin et al., 2000; Hooper et al., 2007; Narayan et al., 2000a and 2000b). Often there are risks to personal safety arising from where and how people in poverty live, and in the nature of the work that they are often forced by necessity to undertake. Finally, there is research that suggests that poverty diminishes a person's sense of psychological well-being, whether revealed in terms of life satisfaction, happiness, or personal sense of failure or shame, and that this process can be exacerbated in more affluent societies (Praag and Ferrer-i-Carbonell, 2008; Ravallion 2012).

Multidimensionality

The various dimensions of poverty considered—lack of income, material deprivation, social exclusion, and psychological well-being—can all be causes and consequences of each other and, unsurprisingly therefore, considerable debate is still ongoing about the reasons for poverty, some of it underpinned by differences in the ideologies of the protagonists. The increasing availability of panel data, which trace persons' circumstances over time, is helping researchers to unravel these causal complexities (Jenkins, 2011; Shepherd, 2011), but the reality is that someone in poverty experiences all of the dimensions simultaneously; the balance between them determines the nature of the poverty experienced and, as Tomlinson and Walker (2009) demonstrate, the impact of the poverty on, for example, child well-being.

While multidimensionality most accurately describes the reality of poverty in people's lives, measurement has proved to be very challenging (Kakwani and Silber, 2008). It should be recognized that multidimensional measurement is different from the simple use of multiple measures as found in Eurostat's Laeken indicators of poverty and social inclusion, or even the HDI for which countries rather than individuals constitute the units of analysis. Data on multiple aspects of people's lives need to be collected and combined, ideally repeatedly over considerable time periods, to establish the duration of poverty and people's trajectories over time. Some methods let the dimensions of poverty 'emerge' from data through quantitative analysis, others hypothesize dimensions and test them against empirical data, and yet others specify the dimensions in advance. Some methods give the dimensions equal weight, some apply weights arbitrarily that can be more or less informed by theoretical understanding, and others derive appropriate weights based on patterns in the data.

All studies of multidimensional poverty to date have been severely constrained by the availability of data, even the specially designed study of the United Kingdom currently being undertaken by Gordon and colleagues is limited by the length of interview that could be afforded (PSE, 2013). An earlier study of the UK (Tomlinson and Walker, 2009) proposed and tested five dimensions of poverty that could be ranked in terms of their decreasing salience as follows: financial pressure (comprising material deprivation and financial strain); deprived neighbourhood; psychological strain (amalgamating anxiety, social dysfunction, and lack of confidence); lack of civic participation; and social isolation. It concluded that the dimensions were all highly significant in shaping the experience of poverty, but that financial pressure was almost five times as important as social isolation. In marked contrast, the Multidimensional Poverty Index (MPI), first adopted by the UNDP in 2010, currently specifies three basic dimensions as a priori (health status, educational attainment, and standard of living), and arbitrarily assigns them equal weight. However, the simplicity of the approach and its limited data requirements enabled multidimensional poverty rates to be calculated for 104 countries (Alkire et al., 2011).

So, while multidimensional conceptions of poverty have theoretical and other advantages over unidimensional approaches, there remains considerable doubt about which dimensions to include, the priority to give to each, and the nature of the associations between them.

Poverty as a Human Rights Issue

A final perspective on poverty that warrants mention is comparatively new and explicitly political. It construes poverty as a human rights issue that requires a new way of thinking, a new language, and precipitates a new set of political demands (Donald and Mottershaw, 2009; Lister, 2008). Concerns with measurement have so far taken second place to political action.

At an international level, action is underpinned by the Universal Declaration of Human Rights adopted on 10 December 1948, which with the International Covenant on Civil and Political Rights and the International Covenant on Economic, Social and Cultural Rights, constitute the International Bill of Human Rights. A network of committees exists, comprised of independent experts and run under the auspices of the UN High Commissioner on Human Rights, to monitor adherence to the bill of rights and subsequent treaties, notably the conventions of the rights of the child (1989), migrant workers (1990), persons with disabilities (2006), and those to eliminate discrimination of the grounds of race (1965) and gender (1979). Furthermore, this framework has favoured the growth of a number of poverty activist organizations that have sought to base their campaigns around the language of rights. Notable among them are ATD Fourth World whose founder, Father Wresinski, was instrumental in promoting a human rights approach to extreme poverty within the UN, and the European Anti-Poverty Network and the Poor People's Economic Human Rights Campaign in the US.

The language of rights broadens the focus of poverty from material inadequacy to social and power relationships, and embraces the way in which people in poverty are treated; it also creates an affirmative agenda based on dignity and respect that, initially in the global South, was built upon participatory action and research (Lister, 2008). The agenda includes recognition of the indivisibility of rights, enshrined in the International Covenant on Economic, Social and Cultural Rights, since the goal of financial adequacy is only likely to be achieved if people in poverty have access to political and civil rights through which to advance their claims and to defend their gains. It also acknowledges the importance of dignity, not only in the context of setting poverty lines and minimum social protection provisions, but also in the delivery of benefits and services, and in the rhetoric of public debate, both giving people in poverty a voice and avoiding the language of denigration that is often so evident in the political construction of poverty, as discussed in

Chapter 1. The UN's own framework emphasizes the importance of empowerment and participation, non-discrimination and equality, and the instigation of an 'international minimum threshold', and aspires to the progressive realization of rights through holding 'all duty-holders, including States and intergovernmental organizations ... to account', and through international assistance and cooperation (OHCHR, 2004).

The broad rights-based perspective on poverty has been credited with stimulating a number of international policy initiatives. Perhaps the most important is the United Nations' Millennium Declaration and Millennium Development Goals to eradicate extreme poverty and to halve, by 2015, the proportion of the world's people whose income is less than one dollar a day and of those suffering from hunger. There is also the United Nations' Decade for the Eradication of Poverty (2008–2017), intended to support the international development goals related to poverty eradication and, most recently, the International Labour Organization Recommendation, approved in 2012, that all governments introduce and maintain a minimum level of social protection including income security, education, and health (ILO, 2012; Voipio, 2010). In 2008 a UN Special Rapporteur on extreme poverty and human rights was appointed, and has subsequently initiated a number of enquiries and reports including ones on participation, access to justice and the penalization of people in poverty (UN, 2011; UN 2012a; UNHR, 2013). Despite such achievements, the focus on rights is not universally welcomed, with some commentators, and indeed governments, demanding that responsibilities be prioritized over rights (Lister, 2008). A countervailing view is that if people are accorded responsibilities they should have the means to carry them out (Wresinski, 1989).

Participative research undertaken within a rights framework frequently contrasts markedly with the sober scientific accounts that demarcate the genre of most policy research. For example, a three-year enquiry by ATD Quart Monde involving seminars and meetings with 1,000 organization members in twenty-four countries concluded that 'poverty is violence', that 'those of us who have come out of a hard place and are still standing know something about survival', and that being 'stuck on the sidelines of life is another kind of violence that walks hand-in-hand with poverty' (Devins, 2013). Another study of extreme poverty observed that:

> down through the ages and throughout the world, the fear of disorder, violence, epidemics and criminality have focused on those furthest from established norms. These people have been disqualified, demonized and degraded to the point of being designated as having no value to the world. The radical inferiority conferred on them meant that victims were no longer considered fully-fledged human beings, but as subhuman, the scum of the earth with no rights. This is how slavery and apartheid were justified.
>
> Godinot with Viard, 2010, p. 13

The political motivation underlying the rights-based approach to poverty has left the issue of measurement largely unaddressed. In terms of definition, the legacy of Father Wresinski is enduring in that many of the UN instruments refer to 'extreme' poverty, which is sometimes problematic. Wresinski considered extreme poverty to be multidimensional and persistent, and to deny people the ability to exercise their rights and assume their responsibilities. However, while he believed that extreme poverty could exist in any country, he considered it to be inherently different from poverty per se in that the pressure of deprivation was so great as to prevent people bettering themselves without assistance (Woden, 2000). Since, for Wresinski, extreme poverty was a poverty within poverty, use of the term in human rights instruments might be taken to restrict their applicability to this form of poverty alone.

Elsewhere, the UN High Commissioner for Human Rights (OHCHR, 2004) asserts equivalence between Sen's capabilities approach introduced above and its own. For Sen, poverty is the failure, or lack of freedom, of people to achieve basic capabilities of a minimum level consistent with that affording them dignity. 'The concern for human dignity also motivates the human rights approach, which postulates that people have inalienable rights to these freedoms' (OHCHR, 2004, p. 9). Poverty, from the human rights perspective, is, therefore, the non-fulfilment of rights to basic freedoms due, in part at least, to inadequate economic resources. Advocates of the human rights approach would further argue that the choice and priority of capabilities to be taken into account should be determined through consultation' including with people with direct experience of poverty, and that methods of relieving poverty should be such as to promote dignity.

Measurement would need to take account of the inherently relative and multidimensional nature of poverty conceptualized as a human right, with lack of income and a lack of access to resources being used as a means of determining whether the non-fulfilment of human rights was a consequence of poverty or something else. Attention would also need to be paid to determining at what level failure to achieve capabilities is taken to be a denial of rights. The programme of research being undertaken by the Oxford Poverty and Human Development Initiative (OPHI, 2013) to operationalize Sen's capabilities approach is possibly the best example of poverty measurement consistent with a human rights perspective. In the meantime, the global community relies heavily on the USD 1.25/day threshold that the World Bank, among others, describes as a measure of 'extreme poverty' (World Bank, 2010).

It should be clear that there can be no perfect definition or measure of poverty. Each is partial, reflecting different conceptions of poverty and exhibiting particular strengths and limitations. Each is likely to tell a different story and so, in seeking briefly in the next section to survey what is known about poverty globally, it is necessary to use different measures.

A BARE ANATOMY OF GLOBAL POVERTY TODAY

Several comprehensive analyses and critiques of global poverty are available and there is no reason to replicate them here (UNDP, 2013; UN, 2013a; Lal, 2013; Collier, 2007). Instead, the twin tasks are to provide context for the subsequent analysis of specific countries while illustrating some of the consequences of different definitions. It is salutary to realize that, despite the rapid economic growth achieved globally over the last quarter century and the many initiatives prompted by the UN's Millennium Development Goals, 21 per cent of the world's population (about 1.22[1] billion people) were still reliant on less than USD 1.25/day in 2010 (World Bank, 2013). It is salutary, too, to realize that this figure is precise only to the nearest one-hundred million people. Also, while it is often claimed that 70 per cent of people in extreme poverty are women, this figure is certainly more 'factoid' than fact, although women, children, and elders are likely to be disproportionately at risk of being poor (GPP, 2013; Green, 2010).

Figure 2.1 summarizes trends in the USD 1.25/day measure of 'absolute' poverty. Because this measure can only be used in low- and middle-income countries, the statistics for Europe and Central Asia exclude all the countries in the European Union; rates of poverty among the remaining countries in these regions are nevertheless very low but show increases in the 1990s following the breakup of the Soviet Union. In marked contrast, poverty rates in Sub-Saharan Africa, although they have declined over the last decade, remain very high. Thirty years ago, poverty rates in the East Asian and Pacific region were comparable with those in Sub-Saharan Africa. Since then they have fallen dramatically, interrupted only briefly by the Asian financial crises in the late 1990s. The decline in poverty in South Asia has been less marked but still considerable and is continuing. However, despite these improvements, about 42 per cent of the world's poverty population still lives in South Asia, while 34 per cent resides in Sub-Saharan Africa. Moreover, notwithstanding decades of pro-poor growth, the East Asia and the Pacific region still accounts for one in five of all people in poverty; China alone accounts for one in eight.

Turning to measures of relative poverty, Figure 2.2 shows the overlap between relative poverty, measured as 60 per cent of median income or expenditure, and absolute poverty defined according to the UN's measure of USD 1.25/day (Garroway and de Laiglesia, 2012). It is obvious that the structure of poverty differs radically between the more affluent countries (belonging to the Organisation for Economic Cooperation and Development, OECD) and less affluent non-OECD countries and between different regions.

---

[1] This figure could be as high as 1.4 billion if the estimate for world population of 6.9 billion in 2010 is taken at face value (GPP, 2013).

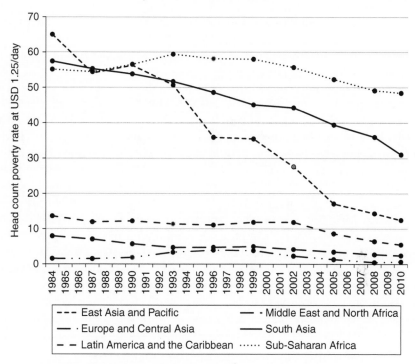

Fig. 2.1. Absolute poverty (1984–2010)[1]

[1] Regional aggregation USD 1.25/day using poverty line 2005 purchasing power parities
Adapted from World Bank (2013)

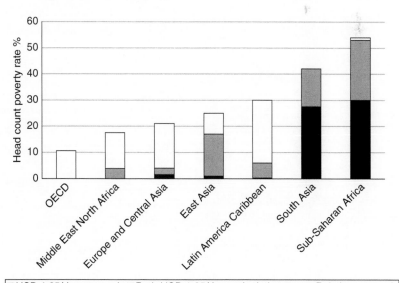

Fig. 2.2. Absolute[1] and relative poverty[2] (mid-2000s)

[1] USD 1.25/day adjusted using purchasing power parities
[2] 60 per cent of median income or expenditure; OECD countries using a different source
Adapted from Garroway and de Laiglesia (2012)

Absolute poverty scarcely exists at all in OECD countries and is rare in the Middle East, Northern Africa, Europe, and Central Asia. It is low too in Latin America where, because of large income inequalities in many countries, levels of relative poverty are high. In contrast, most poverty in South Asia and Sub-Saharan Africa is absolute, subsistence poverty. Moreover, in these countries a sizeable proportion of the people in absolute poverty are also poor relatively, pointing to social exclusion of people experiencing extreme poverty. In East Asia there is a sizable problem of both absolute and relative poverty; most people in poverty are poor in both senses but, with high income inequality, significant numbers who are not income poor in absolute terms are so relative to median incomes.

It is wrong to assume that people in poverty, even extreme poverty, will remain so. Most people experience repeated spells and some only one. Because it is expensive and difficult to measure the duration of poverty, good comparative data are unavailable (but see Foster and Santos, 2012). However, Figure 2.3 presents estimates of chronic poverty, defined as being in poverty on two occasions when poverty is measured according to local thresholds using income or consumption. The incidence of chronic poverty tends to be higher in rural areas than urban ones, as does the prevalence rate (the

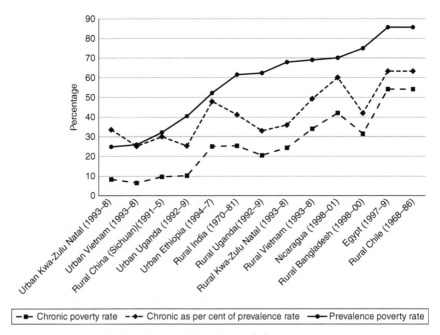

Fig. 2.3. Poverty dynamics and chronic poverty

Adapted from CPRC (2004)

proportion of people who ever experience it, measured at two points in time). Only in areas with extremely high prevalence, typically rural ones, does the number of people in chronic poverty exceed those whose poverty is transient. Thus two thirds of people who experience poverty in rural Chile are chronically poor compared with only a third of those in urban Kwa-Zulu Natal where the prevalence of poverty is much less.

The multidimensional measure of poverty reported in Figure 2.4 combines ten indicators that reflect low educational achievement, ill- health (including child mortality), and poor nutrition and material living standards comprising access to electricity, sanitation, and improved drinking water and selected durables (Alkire et al., 2013). Two levels of severity are calculated: a base-level defined as people who are deprived on at least a third of the weighted dimensions, and a severe measure comprising persons deprived on half of the ten dimensions. As can be seen in Figure 2.4, the basic index tends to yield higher poverty counts than the United Nations' USD 1.25 subsistence line, although not for East Asia and Latin America, whereas the severe measure records lower ones. However, the pattern is inconsistent across global regions. Other calculations show, for example, that while the multidimensional measure of severe poverty indicates that 53 per cent of the world's population lives in South Asia, the UN subsistence indicator suggests that just 41 per cent does so. Correspondingly, the concentration of poor people in East Asia and the

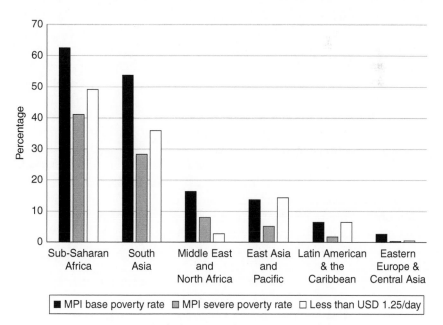

Fig. 2.4. Multidimensional poverty (post-2005)

Adapted from Alkire et al. (2013)

Pacific is less according to the severe multidimensional measure than the United Nations' subsistence measure (15 per cent rather than 31 per cent). While this multidimensional measure does not include subjective components, others that do indicate that people naturally think in relative terms; persons living in poorer areas perceive themselves to be more deprived than objective comparisons would indicate (Pradban and Ravallion, 2011).

It is clear not only that poverty, however defined, affects millions of people worldwide, but also that the choice of definition and measure of poverty is material. Taken individually different measures generate different levels and patterns of poverty that can precipitate different policy responses. Taken together they offer a richer understanding of the experience and complex social construction that is poverty.

COMPETING CONSTRUCTIONS OF POVERTY

As understanding has improved, the scientific construction of poverty has evolved both in terms of definition and measurement; unidimensional, point-in-time estimates of poverty have been superseded by longitudinal multidimensional studies combining objective and subjective perspectives. However, throughout modern history the science has been shaped by political and ideological considerations: how best to bring about change and how most appropriately to conceptualize poverty. Few of the most contentious issues around the conceptualization of poverty have been permanently resolved and it is unlikely that they ever will be while politics is underpinned, as most would agree that it needs to be, by differences in ideology (although see Bell, 2000 and Fukuyama, 1992).

The policy world comprises institutions and interest groups competing for power and influence (Knoepfel et al., 2007). Winning command of the definition of a policy problem and of its causes is usually essential if an institution or interest group is to succeed in its policy mission. Hence, unsurprisingly, definitions of poverty have been used as weapons in ideological debates and as tools by institutions jockeying for influence. While living standards may be a more direct measure of poverty than income alone, income denotes command over resources and an income-based threshold signifies the right and freedom to dispose of those resources as the person sees fit (Atkinson, 1989). Absolute measures minimize the need for proactive government intervention beyond facilitating economic growth, thereby maximizing the scope for market-led solutions. Relative measures focus attention on state-driven post-market redistribution of income. Prioritizing health and education outcomes above social empowerment implies an investment model of growth rather than one based on participative development. The choice of objective over subjective measures is to prioritize state monitoring and control over individual experience and agency.

While much of research undertaken on poverty has been designed to bring about policy change, it has mostly been undertaken by people in relatively privileged positions, either as advocates on behalf of people experiencing poverty or as officials in government charged with the design or monitoring of policy. Except for participative research, a feature of more recent years and possibly still more prevalent in the global South than the global North (although see Bennett with Roberts, 2004), the voices of people in poverty have been quite muted. Facts and statistics, rather than feelings, are often taken to be more important in changing the views of governments and to be more useful in managing policy. But the fact that the World Bank's *Source Book for Poverty Reduction Strategies* gives only 'cursory treatment' to subjective and qualitative measures of poverty while asserting their importance is not a neutral ideological stance (Coudouel et al., 2003, p. 30). Similarly, for officials at the World Bank to question whether people are 'poor, or just feeling poor' (Ravallion, 2012) is, inadvertently or otherwise, to challenge the foundation of the UN's human rights agenda that asserts that 'poverty is not only deprivation of economic or material resources but a violation of human dignity'. It is almost certainly the case that more is known about how much poverty there is than about what it means to be poor, a deficiency that this volume and its companion in small measure both address.

This volume, together with *Poverty and Shame: Global Experiences*, will be read in the light of politico-scientific understandings of poverty and both seek indirectly to influence policy debates. Moreover, the two volumes can be located by coordinates within these debates since they emphasize subjective conceptions of poverty, listen to the voices of those who experience poverty, and connect most readily to rights-based approaches concerned to promote human dignity rather than other policy traditions. However, the focus of attention lies elsewhere since the goal is better to understand the social rather than the politico-scientific construction of poverty, and to explore how this affects the lives of people deemed to be poor. It is this focus that brings the shame of poverty to the fore.

3

Constructions of Shame

While it will be argued that shame is central to the understanding of poverty, shame hardly featured in the previous chapter concerned with the measurement of poverty. It only became evident when the voices of people with direct experience of poverty were heard. In sociology something similar happens. On the one hand, shame is accorded the status as the premier social emotion, in various guises being 'the glue that holds social relationships and societies together' or else 'blows them apart'; on the other, the word is taboo, seldom written about under its real name (Scheff, 2003, p. 258). It is as if the emotion it describes attaches to the word itself and prevents its use. According to Aesop, writing in the sixth century BCE, the Greek god Zeus even forgot to include shame when creating people, and later had to insert 'her' from behind associating shame with sodomy (Gibbs, 2008). Certainly, the term is rarely used in economics despite there being a bourgeoning literature dealing with happiness and well-being. Even within psychology, its host discipline, shame and the other self-conscious emotions, embarrassment, guilt, and pride, have received much less attention than basic emotions such as joy, fear, and sadness (Tracy and Robins, 2007). This is not because shame is deemed to be unimportant. Indeed, Goffman (1955) observed that every social act is influenced by the prospect of shame, however slight the chance of it actually occurring.

So the objective in this chapter is to make shame visible by explaining what it is and how it manifests itself, what causes it, and with what consequences. The academic disciplines largely agree on 'the what and how' of shame but differ on its causes and effects. However, disciplines tend to destroy real-world phenomena of interest by focussing on particular parts of the plot when the whole story is the more important. So it is with shame. The challenge is to rediscover the whole by piecing together disciplinary insights.

SHAME AND ITS ORIGINS

Psychology is the discipline with the most to say about shame, although shame is also an important plot ingredient in much creative writing with insights that closely resemble scientific findings (see Chapters 5 and 6). Psychologists view shame as a self-conscious emotion, more akin to pride and guilt than to joy, fear, or anger. The key point of distinction is that experiencing shame requires both self-awareness, the recognition of 'I', and self-representation—the ability to conceptualize 'me' so as to make possible self-evaluation which, when negative, can result in a sense of shame. Probably because they are cognitively complex, self-conscious emotions develop later in life compared to basic ones, often in the third year rather than within the first nine months as is the case with basic emotions (Mills, 2005; Tracy and Robins, 2007).

Shame entails a negative assessment of the core self, made with reference to one's own aspirations and the perceived expectations of others, that manifests itself in a sense of powerlessness and inadequacy, and the feeling of 'being small' (Tangney et al., 2007a). At a physiological level, shame is recognized by increased pro-inflammatory cytokine activity and cortisol, blushing, gaze aversion, and a slumped posture with head tilted down or to the side (Dickerson et al., 2004; Gilbert, 1997). It has been associated with a range of psychological symptoms including low self-esteem, depression, anxiety, eating disorders, and suicidal ideas (Tangney et al., 2007b).

Shame is usually differentiated from guilt and from embarrassment and humiliation, although these four self-conscious emotions are frequently treated as a 'family' and the distinctions are sometimes recognized as being fuzzy (Elison and Harter, 2007). Guilt and shame are both responses to transgressions that are likely to engender the disapproval of others. In the case of guilt, the transgressions relate to behaviours or transient states that could be changed, whereas with shame they apply to permanent or longstanding attributes, characteristics, and circumstances that cannot readily be altered (Tracy and Robins, 2004). Some people consider that the emotions differ, too, in terms of their external and internal orientation: whereas 'shame typically involves being negatively evaluated by *others* (real or imaginary), guilt typically involves being negatively evaluated by *oneself*' (Wong and Tsai, 2007, p. 210, original emphases). Shame is the fear of exposing oneself to others and may therefore occur more commonly in company, whereas guilt is the recognition of having failed to live up to one's own standards. To the extent that these distinctions are valid, a person feeling guilt has more control, actual or potential, over their emotion and its cause, their errant behaviour, than does the person experiencing shame who needs to change others' evaluation of their character or circumstances. In fact, however, many authors argue that shame also has an internal orientation that is shaped by memories of what others have thought about them in the past, and by self-critical evaluations of self (Ogilvie, 1987). Furthermore, it appears that the internalization of shame focusses less on the distance that a person falls short of their ideal and more on their closeness to some absolute negative image of self.

Humiliation and embarrassment are closer to shame than to guilt. Humiliation differs from shame in that it arises as a consequence of the intended and hostile actions of another, often in public, whereas shame can be sometimes provoked unintentionally, or with limited self-awareness, and the motivation may be positive (Elison and Harter, 2007). While the context of shame is typically one of moral failing, that for humiliation is diverse, requiring only the sense of having been put down. Humiliation, like shame, is an intense emotion, provoking anger and thoughts as extreme as suicide and violence. It is also remembered for a long time, although typically it is not as long-lived as shame. Embarrassment, in contrast, is a mild, short-lived emotion that can even be associated with humour; it is typically triggered when a person fails to meet a social convention. Possibly because it is mild and comparatively frequent, embarrassment seems more acceptable and less stigmatizing than shame so that people are prone to say that they felt embarrassed even though, in reality, they felt ashamed; shame contains a double reflexivity in that shame is shameful.

Dictionaries often suggest that the antonym of shame is pride, but this presents logical difficulties since pride is equally widely construed to be undesirable, suggesting that the opposite of a negative is a negative. Christianity presents pride as a cardinal sin, while Buddhism views it as an impediment to the discovery of true happiness. However, Hart and Matsuba (2007) separate negative hubris, or narcissism, from positive pride, the latter being an emotion associated with a job well done or a moral precept followed that enhances a person's sense of self-worth.

The origins of shame have been traced back into the deep evolutionary past, to dominance structures within primate communities (Fessler, 2007; Wiesfeld, 1999). The physiological attributes of shame, stooping with lowered heads and averted gaze, are directly akin to the acquiescent position adopted among other primates when an inferior individual is threatened by dominant others. However, human hierarchies based on physical power have often been superseded by those founded on prestige, where dominant positions are not taken from others but given by them. Such structures demand complex processes of cognition entailing an awareness of self and an appraisal of one's actions, knowledge by others of these actions, and awareness that others know and make judgements about one's own actions. Shame is felt and signalled when one feels oneself to be negatively evaluated by others. However, whereas in power hierarchies that are underpinned by violence, displays of acquiescence protect against physical harm, within systems based on prestige they demonstrate inferiority without seeming to secure direct benefits for the acquiescent subordinate.

Given that displays of shame in prestige hierarchies apparently yield little personal benefit, the retention of such behaviours presents a puzzle. The resolution to this puzzle comes from anthropology and sociology, with the suggestion that the persistence of shame in human societies stems from the necessity of cooperation in constructing functioning communities (Fessler, 2007). Cultures comprise rules of behaviour and rules for enforcing behaviour and cultural conformity—the ability to abide by cultural rules is used as evidence for identifying those who would make reliable collaborators and leaders. Moral outrage is an important sanction in enforcing conformity and expressions of shame by persons who have transgressed social rules may reduce this, thereby lessening the negative consequences attached to sanctioning for both the individual and the wider society.

ON THE REASONS FOR SHAME

While sociology can help to explain why shame persists, it is important to recognize that sociology itself comprises different theoretical traditions that offer unique but necessarily partial lenses through which to view shame (Turner and Stets, 2005). The two most pertinent traditions are structuralism and symbolic interactionism: the former explores how emotions are shaped by people being embedded in structures of power and prestige, while the latter focusses on how people manage these influences while seeking to maintain a positive self-image.

Turner and Stets (2005) and Scheff (2000, 2003) belong to variants of the second tradition and both prioritize shame and guilt as the most important emotions from a sociological perspective. They do so because they recognize that these two emotions enable the collective community to exert social control over the individual, driving people to conform to social expectations and moral codes and hence promoting social cohesion and solidarity. The driver is the pain that the two emotions impose on the individual, which causes them to recognize the error of their ways and motivates them, to the extent that it is possible, to make amends. The fact that the individual transgressors are moved to change minimizes the cost to the community of imposing its collective will.

Turner and Maryanski (2013, p. 306) conceptualize both shame and guilt as combinations of three basic emotions: sadness, anger, and fear (Table 3.1). Shame is the product of disappointment with self, a sentiment that Turner and Maryanski equate with sadness, accompanied by anger at self and fear of the consequences of social disapproval. Guilt is similarly driven by disappointment with self, but fear of the consequences exceeds the self-directed anger in importance. Although Turner does not explicitly make the distinction that psychologists do—distinguishing guilt as a product of behaviour, in contrast to shame with its focus on self—the greater salience of self-directed anger that he identifies in shame, amounting in some cases to self-loathing, is nevertheless conceptually similar. Scheff (2000, p. 92), citing Lynd's (1958) work, does

Table 3.1. Shame, guilt and alienation

Second-order emotions	Rank order of primary emotions		
	1: Sadness	2: Anger	2: Fear
Shame	Disappointment-sadness (at self)	Assertion-anger (at self)	Aversion-fear (at consequences for self)
Guilt	Disappointment-sadness (at self)	Aversion-fear (at consequences for self)	Assertion-anger (at self)
Alienation	Disappointment-sadness (at self, others, situation)	Assertion-anger at others, situation	Aversion-fear (at consequences for self)

Turner and Maryanski (2013)

affirm that 'guilt is about what one did' and shame is about 'what one is', and also suggests that guilt is closer to the surface than shame which is 'more deeply hidden' and more pervasive. He suggests, too, that whereas guilt 'involves the feeling that the ego is strong and intact', 'shame feels like weakness and dissolution of the self'.

Scheff (2003) asserts that shame is the premier social emotion not just because of its powerful effect on the self, but because at low levels it pervades all social interaction. Scheff (2000, p. 96) presents shame as a family of emotions including 'embarrassment, humiliation and related feelings such as shyness that involve reactions to rejection or feelings of failure or inadequacy'. Such feelings constitute 'a threat to the social bond' that connects individuals to communities and which collectively 'glues' society together. In conceptualizing shame as a family of emotions, Scheff is responding to the strength of the word shame for, unlike French or German, English does not distinguish between 'everyday shame' and 'disgrace shame'. As a consequence people in everyday speech and, in Scheff's view, sociologists of the stature of Erving Goffman frequently use a range of weaker alternatives when they really mean shame.

Scheff portrays individuals constantly monitoring themselves against their own expectations and their perceptions of those of others as a product of which they either feel shame or pride (in the positive sense). For the most part, pride and shame exist at low levels and are reinforced by low-level responses that result in people becoming mutually attuned to each other, reinforcing a sense of attachment built through mutual respect and understanding. Adults often feel uncomfortable with social emotions and so try to avoid encountering and revealing shame, or because of its negative connotations, exhibiting pride since each might attract further opprobrium and discomfort. If individuals lapse and transgress social norms, acknowledging the negative sanctions, this can lead to the reconstruction of social bonds, and indeed their reinforcement, something more easily achieved with guilt than with shame.

Of course, the maintenance of social cohesion and social harmony is seldom likely to be an undisputed social good since the processes of social control can generally be expected to maintain the status quo to the detriment of those in the weakest positions in society. This should be the point at which structural sociologists could make a contribution to understanding shame, but Turner and Stets (2005, p. 259) are sadly correct when they conclude that no theory yet 'adequately connects emotions to the properties and dynamics of social structures'. Barbalet (1998) has sought to construct a comprehensive theory but adopts a very idiosyncratic view of shame, namely as an emotion provoked when individuals claim or are assigned status that they do not deserve. Interestingly though, as will be seen in Chapters 7 and 8, Barbalet's reflections on confidence, resentment. and vengefulness are very much more in accord with people's experiences of shame linked to poverty. People in poverty are likely to lack confidence in relation to those with greater material resources, and are prone to feel resentful and vengeful at being denied the basic right to an adequate quality of life. They are often on the receiving end of such emotions when others accuse them of 'living off benefits' and 'choosing an easy life'. Moreover, the behaviour induced by shame can even reinforce inequalities and strengthen stratification in society. Scheff (2002) reanalysed the language used by protagonists in Paul Willis's (1977) classic ethnographic study of education in a town in the UK West Midlands, and found not only that teachers guided working class youths into working class jobs, but that the youths themselves, feeling shamed and humiliated by the teachers' perceptions of their abilities, tended to reject the education system in defiance, thereby condemning themselves to low-status jobs.

Turner and Stets (2005, p. 19) suggest that secondary, self-conscious emotions such as shame and guilt are universal just like basic ones, arguing that there is a 'a hardwired propensity' for them arising through hominid evolution, but that their expression is moderated culturally. Anthropologists and cultural psychologists recognize distinctions between more collectivist cultures, like China, Japan, and South Korea that promote interdependent concepts of self, and more individualistic ones, such as the UK and US, that view self as being inherently independent of others (Wong and Tsai, 2007). Social pressures to conform and collaborate are naturally heightened in collectivist cultures and thus it might be expected that the salience of shame is enhanced, which appears to be the case. Li et al. (2004), for example, report 113 terms in Mandarin relating to shame, many more than are available in English, and Chinese children become familiar with the concept of shame much earlier than in Britain or the US (Shaver et al., 1992). Within collectivist cultures other people's feelings become as important and meaningful as one's own, and it is quite possible to feel personalized shame on account of what somebody close to one does or is (Tsai, 2006).

The distinction between shame and guilt—the former being the perception of a negative evaluation of self made by others, the latter the negative assessment of one's behaviour made by self—is accompanied in mainstream Western psychology by the normative assessment that shame is generally bad and guilt is good (Smith et al., 2002). This is because shame is found to be associated with low self-esteem and negative psychological and physical consequences, whereas guilt reflects high self-esteem and also leads to reparative action which shame does not (Tangney and Dearing, 2003; Wong and Tsai, 2007). However, in collectivist societies shame is not only more salient but frequently considered to be positive. Confucianism, for instance, teaches that individuals can and should be expected constantly to appraise and improve themselves, and that the experience of shame is one mechanism by which this can be brought about; Chinese parents use shame much more assiduously than would be the case in, for example, the US (Fung et al., 2003). The concepts of shame and guilt are also less readily differentiated in collectivist cultures, with shame being associated with actions that might be the source of guilt elsewhere (Bedford, 2004).

The difference in emphasis between collectivist and individualistic cultures may revolve around notions of what individuals can do to avoid being, and continuing to be, shamed. Within both types of culture, shame attaches to the self. Within collectivist cultures, the self is the product of a person's relationships and actions and is amenable to change. Imposing shame on the self who transgresses may result in a change in behaviour, which would simultaneously change the self and release it from shame. However, within individualistic cultures the self—character—is taken to be largely fixed and is differentiated from behaviour and actions. Therefore, although shaming might change behaviour, it would not be expected to affect the self or, thereby, the shame that the self experiences. Guilt, on the other hand, which is more clearly differentiated from shame in individualistic cultures than in collectivist ones, can be absolved through action: repentance and (ideally) a change in behaviour.

To summarize, shame is a self-conscious emotion that seems to be universal across cultures and probably evolved, associated with the need to organize effective social living, as a mechanism to subjugate the possibly divisive interests of the individual to the collective good and will of the community. However, the salience of shame may be greater in more collectivist societies than in more individualistic ones. Within the former, unacceptable individual behaviour may be perceived to undermine the standing of the entire family, clan, community or caste and thereby cause shame to be experienced by all members of the social group. Members of the social group may correspondingly feel that it is appropriate to shame fellow members who transgress social norms with a view to achieving the collective goal of bringing them into line (which may also reduce the indirect shame felt by all members of the group).

The experience of shame in more individualistic societies is similarly shaped by perceptions of the views of salient others, but it is more circumscribed in its influence, generally affecting solely the individual who transgresses the social norms. It may also be that the expression of shame is less in more individualistic societies than in collectivist ones, and the sanctions through which it is applied are weaker or, at least, less overt. Equally, there is much less agreement as to whether shame has a positive effect, notwithstanding populist calls 'to name and shame' those who transgress social norms, including sex offenders, people dependent on benefits, and, more rarely, rich persons and companies evading taxation (Pawson, 2002; Teichman, 2005).

THE CONSEQUENCES OF SHAME

The prevailing view is that shame can bring social benefits through the mechanism of imposing or threatening psychological pain on individuals who transgress, or consider transgressing, social norms. Individuals who adopt exemplary behaviour in order to avoid the constant threat of being shamed, gain to the extent that the direct benefits conferred by engaging in socially approved behaviours exceed those associated with disreputable ones; additionally, they stand to benefit indirectly from social acceptance and engagement (Goffman, 1955). These indirect benefits are, according to Scheff, very powerful since what is threatened is loss of the 'social bond', a person's membership of society, their passport to human intimacy, and protection against being made a social outcaste. This, then, is the glue that binds people and society together.

Shame works positively for society on occasions when it is acknowledged by the individual who is shamed, and when the individual can address the source of their shame. However, shame is directed at character and long-term traits that are often difficult for the individual alone to alter. Moreover, where the long-term traits relate to repeated behavioural transgression, these might be explicable in terms of structural constraints that limit the opportunities that people have to choose to do 'the right thing'. Furthermore, the expression of shame is itself often considered shameful, an admission of shame that is likely to trigger another round of shaming such that individuals may 'sanction themselves' against exhibiting shame (or indeed other negative emotions that might also elicit shame) (Turner and Stets, 2005, p. 158). It follows, therefore, that individuals may seek to conceal their shame from others, a strategy that can provoke accusations of 'shamelessness'. They may even try to hide the shame from themselves.

Shame, of course, impacts on individuals as well as having societal effects. Tangney et al. (2007b) document the negative consequences of shame and contrast these with frequently positive reactions to guilt. They confirm the propensity of individuals to deny or hide shame and to avoid shame-inducing situations, and demonstrate these responses biochemically through measurements of hormone levels (pro-inflammatory cytokine and cortisol production are associated with deference and self-concealment, Dickerson et al. (2004)). In contrast to guilt, which prompts reparation and apology, shame more often results in defensiveness and interpersonal separation and distancing. Shame also causes people to turn in on themselves, focussing on their own hurt rather than empathizing with the other, as more readily happens in the case of guilt when an offender appreciates that they have wronged someone (Tangney et al. 1994). The lack of empathy is often combined with anger, which frequently manifests itself in destructive ways, and with the propensity, rightly or wrongly, to blame others for their predicament. Tangney et al. (2007b, p. 352) succinctly characterize the negative dynamic that can ensue:

> Desperate to escape painful feelings of shame, shamed individuals are apt to turn the tables defensively, externalizing blame and anger outward onto a convenient scapegoat. Blaming others may help individuals regain some sense of control and superiority in their life, but the long-term costs are often steep. Friends, co-workers, and loved ones are apt to become alienated by an interpersonal style characterized by irrational bursts of anger.

Given the observation that shame imposes psychological pain, it is not surprising that the psychological consequences can be severe; the aforementioned list of low self-esteem, depression, anxiety, eating disorder symptoms, post-traumatic stress disorder, and suicidal ideation have all been associated with shame across diverse age groups, populations, and cultures (Furukawa et al., 2012; Tangney and Dearing, 2003). These personal costs are, as noted above, generally theorized to be offset by the gains to society arising from greater conformity to social norms. The empirical evidence for this, however, is not secure. Indeed, Tangney et al. (2007b, p. 354) conclude that there is 'virtually no evidence supporting the presumed adaptive nature of shame'. They report studies of children, adolescents, college students, and prisoners where shame, unlike guilt, does not produce reparative changes in attitudes or behaviour. Moreover, there is evidence of shame seemingly making matters worse. Studies of children, young people, and adults reveal that those subject to feelings of shame were more, not less, likely to anticipate future involvement in illegal activities, drug and alcohol use, and other antisocial behaviours (Dearing et al., 2005; Stuewig and McCloskey, 2005).

Scheff (1997) portrays two scenarios in which shame results in negative outcomes for both individuals and societies, each being a product of attempts to hide shame (Figure 3.1). In the first, a scenario that Scheff variously terms 'overt, undifferentiated shame' and 'underdistancing', a person feels the pain of shame but disguises the fact. They may do this by, for example, averting their gaze or hiding their face, or linguistically by referring to feeling stupid,

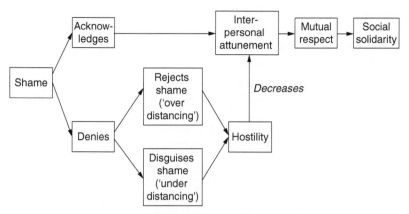

Fig. 3.1. From Scheff's model of shame and solidarity
Adapted from Turner and Stets (2005)

awkward, or silly. The second scenario, 'bypassed shame' or 'overdistancing', describes the situation in which neither the pain nor the shame is acknowledged. The denial or repression of shame, Scheff suggests, leads to the anger that may result in actions and antisocial behaviour that fracture social relationships and erode mutual respect and solidarity. It may also be the case that the lack of acknowledgement of shame promotes a negative response from the wider community, one that is less condoning of further transgression so that the breakdown of relationships is both quicker and more permanent.

Scheff has sought to illustrate these processes (rather than empirically to establish them) as they affect whole societies and as they apply to individuals. For example, Scheff and Retzinger (1991) explain support for the rise of Hitler in Germany in terms of the collective shame and rage stemming from the humiliation of the Versailles Treaty at the end of World War I and its political and economic aftermath. Equally, he presents the suppression of feeling that is characteristic of depression as an attempt by individuals to manage the pain of shame (Scheff, 2001), and as an element in the dynamic of some episodes of domestic violence (Jury, 2009; Scheff, 1995). Most relevant to economic disadvantage, he reinterprets Sennett and Cobb's classic 1972 study of working class life in terms of the lack of respect felt by working class men in relation to their bosses and significant others, such as school teachers (Scheff, 2002). Not only do school teachers fail to respond to working class children, by interpreting class differences as indicative of lack of educational potential, but working class men blame themselves for their class position resulting in a lack of self-respect that they convey to their children.

The crux of Scheff's thesis is that shame that is acknowledged can bring positive benefits, whereas shame that is repressed is likely to be socially and personally destructive. Some scholars have suggested that shame has been becoming less prevalent over the centuries and less socially acceptable in Western countries (Elias, 1969, 1982; Fernández-Villaverde et al., 2010). Public executions, the exhibiting of miscreants in village stocks and the branding of criminals are, in much of the world, embarrassments of history. The shame attaching to premarital and extramarital sex is much reduced, while the use of shame as a deliberate and explicit element in policy, manifest in bricks and mortar in the Victorian Poor Law Workhouse, is ostensibly less (or at least less visible). This process has been linked to the rise of modernity and individualism that both cause shame, a collective self-conscious emotion, to be superseded by an individualistic one: guilt (Benedict, 1946). Scheff (2003, p. 255), however, argues that guilt 'does not so much replace shame as serve as one of its many masks'; it (shame) 'does not disappear' but instead 'goes underground', increasing the likelihood that it will be repressed and hence destructive in its consequences.

Shame remains prevalent in many collectivist societies and retains positive connotations; it may achieve more social and personal benefits as a consequence of less often being repressed. Bagozzi et al. (2003), for example, contrast the positive consequences of shame on the performance of sales staff in the Philippines (a collectivist culture) relative to those in the Netherlands. Similarly, Wallbott and Scherer (1995) report, based on analysis of thirty-seven countries, that shame has far fewer disruptive consequences in collectivist cultures than in individualistic ones. However, there is increasing evidence that shame may have negative personal and social consequences even in collectivist cultures (Breugelmans and Poortinga, 2006; Fontaine et al., 2006). Furukawa et al. (2012), for example, compare the experiences of school children in Japan, South Korea, and the US and find that although the prevalence of experiencing shame is much higher in Japan, the psychological implications of experiencing it were similar across cultures. In each country, children exposed to shame were more likely than other children to experience anger and to externalize blame, but they are no less likely to behave aggressively or to exhibit other troublesome behaviour. The hurt associated with shame did not change behaviour even in Japan, the most shame-orientated of the three countries.

Scheff (1997) suggests that how people cope with shame has partly to do with their level of self-esteem. When self-esteem is high, people are generally well-able to acknowledge and discharge shame, whereas if it is low the pain of shame may be overwhelming. In the latter case people often repress their sense of shame, and thereby risk entering the self-destructive cycle of repressed shame, anger, and further repressed shame that may lower their already low self-esteem. Turner and Stets (2005) suggest that this cycle of shame and anger can be transmitted across generations, citing the example of abusive parents who shame their children with angry words, forcing them to deny their shame and causing them later to become, as parents, hostile to their own children. They also point to social structures and cultural taboos that both generate shame and force individuals to hide or deny their shame.

While the overall prevalence of shame may have declined, some argue that shame associated with poverty may have increased and its negative consequences exacerbated by the lower salience of shame generally (Gaulejac, 1989; Jo, 2013). With economic development and growing individualization, social status has increasingly come to be associated with achievement, rather than with ascribed characteristics such as age, birth right, and gender. Most recently, wealth, expenditure, and consumption have emerged as the predominant measures of personal success, the concomitant being that poverty has come to be viewed as a conspicuous indicator of personal failure. Moreover, the prevailing belief, not dissimilar to that associated with the concept of a well-governed society as envisaged by Confucius (see Chapter 1), is that social mobility guarantees success for those with ability and application, implying that those in poverty must lack at least one of these qualities (Wilkinson and Pickett, 2010). The reality, of course, is that opportunities are structurally determined and inequality is persistent such that the winners, the rich, remain winners as do their children, while those who lose out, those in poverty, are potentially exposed to multiple burdens of shame (Goldthorpe, 2013). Not only are people in poverty poor, and therefore unable fully to participate in the society of which they are nominally part, their lack of success is attributed to their own personal failings since the structural hurdles that they face either go unnoticed or are not admitted (Chase and Walker, 2013; Ferragina et al., 2013; see also Chapters 7 and 9). Furthermore, the limited prevalence or acknowledgement of shame in general may well make the shame to which they are exposed through economic failure more painful to bear, thereby increasing the desire either to repress or to conceal it.

So while shame is thought to have persisted in the species over hundreds of thousands of years, seemingly selected as an attribute that enables communities to prosper through subtle mechanisms of social control, it invariably causes hurt and, apparently, seldom brings direct benefits to the person who is shamed even in collectivist societies which are more likely to view shame positively. Moreover, if Scheff is to be believed, it has the potential to destabilize societies and even to trigger wars. Nevertheless, even in Western societies there are calls for the explicit application of shaming as a means to curb undesirable behaviours, and economists have sought to build models to illustrate how this might be done.

THE USES OF SHAME

Much of the classical economic thinking on human behaviour takes little account of emotions (Boulding, 1987). The presumption is that people rationally choose what to do on the basis of what they think is best for them on the basis of assessments of the likely outcome of each option. Decisions are presumed to be made without reference to others or influenced by emotions. Reality, of course, is very different, with individual preferences and choices being shaped through interactions with others: seeking their approval, avoiding their disapproval, and even wanting to behave like some people and not like others. Charity, and even taxation, is not easy to account for using a self-centred individualistic model of well-being, whereas both become more comprehensible through reference to notions of shame and pride that one might feel about the existence of social problems and pride in having done something about them. Boulding (1987, p. 16) recognizes the two kinds of pride: describing positive pride as 'negative shame' he goes so far as to conclude that 'there is perhaps nothing more crucial to the understanding of the overall dynamics of a particular society than the marked differences' in the 'creation, destruction and distribution of various forms of pride and shame'.

In the twenty-five years since Boulding's reflections, behavioural economics has sought further to investigate the role and implications of emotions in explaining economic and other forms of social behaviour. Dawnay and Shah (2005), in a recent review of the field, included among seven basic principles three that appertain to social emotions. They note, first, that people are generally motivated to do the right thing and that, in such circumstances, offers of money can be demotivating or punishments actually release people from guilt and shame. Secondly, like Boulding, they recognize that people are influenced by the behaviour and attitudes of others to do some things and desist from others. Thirdly, they appreciate that individuals have expectations with respect to their own values that are resistant to change, especially if they have been publicly expressed. Equally, if people make a public commitment to change they are more likely to do so than otherwise, and especially if others support their intentions. Notions of self-respect, shame, and pride are key elements in this dynamic.

These insights have been used to show how changes and variations in behaviour are explicable in terms of the incidence and prevalence of shame and, in turn, to develop models as to how shame might be deployed most effectively by institutions, governments, and firms to change the behaviour of individuals. Fernández-Villaverde et al. (2010) interpret the growth in pre-marital sex and in the incidence of out-of-wedlock births characteristic of many Northern countries in terms of a lessening of shame as a sanction. Historically such behaviour was strongly sanctioned by families who might disown their own daughters, the law which often curtailed the rights of illegitimate children, and the church that often bore the cost of caring for unwed mothers and abandoned children. With the arrival of effective contraception the risk of illegitimacy was much reduced, socialization and shaming by parents and by the church and governments were reduced, and premarital sexual activity increased. Similarly, research has shown that people behind with their housing mortgage payments are more likely to default when they believe many others are doing so, especially if they are personally known to them, because shame attaching to default is perceived to be less (Burke and Mihany, 2012; Seiler et al., 2012). In contrast to the lessening of shame, Biewen and Steffes (2010) report that the stigma attaching to unemployment rises and falls in opposition to the economic cycle: when unemployment is low, stigma is high and spells of unemployment (counter-intuitively) increase in duration. The authors focus on the perceptions of employers, citing experimental work showing that employers discriminate according to the length of unemployment (Oberholzer-Gee, 2008), which, if correct, illustrates the powerful negative influence of shaming in directly reducing life-chances, and probably increasing the degree of shame felt, and further eroding self-confidence.

The management literature includes much discussion on how emotions can be managed within the workplace to enhance performance, although the role of shame is still somewhat neglected (Stiles, 2008; Williams, 1993). Management gurus have generally seen shame as being critical in self-regulation, but have only recently explored its role as a tool to improve motivation and performance rather than as an unwelcome consequence of poor management. Scenarios that use the threat of shame arising from being seen to let the group down are common, as is setting performance targets to place employees in competition with their peers. The challenge for management is to avoid employees viewing the goals as unattainable for reasons of either ability or factors beyond their control, for this could lead individuals either to refuse to accept the goals or not to try to attain in order to avoid the shame of failure. Management is also encouraged to avoid the fundamental attribution error which attributes poor performance to ability and other stable personal characteristics irrespective of the actual causes, for this again increases the risk of shaming (Ross, 1977). More generally the guidance offered to employers instigating performance management systems that are underpinned by sanctions and the threat of shame is to try to balance positive and negative stimuli through organizational support that includes encouragement and, where appropriate, training (Eisenberger et al., 1986).

Turning to the policy sphere, one of the increasing attractions of attempting to use shame to change behaviour is the prospect that it could be cheaper than many other sanctions (Teichman, 2005). There is much discussion within the legal field concerning the merits of shame-inducing sanctions, including publicizing the names of offenders in newspapers or on community television, the requirement for offenders to wear stigmatizing t-shirts in public places, or for persons convicted of drink driving to display notices on their cars (Notes, 2003). Perhaps most contentious has been the registration and publication of the names of sex offenders living in a neighbourhood (often called Megan's

Law in response to the public outrage following the brutal murder of Megan Kanka in New Jersey in 1994) that was first introduced in California in 1947, enacted by the US Federal Government in 1994, and has now been adopted by the UK, Australia, and Norway among other jurisdictions. Originally intended to protect children, Megan's Law has come to be recognized primarily as a device for shaming offenders that sometimes incites aggressive and violent responses from communities (Teichman, 2005).

Some have argued that shame worked best as a punishment and disincentive in traditional tightly knit communities, where it was not only difficult for offenders to hide but where reparation was possible because contrition and changed behaviour would not only be recognized but welcomed and supported, conditions that have largely been destroyed by modernity (Massaro, 1991). However, others argue that in the modern world such sanctions operate differently and primarily through the internalization of shame, rather than through its external imposition, with the sanctioned being deterred by the risk of alienation and by the fear of their past being exposed (Notes, 2003). Equally, in the media and Internet age, it could be argued that shame is both identified and exerted through the 'court of public opinion' (Heller, 1985). By actively or even passively participating in debates, the public may feel that they are expressing their contempt and indignation, directly influencing the judicial process, fulfilling their citizen duty, and even strengthening their attachment to social values and encouraging others to do the same. Sometimes such processes may generate a disproportionate response resulting in 'witch hunts' and 'moral panics' seeking to shame and typically punish groups thought to be a social threat (Ben-Yehuda and Goode, 1994); this has been reported in the context of Megan's Law (Teichman, 2005).

Economic modelling suggests further limitations to the legal use of shame-inducing sanctions. It would appear, for example, that increasing the prevalence of shaming penalties reduces their effectiveness because sanctions become less unusual and discriminating and the public becomes less willing to invest energy in enforcing them (Harel and Klement, 2007). It seems likely that sanctions that are long lasting are also counterproductive and may increase crime rates if the stigmatizing of offenders makes it more difficult for them to go straight, for example, because criminal records need to be declared to potential employers. They could also encourage people to join with other stigmatized individuals who may be willing to ignore the offender's record or even to accord status based on it (Blume, 2002). Teichman (2005) accepts that shame-inducing policies probably have limited preventative value, but nevertheless contends that they can still be justified as a means of punishment in the context of sex offenders, both because they inflict suffering on the criminal and may be cheaper than other forms of legal sanction.

FROM SHAME TO POVERTY

Shame, then, is a very powerful self-conscious emotion that sometimes appears to operate by stealth, labelled as embarrassment, discomfort, shyness, or even as guilt. It is found universally across different cultures but tends to be more evident and respected in collectivistic societies than in individualistic ones. Scheff, one of the comparatively few sociologists who have studied self-conscious emotions, contends that the threat of shame binds societies together, for what is at stake is an individual's continued belonging to the family, group, and culture of which hitherto they have been a part. Shaming and its normal consequence, being shamed, constitute the symbolic breaking of the social bond that holds society together, with the degree of damage imposed on the social bond varying according to the nature of the sanction imposed. Ironically, society is held together by the absence of active shaming. When shame is actively employed it can unintentionally trigger the social breakdown that it arguably exists to prevent. Indeed, shame is generally only imposed when society is under threat because social norms have already been transgressed.

The importance of shame to the collective is matched by its destructiveness for the individual and, in collectivist cultures, for the social units of which the offending individual is part. Psychologists demonstrate that people experiencing shame not only feel small and humiliated, they are likely to experience social isolation which is either forced upon them, a form of exile, or chosen by them so as to avoid the possibility of public shaming. They are also prone to feelings of anxiety, depression, suicidal thoughts, and even suicide. In extreme cases, their lives might equally be at risk because of the shame indirectly felt by members of their family or clan.

Shame, then, lies at the interface between the needs of the collective and the wants and freedom of the individual. Deep in prehistory, the human species probably inherited the emotion of shame shared with other primates that served as a device for reconciling the need for communal living with status hierarchies underpinned by physical force and violence. Shame is still one of the tools that society uses to impose its will, usually through the exercise of social power by more privileged individuals and groups. These processes have been illustrated above in the context of business and punishment and will be reconsidered in Chapter 4 with respect to policies to address poverty.

A further irony that has been revealed is that the pain experienced by individuals who are shamed does not generally translate into direct social benefits. While it is probable that people generally behave well, both to avoid shame and because they have internalized the social values policed by shame, there is limited evidence that those who experience shame behave better as a consequence. Rather, the suggestion is that shaming stokes anger and resentment and is counterproductive, driving people from society rather than reintegrating them into it. In part, this is likely to be due to the fact that unlike guilt, which is focussed on specific aspects of behaviour, shame attaches to personal characteristics and conditions that are not easily amenable to immediate or even to long-term change. Moreover, insofar as is currently known, these negative social outcomes apply just as much to collectivist societies as they do to individualistic ones.

The negative personal and social consequences of shaming are not widely appreciated. It is not in the interests of people who are shamed to share their pain with others, especially those who are shaming them since this is likely to trigger further shaming. Those witnessing or fearing social transgression may feel obliged to do something about it and social convention suggests that shame is an appropriate tool. Moreover, its use may well engender a sense of moral rectitude as a consequence of doing one's social duty. Likewise, it is likely to reinforce an individual's social and moral position as being better than the person being shamed, and also instil a sense of pride—positive and very possibly negative. In such circumstances, there is little chance that social beliefs as to the positive nature of shame will be challenged.

The expectation that adults should be able to make their way in the world and to provide and care for their children and families financially and in other ways is a universal and longstanding social norm that underpins economic production and social order. The existence of poverty is frequently taken as evidence that this norm has been transgressed. This is illustrated by the belief that poverty is a consequence of personal failings, a social construction that, as documented in Chapter 1, is prevalent across cultures and has existed throughout history. The argument developed in Chapter 4 is that people in poverty are frequently, if not invariably, subjected to shame as a social sanction for transgressing the norm of self-sufficiency. Moreover, for reasons explained above, the consequences of this shaming are likely to be personally painful and socially destructive. Shame has positive consequences largely to the extent that it remains a threat. Once imposed it has to be acknowledged by the victim, who needs to be in a position to change their circumstances. Given that shame tends to be imposed indiscriminately on all who experience poverty, most cannot acknowledge a justifiable cause for being shamed. Instead, they internalize the shame thereby risking social isolation, loss of agency, anger, depression, and despair that all compound the problems of managing with inadequate resources (see Chapter 8).

4

Poverty, Shame, and Stigma

Having largely segregated the discussion of poverty and shame in Chapters 2 and 3, it is now important to bring the two concepts together. It is, after all, the poverty–shame nexus, with its implications for understanding the nature of poverty and the effectiveness of antipoverty policies, that constitutes the rationale for this and the companion volume *Poverty and Shame: Global Experiences*. Two observations introduced in Chapter 1 provide an important backdrop to the ensuing discussion. Firstly, poverty is inherently political because it poses a threat to the status quo. Secondly, because poverty is often taken to be the result of individual failure, a powerful social construction, it is replete with possibilities for shaming.

Hitherto, shame has featured only intermittently in policy discussions related to poverty. Stigma, on the other hand, has been an abiding concern variously championed as an important policy tool, a factor explaining policy ineffectiveness, and the rationale for preferring one policy regime to another. Taking stigma as the starting point, the argument developed is that shame is integral to poverty, shaping both the experience and its dynamics, and that stigma—shame bureaucratized—is an important conduit in the shaming process. This argument is then encapsulated in a simple model which is to be evidenced in Chapters 5–11 and supported in detail by empirical evidence assembled in *Poverty and Shame: Global Experiences*.

STIGMA

Stigma was originally a sign marking a person as being different, typically inferior. In ancient Greece, slaves and criminals were often branded, their skin cut or burned. In ancient Rome, convicted prostitutes were forced to wear a *toga muliebris* as a badge of shame (McGinn, 1998). In Genesis, Chapter 4, Cain is cursed with a mark for killing his brother. In Medieval Europe, Jews were, at varying times and in various places, required to wear particular forms of clothing or yellow patches which much later, under Nazi occupation,

became a six pointed yellow star (Roth, 2003). Women who had consorted
with German troops during World War II sometimes had their heads forcibly
shaved as a mark of betrayal and shame (Simonsen and Ericsson, 2005).

It is already clear that shame and stigma are intricately connected to the
point whereby they can be treated as being almost synonymous. Equally, they
are rarely juxtaposed or differentiated. Scheff and Retzinger (2000) note that
in the most influential sociological treatise yet written on stigma, Goffman
(1963), only mentions shame twice in passing whereas, in their view, shame
was 'a central subject' of the book. Conversely, Tangney and Dearing's (2003)
book *Shame and Guilt* includes a single mention of stigma in relation to
mental illness. Stuenkel and Wong (2012, p. 52) appear to imply that use of
the term stigma has actually superseded shame when they write that 'in the
past, the words shame and guilt were used to describe a stigma—a perceived
difference between a behaviour or an attribute or an ideal standard'.

Goffman (1963, p. 14) links stigma to social identity, the mix of roles,
attributes, and sense of self that defines someone as a person. Stigma is
something that disqualifies someone from full social acceptance as a person:
'abominations of the body', 'blemishes of individual character', and 'the tribal
stigma of race, nation and religion' to adopt Goffman's rather dated language.
The stigma can be self-evident and the person 'discredited', or concealed
and the person 'discreditable'—permanently at risk of being found out. Either
way, 'by definition . . . the person with a stigma is not quite human' (Goffman,
1963, p. 15).

For Goffman stigma is relational, it is inherently social. A stigmatized
individual is not accepted fully into society in that those with whom they
have dealings do not accord them the respect that they would otherwise
expect, and that any person (including the person stigmatized) would normally, anticipate. The rationale for stigmatizing someone, a judgement that
the person does not live up to a social ideal, may or may not be well-informed.
Indeed, people who are stigmatized are often at the receiving end of prejudice,
discrimination, and indiscriminate labelling. To the extent that the person
recognizes, 'if only for a few moments', that they do fall short of some societal
ideal then 'shame becomes a central possibility' (Goffman, 1963, p. 18).

Writing later, social psychologists such as Dovidio et al. (2000) also recognize the relational imperative of stigma, distinguishing between the people
stigmatizing and those who are stigmatized, between personal and group-
based identities as bases for stigma, and between motivations and reactions.
People stigmatizing, 'stigmatizers', are considered to differentiate others primarily on the basis of group or category membership, paying relatively little
attention to the individual attributes of the persons being stigmatized (Brewer,
1988). The process of differentiation and categorization is, of course, inherent
in the way that people organize knowledge and define the world (Link and
Phelan, 2001). The crucial point is that individuals and societies categorize

according to some characteristics and not others: skin colour often, eye colour more rarely. Moreover, once categorized other attributes are presumed, almost irrespective of the truth, to apply to all people in the group; the process of stereotyping. Often those other attributes are deemed to be very largely negative and are frequently used to distinguish 'them', the categorized other, from 'us'. This is certainly true in stigmatizing relationships where, because of power differentials, stigmatizers are able to impose a loss of status on their targets that is frequently achieved or exacerbated through discriminatory practices.

Whether and how those who are stigmatized, 'victims', respond in terms of behaviour, affect, and cognition will partly depend on whether the stigma attaches predominantly to the group (the norm) or to the person. Where groups rather than persons are stigmatized, group members have less agency at their disposal; they are tarnished with the brush of others. Moreover, where a group is stigmatized members that prioritize their social identity relative to their personal one are most likely to experience anger and probably pressure to repress it. They may pretend to ignore the stigma (passing). They may try to minimize its effect (covering). They may even seek to challenge it. A common strategy is to retreat socially so as to avoid it and to conceal both the pain and the associated anger (Stuenkel and Wong, 2012). What they cannot easily resist are the results of active discrimination that occurs at structural, individual, and intrapersonal levels (Link and Phelan, 2001).

While much of the sociological and psychological literature on stigma focusses on one person acting in stigmatizing and discriminatory ways towards another, the reasons that they do so, and can do so, effectively lie outside the individual and are structural or systemic by nature (Fiske, 1998). People are 'expected' to behave in discriminatory ways against certain groups according to the norms of the institution or society at large, expectations reinforced by the abusive labelling of the other: 'Nigger', 'Cripple', 'Slacker', 'Scrounger', or 'Benefit Bum'. Structures systematically exclude opportunities for equal engagement that might challenge stereotypes or enable positive interaction while reinforcing, through circumscribed access, inequality, status loss, and negative mythologizing. Moreover, the negative views of the powerful stigmatizing majority may be internalized by the people targeted, who come to expect that they too will be discriminated against because of their membership of the group. In turn, this may negatively affect their self-confidence and constrain their decisions and behaviour. To the extent that their constrained behaviour can be negatively interpreted by the stigmatizing majority, the divisive, discriminatory processes are reinforced and perpetuated (Link and Phelan, 2001).

The term stigma has attracted opprobrium in some academic and campaigning quarters for its focus on individual-level cognitive processes and its failure to address and indeed to challenge the structural causation (Holley et al., 2012). However, to the extent that stigma differs from shame, the differences lie in the underlying intent and the structural processes that lead to either shame or stigma. The threat of shame aims to ensure that individuals conform to group attitudes and behavioural norms by preventing behaviour that might threaten the group as a whole, and that therefore would need to be controlled by explicit shaming, ostracism, and exclusion of the offending individual. Shame purports to ensure social cohesion and inclusivity and, while explicit shame is best avoided because its effects are unpredictable, the hope would be that shaming could still cause the offender to change, to repent, and to be readmitted into the group. Stigma, in contrast, serves to differentiate between groups, the 'us' and the 'them', the acceptable and the unacceptable, rather than to ensure cohesion between them. Whereas shaming is generally a knowing act designed to bring about positive change, albeit one that is sometimes an instinctive product of social conditioning, the act of stigmatizing is at best unconscious, invariably divisive, and at worst malevolent. Moreover, if Link and Phelan (2001) are to be believed, discrimination is an integral component of stigmatization that necessarily hurts the person affected even when it is without active intent, and may materially add to their loss of status.

Whether the consequences for the person shamed or suffering stigma are so clearly distinguishable is a moot point. In Chapter 3 it was apparent that, regardless of good social intent, the consequences of shame for the shamed individual are usually overwhelmingly negative. To the extent that shame works positively, it is through the threat of shaming rather than its imposition as a sanction. But even the threat of shame can have negative consequences as exampled, in the context of poverty, by the pretence that things are fine and the desire to behave 'as normal', which can lead to indebtedness and to personal financial catastrophe. Moreover, the individual reactions to stigma described above are remarkably similar to those associated with shame: denial, pretence, retreat, anger, and depression.

From the viewpoint of the recipient of shame or the target of stigma, the feelings and processes might seem identical. However, one distinction is the extent to which people targeted both share the values of the group that shames or stigmatizes them. A person who is ashamed certainly feels that they are not what they would want to be, and very often their aspiration would be to be as others in the group. This is not universally true of people who are stigmatized; they may be proud to be black, gay, or a migrant and still be subject to discrimination and stigma. If they are not proud of whatever it is that distinguishes them from the other, then stigma is likely to be experienced as shame.

It is possible that poverty is a special case that unites stigma and shame. Stigmatizing discourse asserts that 'people choose to be poor' (Anok, 2008; Yahoo, 2013). However, while not everybody would admit to the desire to be rich, very few are likely to assert that they want to be poor (leaving aside St Francis and others of similar persuasion). If this is the case (something to be demonstrated in Chapters 7 and 8 and in *Poverty and Shame: Global Experiences*), then a person stigmatized for being poor is likely to experience stigma as shame; they might not want to be rich but they certainly do not want to be poor.

Moreover, in structural terms, shaming imposed through the power of the state is likely to feel indistinguishable from stigma. As explained in Chapter 1, attempts to reduce or eliminate poverty are generally accompanied by the rationalistic desire to do so at minimum cost while not destroying incentives to work or generally to do the right thing. The focus on incentives is premised on negative beliefs about human behaviour, namely that people are naturally lazy or at least prefer leisure to work, and that they would generally choose to rely on others rather than to look after themselves. While parents might shame recalcitrant offspring into helping around the house or finding a job, shame in the hands of the state risks rapidly being transformed into stigma. The population is repeatedly divided into bureaucratically defined, more or less arbitrary, groups of 'them' and 'us': poor and non-poor, indolent and worker, claimant and taxpayer to which higher or lower status is attached or, indeed, deliberately accorded as part of the shaming process. The status differentials are reinforced by characteristics that are either intentionally or inadvertently ascribed to the groups. For example, 'the poor' are considered to be at best inadequate and at worst feckless, lazy, and criminal. In contrast, those who are not poor are deemed to be industrious and resourceful. Shame, as noted in Chapter 1, when used by government to deter illicit applications or to distinguish deserving from undeserving claims, can very easily become generalized as stigma applied in an undifferentiated way to all people in poverty and especially to those receiving welfare benefits. This construction of stigma then provides a rationale that can underpin institutional discrimination manifest, for example, in the imposition of arduous conditions, expectations, and duties on people in receipt of benefits that would not be applied to people in otherwise comparable situations.

To encapsulate the argument so far, shaming that is backed by the power of the state becomes stigmatization. People in poverty are stigmatized in political discourse by being considered a problem while policies that are put in place specifically to address poverty are likely to be stigmatizing. People in poverty are liable to feel ashamed of their circumstances, including the receipt of stigmatizing welfare benefits, and may well be discriminated against as a result of receiving benefits and during the process of claiming them.

POVERTY, STIGMA, AND POLICY

Although Lister (2004) has written about stigma attaching to poverty per se, most attention has focussed on that associated with claiming welfare benefits and, more specifically, with means-tested benefits where the eligibility is established on the basis of financial need. Correspondingly, most research has been undertaken in liberal regimes where means-tested benefits are most common (Baumberg et al., 2012; Manchester and Mumford, 2012; Moffitt, 1983; Page, 1984; Pinker, 1971; Spicker, 1984)

This policy related literature reflects some of the characterizations and distinctions introduced in this chapter, such as the relational or recursive nature of stigma and the difference between 'personal' or 'felt' stigma experienced by the targeted individual and 'social' stigma, the process of stigmatizing by others (Baumberg et al., 2012; Walker 2005). It also adds 'institutional' stigma: that arising from the process of claiming benefits, both as the description of a process and as a policy intention. All three are, of course, closely interrelated.

Personal Stigma

In the context of policy, Baumberg et al. (2012, p. 6) define personal stigma as 'a person's own feeling that claiming benefits is shameful', the implication being that the claimant accepts that the act of receiving benefit is something disreputable. Similarly, Walker (2005, p. 197) characterizes this form of stigma as 'a sense of personal failure', shame arising from a person's belief that receipt of benefits is something that should be avoided and that they have transgressed social norms in receiving them. He also notes that the sense of shame can be heighted by lack of privacy and by probing questioning by officials, and so is affected by manifestations of institutional shaming.

Why receipt of benefits should be seen as unacceptable is an open question. Both Spicker (1984) and Stuber and Schlesinger (2006) suggest that this has to do with a lack of reciprocity between the recipient and the taxpayer as giver, and both contrast benefit receipt with the giving of gifts. While gifts may be freely given, the giver often expects a gift in return and the recipient may be embarrassed if they do not reciprocate. Moreover, as is demonstrated in Chapter 7, people may feel ashamed if they cannot afford to reciprocate. This sense of shame is likely to be reinforced by social sanctions, including loss of status, and conceivably by the ending of a relationship. Charity is giving with the explicit expectation that nothing, except gratitude, is required from the recipient in return. (An exception, noted in Chapter 1, is that charitable givers of a religious persuasion may expect their reward in the afterlife.) Charity thereby demeans the recipient while serving to enhance the status of the giver. Moreover, as Simmel (1950, p. 393) notes, the requirement for gratitude has 'a taste of bondage' about it since it is so difficult to redeem. In effect, charity (to cite Frenkel-Brunswick, 1950, p. 307) 'often has the function of keeping the underprivileged in their place, kindness acting in effect as a humiliating factor'. If benefits are seen as charity, as an unreciprocated gift, then they are likely to be similarly stigmatizing.

Research on the take-up of welfare benefits—the proportion of persons eligible for benefits that claims and receives them—is generally consistent with the existence of stigma. It indicates that often between 20 per cent and 60 per cent of people fail to take up benefits to which they are entitled, reducing the effectiveness of schemes in tackling poverty (Hernanz et al., 2004). Stigma is, of course, not the only reason for the low take-up of welfare benefits and is difficult to isolate from other factors. However, the evidence, limited but wide-ranging in its coverage of industrialized countries, indicates that take-up rates are typically higher for insurance benefits than for means-tested ones. This has been interpreted as indicating that benefits based on an exchange relationship, benefits in return for a lifetime of contributions, are less stigmatizing than ones for which eligibility is determined by financial need (Oorschot, 1991, 1998). The latter may smack of charity, impart shame associated with economic failure, or both (Corden, 1995). It could also be that institutions promote means-tested benefits less effectively, either because it is technically difficult to do so or because they are assigned lower priority; a form of institutional stigma (Walker, 1978; Robles, 2013).

While stigma needs to be negotiated in order to claim welfare benefits, it does not mean that recipients are necessarily immune (Corden, 1995). Studies dating back over sixty years have found in both Britain and the US 'the mere process of applying for, or receiving, . . . benefits can induce feelings of stigma' (Page, 1984, p. 54). 'It's the shame, the stigma of it' as one UK benefit recipient said of means-tested Supplementary Benefit in 1978 (Richardson and Naidoo, 1978, p. 27), a view known to be echoed today in countries as diverse as Uganda, Pakistan, India, South Korea, and Norway and even among a minority of recipients of the respected Chinese Dibao system (Chase and Bantebya-Kyomuhendo, 2014; Gubrium et al., 2013; Zhou, 2012). In addition to the charity-like nature of many welfare benefits, Spicker concludes that felt stigma is exacerbated by degrading treatment, loss of rights, and the targeting of assistance on poverty thereby labelling recipients as being poor. 'The poor person', Simmel (1908, p. 140) notes, 'sociologically speaking, is the individual who receives assistance because of the lack of means'. Benefit receipt is, therefore, the stigmatizing badge of poverty.

Social Stigma

In the same way that feeling ashamed is partly a product of being shamed, so felt stigma is a response to the social stigma conveyed by others. Social stigma is a process entailing attitudes, thoughts, and actions on the part of the majority group, and the perceptions and responses to these by the people stigmatized, which both frame their felt stigma and may also serve to fuel further stigmatizing. However, methods used by social scientists to measure social stigma sometimes appear to transform it inadvertently into a state: the state of public opinion, or even what survey respondents report other people think about the stigmatized group (Baumberg et al., 2012).

In the context of poverty and welfare receipt, social stigma is frequently underpinned by attitudes towards need, deservingness, and personal responsibility that are coupled with other traits that have come to be perceived as negative in many societies (Loseke and Kusenbach, 2007; Oorschot 2000, 2006). As elucidated in Chapters 1 and 2, poverty is inherently challenging to people who are not poor since the concept carries with it a moral imperative to respond to people in need. While poverty may be dismissed as an inevitability about which nothing can be done ('The poor you will always have with you', Matthew 26:11), the history of charity, Zakat, and welfare benefits speak to the power of poverty's moral obligation. Yet people typically do not find it easy to part with their money, require justifiable reasons for doing so, and are keen to find ways to limit and ration their spending. The evidence from across Europe is that the public, while moved by severe and genuine need, are intolerant of those people whose poverty might be held to be avoidable (Oorschot 2000, 2006). They are quick to generalize and readily view most poverty as being self-inflicted, accepting the stereotype of the 'poor person' as being either a rogue or an inadequate. As evidenced in Chapter 9, and in Chase and Bantebya-Kyomuhendo (2014), people are willing to debate whether poverty is caused by structural or personal failings but tend to prioritize the latter; in private, this is even so in countries such as China and Norway where public discourse tends to be most inclusive and least discriminatory.

In European countries and the United States, research suggests that the public is generally most sympathetic towards people who can be seen to have contributed to society in the past such as elderly persons and those who have become sick (Larsen and Dejgaard, 2012; Lind, 2007; Walker, 2008). This, of course, echoes the higher take-up rate of contributory benefits, reflecting the fact that shame and personal and social stigma are products of shared values and attitudes. Oorschot (2006) interprets these attitudes as being a reflection of the aforementioned importance of reciprocity, but in this case the preparedness to give is conditional on evidence of prior commitment rather than the prospect of future reciprocity. The public are less supportive of unemployed claimants (despite most having a history of employment and contributions) and of lone mothers (especially in the United States and Britain). For persons who are unemployed and lone mothers, lack of evidence of reciprocity is compounded by moral opprobrium: unemployment taken as 'evidence' of indolence; out-of-wedlock pregnancy as indicative of irresponsibility if not immorality.

Stigma attaches to those benefit recipients who are perceived not to be deserving in terms of the severity and cause of their need. But judgements also appear to be influenced by factors unrelated to need. Identity, in particular, is important. 'Welfare' in the United States has traditionally been heavily stigmatized because it is widely identified with receipt by African Americans who, in turn, have been stigmatized as being more irresponsible and lazy than white Americans (Gilens, 1999; Neubeck and Casenave, 2001). Correspondingly, in Europe migrants have consistently been rated among the least deserving groups with certain subgroups, including Roma, being particularly heavily stigmatized (Oorschot, 2006). In China, migrants from rural areas and former prisoners receive little sympathy as recipients of Dibao social assistance, while on the Indian subcontinent caste provides a finely tuned basis for discrimination in access to, and support for, public provision (Pellissery, 2009; Yan, 2014c). It seems that people identify with the persons most like themselves and are prepared to look favourably upon them even to the point of supporting spending public money. Research in the Nordic countries, where poverty rates are particularly low, suggests that the fact of being poor can itself distance a person in the mind of the public, reinforcing the notion that persons in poverty differ from the majority, strengthening notions of 'us' and 'them', and reducing support for social assistance relative to other public services (Gubrium and Lødemel, 2014c; Larsen, 2008). It may also be that those who do identify with benefit recipients are people who perceive themselves as potentially needing to claim benefits so that identification is tied directly to self-interest.

To the extent that the general public do not identify with benefit recipients, the repeated pattern is one of stereotyping and prejudice. All recipients tend to be classified as 'wasters', 'scroungers', 'workshy', and 'lazy' or, more pejoratively, as 'stupid' or 'parasites' or worse (Baumberg et al., 2012). They are ascribed the perceived characteristics of other stigmatized groups such as criminals, ethnic minorities, and people who are mentally ill. Beliefs about the negative causality of poverty are compounded and benefits themselves imbued with the power to corrupt. In Britain and the US, in particular, they have been blamed for the breakdown of families and the community, the supposed growth of an 'underclass' and a 'culture of poverty', increases in teenage births and promiscuity, drug abuse, worklessness, and the birth of 'a something for nothing' society (Larsen, 2008; Larsen and Dejgaard, 2012). Across Europe, the degree of negativity towards benefit recipients varies but tends to be directed mostly towards those in receipt of residual, means-tested, social security schemes. Negativity has tended to increase over time and has seemingly not lessened in the context of the global recession of 2008 and the subsequent era of austerity (Diamond and Lodge, 2013; Svallfors, 2012; Taylor-Gooby, 2013).

The social stigmatization of benefits does not occur in isolation; it reflects and fuels institutional stigma and is frequently mediated by public debate conducted in the mass media, and more recently through social media (Baumberg et al.,

2012). Individuals who are not poor or in receipt of benefits both reproduce and help to shape social stigma in their discourse with peers and in their (often rare) direct encounters with claimants and people in poverty. People having authoritarian personalities are more prone to stigmatize; those who are less successful may direct their resentments against others; persons occupying low-status positions may seek to build self-esteem by disparaging those perceived to be of even lower status; past experience of benefit receipt may foster empathy and solidarity or be used to construct a self-justifying and protective narrative that blame others for remaining poor (Alicke and Sedikides, 2009; Baumberg et al., 2012; Bos and Stapel, 2009; Chase and Walker, 2013; Hoggett et al., 2013). How social stigma is felt personally by benefit recipients and people in poverty depends in part on whether they absorb or reject the majority critique, of which more in Chapters 7 and 8.

Institutional Stigma

Institutional stigma is evidenced in the framing, structure, and/or delivery of benefits. It can be an intentional component of policy or an inadvertent element that may or may not reflect underlying social norms or political ideology. In democratic, pluralistic societies it is likely both to mirror and simultaneously influence social stigma while directly shaping the stigma experienced by benefit recipients.

Britain offers perhaps the most longstanding example of institutional stigmatization in the framing of antipoverty programmes, but it is, to borrow a biological term, a 'type specimen' that best exemplifies the process rather than being an exception. Chapter 1 made reference to the seventeenth-century distinctions between 'the impotent poor' and 'the able-bodied poor' who were considered to be deserving and 'rogues and idlers' who were to be made to work in 'Houses of Correction'. Stigma was to a large degree intentional, a deterrent to those that might consider abusing the perceived generosity of the Poor Law Guardians, although in time the stigma of pauperism came to contaminate all those who approached the state in need (Himmelfarb, 1984).

Similar distinctions between deserving and undeserving remain evident in the twenty-first century as illustrated by an important campaign speech given in 2010 by David Cameron, the current Conservative Party Prime Minister. In the speech, entitled 'A New Welfare Contract', he asserted that 'people who are able to work, and people who choose not to work, you cannot go on claiming welfare like you are now'. The previous Labour government had 'modernized' the language of deserving and undeserving, juxtaposing the right to receive benefit against responsibilities. Responsibilities translated into increased work-related conditionality, the modern equivalent of 'Houses of Correction', but also increasingly embraced people with disabilities who would have been considered deserving in the seventeenth century (Walker and Chase 2013). The Labour government also made explicit the idea that 'welfare benefits' were both a problem, in that their expense inhibited economic growth, and indeed the problem: 'the enemy within' which 'erodes the wider moral order of society' in creating dependency and worklessness (Field, 1997, p. 20). Benefit recipients were therefore doubly stigmatized: they cost their fellow citizens money while also being morally corrosive.

Although implemented by a coalition government that did not include the Labour Party, major welfare reforms of 2013 sought to address both supposedly problematic aspects of benefit receipt. This political consensus was initially shaped by focus groups conducted by the Labour Party when in opposition in the 1990s. These revealed antipathy towards benefit recipients that emboldened Labour, in search of political advantage, to juxtapose spending on welfare against that on education and health (Mattinson, 2010). Subsequent discourse, elaborated by the media, further confounded the social problem of poverty with political concern about spending on welfare and further confused the public as to what was cause and what was effect. In recent focus groups, members of the electorate drew on the negative framing and language used by politicians that was, in turn, seeded by focus groups conducted two decades earlier (Baumberg et al., 2012; Chase and Walker, 2014c; Walker and Chase, 2013). People receiving benefits describe what it is like to be on the receiving end of such stigmatizing discourse (Chase and Walker, 2013):

> there's a stigma isn't there, there's a stigma attached to it. You know . . . living on a council estate, being on benefits, ra, ra, ra . . . it's like the image portrayed in the media and stuff—you're this kind of ASBO-hoodie. (Mike)

> it comes across in theory as scroungers on the dole, or on the DLA, you know . . . 'I can't get enough money on the dole so I'll go on the sick' . . . Again it's a stigma, it makes you feel like scrounging . . . I'm not scrounging . . . I'm asking for what I put into the system. (Trevor)

The belief that spending on welfare is excessive is a perspective that is of course not limited to Britain. It is a view inherent in the so-called Washington consensus that fuelled support for the structural readjustment policies that sought to reduce state and welfare spending and were imposed on developing countries by the World Bank, IMF, and other 'donors' during the 1980s (Surender, 2013). It also shaped the influential OECD 'Jobs Study' in 1994 (OECD, 1994) that contrasted 'active' (i.e. conditional) employment policies with passive unemployment benefits, and advocated the former over the latter. Even in Germany, where the right to benefit is enshrined in the constitution, the Hartz IV reforms reduced financial support for unemployed people and increased the proportion reliant on means-tested social assistance. In China, at the same time that the Dibao system of social assistance is being expanded to cope with the consequences of economic liberalization, it is promoted as 'a program that costs little', akin to British reforms that are being marketed as 'giving value for tax payers' money' (Pellissery et al., 2013).

In other settings, the framing of welfare provision may engender feelings of neglect. In affluent social democratic countries where poverty is rare, discourse can be exclusionary, intensifying the sense of frustration and isolation felt by the small numbers needing to apply for social assistance. In India and Pakistan, the enormous social distance between the governing elite and the many millions in poverty makes access to state support seem almost random or brokered by nepotism and patronage that can lend further stigma to receiving benefits intended 'only for the poor'. Such provision, seen to be 'for the poor', is often as a direct consequence poor in quality and becomes the badge of poverty, a publicly witnessed confession of failure. This may be intentional. In Korea, governments resisted the introduction of generous social assistance for fear that it would weaken the collective impetus for economic development. In Germany, insurance benefits have until very recently been clearly differentiated from social assistance to reward sustained employment. In the US, demands to universalize healthcare and even 'Obamacare' (the 2010 Affordable Care Act) were resisted by the private health insurance industry keen to ensure that a differential quality of service was retained between public and private care that people are prepared to pay for. Sometimes, differential quality is simply a reflection of the lack of political and consumer voice of welfare recipients and people in poverty.

The stigma of antipoverty provision is often exacerbated by its structure. Contributory provision is frequently juxtaposed against means-tested social assistance: the former serving the majority or, in the developing world, solely the elite, the military, and civil servants; the latter being for 'the poor'. Whereas contributory and rights-based provision can be seen as a celebration of citizenship and the exercise of rights, means-tested provision may smack of charity. Social assistance is also often based on discretionary decisions that may appear arbitrary to the recipient, and hence be disempowering. Social assistance recipients across diverse countries talk about being treated as numbers, feeling dehumanized, being in a vacuum, needing to negotiate endless checks and limitless forms, and battling against a system that seems to be against them (Chase and Bantebya-Kyomuhendo, 2014; Narayan et al., 2000a, 2000b). Conditional cash transfers, which have been recently introduced in a number of developing countries and in parts of the US and Europe, require recipients and/or their families to participate in education and health prevention activities in order to receive income support. Such policies run the additional risk of conveying to benefit recipients and the general public that people on low incomes need, on account of personal inadequacy or wilfulness, to be forced to act in their own self-interest or the interests of their children, whereas the lack of engagement might equally be attributable to the lack of resources necessary to participate in education or health.

The pitching of eligibility and the structuring of means testing and access can also create stigma and be necessarily discriminatory. In China, Dibao is targeted at people who are very poor and, until very recently, has only been available in urban areas (ILO, 2013). In Mexico, *Oportunidades* is differentially targeted in rural and urban regions: in the former, entire communities are deemed eligible or ineligible irrespective of the circumstances of particular residents, while in urban areas a household means-test can mean that neighbours differ in their individual entitlement (Robles, 2013). In Pakistan, modelling of state schemes on Zakat and Sharia law means that non-Muslim groups are excluded, while women beneficiaries are often restricted in their ability to pursue claims without the active support of male relatives (Choudhry, 2013). In South Korea, a family means-test entails applicants demonstrating to officials that their kin are either unprepared or unable to support them financially, while employment search requirements mean that they need to document that employers have refused to recruit them and to give the reasons why (Jo and Walker, 2013). In Norway, a trajectory of increasing support towards employment creates a status hierarchy among benefit recipients that is humiliating to those towards the bottom (Gubrium and Lødemel, 2014c). In Britain, the move to web-based application, 'digital by default', risks further stigmatizing those without Internet access or unable to use it.

Delivery, too, can create stigmatizing settings and discourse. In Uganda, under-resourcing of state primary education has made it the option of no choice, a symbol of parental failure denying children educational success (Bantebya-Kyomuhendo and Mwiine, 2013). Under-resourcing can lead to lack of privacy and poor facilities and to confrontation between overstretched staff and stressed beneficiaries. In such circumstances, and more generally, welfare recipients may be stigmatized, deliberately or inadvertently, through the actions and language of staff (Lipsky, 1980). Staff typically distinguish deserving from undeserving, good from bad, allocating more time to the former than the latter which may be further subdivided into groups that might be derogatorily labelled, in Britain, 'wasters', 'unemployables', 'nutters', or those deemed to be 'at it' (i.e. committing fraud) (Wright, 2003). Claimants in countries as different as Norway and the UK, China and South Korea, report being looked down on by staff, being presumed lazy and dependent, and considered 'guilty' without the need for evidence (Finn et al., 2008; Gubrium et al., 2013). Similarly, the *Voices of the Poor* study that drew on the experiences of 40,000 people in 23 countries (Narayan et al., 2000a, 2000b) reveals that men, women, and young people in Kenya said that they were 'treated worse than dogs' at health clinics; in Bangladesh, dishonest officials reportedly discriminated against applicants who could not afford to offer bribes; in the Ukraine, unemployed respondents believed that humiliation experienced at the unemployment office was deliberately 'designed to chase the unemployed away', while in Russia 'even the most needy were humiliated to take poor-quality goods provided by the welfare office'.

Uses and Consequences of Stigma

While stigmatizing discourse and processes can emanate from the framing, structure, and delivery of policy, this is not to say that all public policies stigmatize recipients. Welfare provision and welfare regimes based around principles of universality, social cohesion, and social solidarity are frequently juxtaposed against targeted, means-tested provision with claims, empirically legitimated, that the former do not result in stigmatization (Hernanz et al., 2004). However, policies that address poverty or which are directed at people who are poor rarely escape being stigmatizing. This may arise simply through association. Provision may be stigmatized because it is for, or used by, people who are poor. This simple process may in turn be exaggerated by a self-perpetuating dynamic arising from the fact that stigmatized provision can further stigmatize users which may, in turn, increase the stigma associated with provision. Stigma can also occur through omission, as when residual policies are neglected because they do not serve the social mainstream and lack powerful interest groups to promote or defend them. If so, the same dynamic of stigma through association may set in. Finally, stigma may arise inadvertently though ignorance, neglect, or carelessness in the policy design process. Sometimes this occurs when dignity of treatment is overlooked as a result of attempts to direct resources quickly or cheaply to persons in need (Oorschot, 1998; Walker, 2005).

Often, though, stigma is more or less deliberate, used in an analogous way to that suggested by the proponents of employing shame to modify behaviour as reviewed in Chapter 3. Murray (2009, p. 1) recites the logic:

> Stigma is the only way that a free society can be generous . . . Stigma does three things. First, . . . children are taught that accepting charity is a disgrace, they also tend to be taught the kinds of things they should and shouldn't do to avoid that disgrace. . . . Second, stigma encourages the right kind of self-selection . . . people ask whether the help is really that essential. . . . Third, stigma discourages dependence—it induces people to do everything they can to get out of the situation that put them in need of help.

The difference from shaming evident in this quotation is the divisive, non-negotiable nature of stigma: right versus wrong; independent versus dependent; charity, a disgrace. Murray (2009, p. 2), a writer on the American political right, goes on to contrast the merits of stigma ('indispensable') with what he considers the limitations of 'the European model' based on 'a right to social assistance', namely welfare dependency.

While actual policies are generally less crisp and clinical in their use of stigma than Murray's rhetoric would suggest, at an operational level stigma will suppress demand and may possibly deter some elicit claims. At a political level, it may achieve a degree of reconciliation between left and right as was the case with the passage of the Personal Responsibility and Work Opportunities Reconciliation Act (PRWORA) in the United States, maintaining some support for people in poverty but not too much (Wiseman, 2003). At an ideological level, it can, by defining and juxtaposing success and failure as products of individual morality and economic effort, legitimate many variants of capitalistic endeavour: the American Dream; China's post-liberalization mantra of letting 'some get rich first'; South Korea's developmental doctrine of 'growth first'; Norwegian desires that generous state spending should not support divisive antisocial lifestyles; and even the perpetuation of clientelism and nepotism underpinning state support in India or Pakistan. In Britain, the 'type specimen', stigma is operative at all three levels: variably low take-up of benefits; shared policy discourse from which politicians profit electorally by scapegoating benefit 'scroungers'; and a predominant focus on avoiding disincentives that might conceivably deter people from working.

The ubiquitous association of stigma with policies that address poverty suggests that it must be socially beneficial. Whether a cost–benefit analysis—yet to be undertaken—would confirm such a conclusion is far from certain. For stigmatizers, social stigma can serve as a narrative of self-justification that maintains and, in operation, reinforces the pattern of inequality which defines the status quo—'we have earned our privileged place in society'—while weakening the moral imperative to assist those who are less fortunate since 'they have only themselves to blame'. To the extent that stigmatizers constitute the majority, democratic politicians stand to gain electorally by pandering to the discriminatory views of the stigmatizers, with the result that the *modi operandi* of institutions are likely to reflect popular negative attitudes towards both welfare benefits and the people that rely on them.

However, such sectional benefits of stigma are likely to be offset by the negative consequences among stigma's targets victims that can have profound societal implications. To the extent that people experience stigma as shame, the most likely outcome since they are apt to covet economic success as much as anyone, the psychic pain that they feel is likely to be severe. Furthermore, the sense of shame is likely also to be prolonged because most people in poverty will generally already be doing as much as they can to escape from poverty. Moreover, generally lacking the social esteem and moral support needed to be brazen in the face of their detractors, the best that most can do in response to stigma is to bear the shame as an additional consequence of poverty, perhaps putting up the pretence that everything is fine in the knowledge that it is not. Other strategies, such as retreating into social isolation so as to avoid the pain associated with exposure or internalizing the shame as anger, depression, and despair, tend to lessen still further people's chances of escaping from poverty.

An alternative positive response, which, as is reported in Chapter 6, features as a repeated theme in world literature, is for the people targeted by stigma to reject the analysis and convert the shame into the fuel of protest. Goffman (1963) writes of some groups turning the stigma into a badge of pride with Gay Pride, 'Black is beautiful', and even the Black Panthers serving as examples. Historical examples include trade unions and the vanguard working class, whose collective actions are often credited with triggering the birth of the traditional Western welfare state. Dalits, in India, have campaigned around the word 'Humiliation', transforming it from the experience of abuse into a rallying cry for action. Community development programmes globally seek to empower people to work collectively to promote their joint interests, and organizations such as ATD Fourth World exist explicitly to give direct voice to 'activists' living in extreme poverty by taking them into the decision making arenas of the world. Important though these counterexamples are, they illustrate the need for some in the stigmatized group to have secured the degree of economic success and political influence necessary to change public attitudes and policy agendas.

Economic success and political influence are just what individuals in poverty generally lack. Moreover, stigma brings with it discrimination and rejection. People in poverty are deemed by the majority to live on 'the wrong side of the track'. Avoided socially because they cannot afford to reciprocate, to stand a round of drinks, or to buy a suitable wedding present; employers fail to hire them, potential in-laws rebuff them, landlords refuse to house them, banks will not to deal with them, moneylenders abuse them, officials lecture and coerce them, bailiffs evict them, and politicians chastise them. While the distinctions are not always as clear cut as this litany of social exclusions might suggest, stigma divides, creating a social fault line between 'the poor' and 'the non-poor', the benefit recipient and the taxpayer, that shapes experience and constrains opportunity. Indeed, Waxman's (1977) recognition of stigma allows him to reinterpret and partially to rehabilitate Oscar Lewis's account of a culture of poverty. Lewis (1968) had argued that people in poverty, 'the slum', choose to live by different rules framed by different social norms. Waxman argues that to the extent that this is true, it is because the stigma experienced by slum residents condemns them to 'getting by' rather than 'getting on'. He notes, too, that the 'us and them' discourse adopted by cultural theorists like Lewis itself adds to the stigma of poverty and welfare receipt. More prosaically, activation policies designed to provide counselling and support on both sides of the employment divide have sometimes proved impossible to implement because of recipients' insistence on hiding their status as welfare recipients for fear that employers and fellow workers would discriminate against them (Walker and Kellard, 2001).

In sum, governments have over many centuries sought to employ stigma as a means of rationing benefits and encouraging personal independence, doing so for reasons of ideology, opportunistic reactions to discriminatory public opinion, or pragmatic operational concerns. Despite this, there is little reason to suspect that stigma has done much to enhance the effectiveness of policies designed to address poverty. Rather, it has probably increased the misery and possibly the persistence of poverty by adding discrimination to the debilitating effects of the shame that people often or invariably feel as a consequence of their poverty.

MODELLING THE POVERTY–SHAME NEXUS

The literature reviewed in this and Chapters 1–3 leads inexorably to Amartya Sen's assertion (1983, p. 159) that shame lies at the 'irreducible absolutist core'. It is an idea that also occurred to Adam Smith, writing in the eighteenth century, and is exemplified in the disgust expressed by Seneca and the Roman elite towards people living in poverty during pre-Christian times. Shame is posited by Sen to be inherent in poverty. Not only is poverty itself demonstrable evidence of personal failure, it also prevents a person from being able to participate in society in a manor appropriate to prevailing norms and customs. People in poverty lack the resources necessary to reciprocate, to support wives and husbands, to bring up children or even, adopting the language of stigma, to be fully human. Moreover, should they fail to appreciate the degree of their inadequacy and the depth of their degradation, society takes it upon itself to shame them into changing their ways or, with similar intent, to stigmatize them, thereby reinforcing social divisions of 'us' and 'them' and often actively discriminating against the them, 'the poor'.

Figure 4.1 captures these and other ideas discussed in a simple graphical model. It suggests, following Sen, that shame is a universal concomitant of poverty. People in poverty generally feel ashamed at having failed to live up to society's expectations that, for the most part, they have internalized as their own. They are also shamed by those around them, sometimes deliberately by way of reproach and, at other times, inadvertently as when people act out of pity or ignore poverty and those who experience it. They similarly suffer stigma, bureaucratized shame manifest in the framing, structures, and implementation of policy that is often reinforced by the discriminatory actions of others: neighbours, employers, and financial institutions.

Moving beyond Sen and connecting with psychosocial theorizing, the evidence reviewed in Chapter 3 points to shame lowering a person's sense of self-worth that, in turn, limits their agency and overall self-efficacy. This process may be particularly acute if the shame that they experience is a

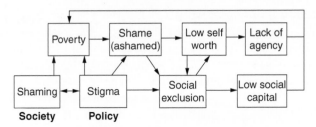

Fig. 4.1. Model of the poverty–shame nexus

response to indiscriminate shaming or stigma that demands of them actions that they have already taken or that seem unfeasible given their circumstances. Individuals' attempts to manage shame may be counterproductive: anger; depression and despair; overindebtedness; or even, on occasion, to sustain an income, criminal behaviour. A perhaps more common response is to choose social isolation and to avoid associated social obligations, a strategy that is sometimes enforced by others as social exclusion. This not only further lowers self-esteem but also reduces social capital that might have been called upon in times of crisis or exploited to generate economic opportunities. Low self-esteem and limited social capital potentially introduce the negative feedback loop shown in Figure 4.1, through which shame serves to perpetuate poverty by reducing human agency.

While undoubtedly oversimplified, the model encapsulates many insights derived from the various literatures that claim the concepts of shame and stigma as their own. The potential contribution is to show how they add to understanding poverty both as a real world experience and as a policy problem. The remainder of this volume seeks to explore the utility of this model as a lens through which to interpret the poverty experienced in very different economic and cultural settings.

5

Cultural Conceptions
of Poverty and Shame[1]

So far the argument has been global and largely undifferentiated, suggesting that shame is a universal concomitant of poverty. Fear of shame and social rejection encourages individuals to adhere to social norms. These norms naturally tend to prioritize personal competence and the economic, social, and cultural resources necessary to fulfil the multiple roles that people are expected to play in society. Poverty provides demonstrable evidence of economic failure, typically in the role of worker but with implications for performance in other roles including those of partner, parent, and citizen. Moreover, poverty is often accompanied by social and institutional stigma with the associated discrimination and loss of social status that materially increase the sense of shame associated with being poor. This shame hurts and is part of the experience of poverty. Moreover, shame, being among the most pernicious of the social emotions, creates a sense of powerlessness and lack of agency. For some, this can be all encompassing and totally destructive. For others it may constitute an ever-present threat or obstacle that has to be negotiated. Furthermore, to the extent that policies designed to tackle poverty deliberately or inadvertently stigmatize, adding to the shame experienced by people in poverty, they are likely to prove counterproductive by eroding individuals' agency.

The aim in this chapter is to begin to put these hypotheses to the test. However, the task of establishing whether or not shame is universally associated with poverty is a daunting one. It seems self-evident that conceptions of poverty are likely to vary over time and across cultures. Indeed, the truth of this was demonstrated in Chapters 1 and 2. Equally, while the psychology literature reported in Chapter 3 indicates that shame is found universally across different cultures, there is also evidence that it is accorded greater import and deployed more knowingly in collectivistic societies than in individualistic ones. Nevertheless, the persistence of public discourse that associates poverty with personal failings rather than with

---

[1] This chapter draws heavily on the following publications: Bantebya-Kyomuhendo and Mwiine (2014a); Chase and Walker (2014a); Choudhry (2014a); Gubrium and Lødemel (2014a); Jo (2014a); Pellissery and Mathew (2014a); and Yan (2014a).

structural determinants, combined with the political challenge that poverty invariably presents to the status quo, make poverty pregnant with possibilities for shaming and shame. Furthermore, current research suggests that consequences of imposing, as opposed to threatening, shame may be similarly damaging for individuals in both types of society.

Rather than drawing evidence selectively from around the globe, a strategy that enables one to appear to demonstrate the validity of any premise, the approach adopted is to draw heavily on carefully coordinated fieldwork undertaken in a limited number of contrasting settings: rural Uganda, India, and Pakistan; small-town Norway; urban Britain, Norway, and Pakistan; and metropolitan China and South Korea. The fieldwork and national analyses were undertaken by Grace Bantebya-Kyomuhendo, Elaine Chase, Sohail Choudhry, Erika Gubrium, Ivar Lødemel, JO Yongmie (Nicola), Leemamol Mathew, Amon Mwiine, Sony Pellissery, YAN Ming, and Robert Walker. While the small number of locales cannot adequately reflect the true extent of global diversity, they nevertheless embrace Christian, Islamic, and Confucian traditions; reflect established parliamentary democracies, fragile political systems, and communist regimes; and include places in some of the richest countries in the world as well as some of the poorest. What is lost in coverage is compensated for by in-depth analysis that builds on insights gained from teams of local researchers working closely together to a shared brief, not adopting a standardized format but seeking instead to compare like with like while being sensitive to cultural nuance and difference. To the extent that a poverty–shame nexus is found to exist in each of these very different settings, it adds credence to the idea that shame is everywhere associated with poverty.

Assembling and analysing detailed information from each of these settings was made possible by members of the research team working together to a common template in the places that they know best. Much of the empirical evidence that informs the arguments developed in this book therefore derives from detailed information gathered in the different settings by other members of the research team. This original evidence is assembled in the companion volume, *Poverty and Shame: Global Experiences*, edited by Elaine Chase and Grace Bantebya-Kyomuhendo (2014). Additional material is available in a further volume, edited by Erika Gubrium, Sony Pellissery, and Ivar Lødemel (2013). The relevant sources used are cited in a footnote on the first page of this and subsequent chapters so that the reader can refer to them for further information or, indeed, to check this author's interpretation. Some references quoted in the sources—for example, literature from Norway, Uganda, or China—may be quoted in the text even if these references have not been directly consulted by the author of this book.

Before engaging directly (in Chapter 7) with the shame that people in poverty may experience as a consequence of being poor and the day-to-day processes that shape this experience, there is value in considering the juxtaposition of poverty and shame within the dominant values that frame the beliefs and values of most people and, as such, help to distinguish one culture from another (Abercrombie et al., 1990; Oorschot et al., 2008; Zetterholm, 1994). Characterizing such values is by no means easy. Cultures are neither static nor homogenous, yet are palpable and enduring. Their durability is partly attributable to education, formal and informal, that transfers understanding from one generation to the next, while their tangibility results in part from repetition and cross referencing between different components of culture. The educative process is captured in this volume through the medium of creative writing and, in countries with strong oral traditions such as India, China, and Uganda, through the analysis of proverbs. The samples were constructed with the advice of leading local literary scholars and critics but were seeded by, though not restricted to, the language syllabi used in secondary schools; texts chosen by elites for study in school constitute an explicit component of the formal process of cultural reproduction. Samples of approximately thirty volumes were drawn from each culture, typically spanning the last 150 years or so.[2] This literature was supplemented by analysis of a similar number of films each from India, South Korea,[3] and the UK, countries with thriving indigenous film industries. The films were selected with the assistance of local film studies academics, and each film was subjected to detailed content and targeted semiotic analyses. Films were frequently based on indigenous books, an aspect of cross referencing, and there were sometimes cross-cultural references; for example, Indian films initially produced in Hindi were often remade for Bengali or Malayalam speaking audiences and vice-versa, while occasionally the influence of British film was also apparent (Pellissery and Mathew, 2014a).

The argument is not that these media provide an accurate account of individual experiences of poverty or shame. Nor is it suggested that the media will necessarily be directly accessed by people facing poverty or that they will immediately be affected by them. Rather it recognizes that societies are more than the sum of individual experiences and help to mould such experiences through the practice of culture and the workings of social institutions. Shame is internally felt but externally imposed and poverty is both a social and political construction. Treated as cultural artefacts, literature, film, and oral tradition provide means of accessing dominant values that partially shape social understandings of poverty, its causes and consequences, and help to determine the part that shame plays in the experience and perpetuation of poverty. Therefore, the analysis undertaken and reported in this book is not the product of literary criticism but rather follows in the tradition of social scientists who view literature and film as lenses through which to glimpse social meanings (Coser, 1963; Lewis et al., 2008; Sutherland and Felty, 2010).

---

[2] In Uganda, one novel and three plays were reviewed, the only indigenous literature considered to be relevant.

[3] Only film was analysed in South Korea.

In each case, the texts chosen were read in detail and their content coded hierarchically with subtopics nested within larger topics and relationships between topics determined by colocation, textual reference, and implication. The analysis was contextualized by reference to historical period and the known intentionality of authors as pioneered by adherents of the 'New Historicism' approach (Gallagher and Greenblatt, 2000). Films were similarly analysed but attention was also paid to the visual imagery, notably settings, costume, and gesture, insofar as this appertained to the characterization of poverty and shame, and the relationships between them.

This form of analysis generates all manner of insights, but the aim in the remainder of this chapter is to focus on what it reveals about the social coincidence of poverty and shame. Is it the case, for example, that authors and filmmakers present shame as an inherent part of being poor? Is shame manifested in similar ways or does it differ across cultures, within nations, and according to different authors? Are the consequences of any shame associated with poverty always depicted as negative or are there occasions when the effects are portrayed as beneficial? First, however, it is necessary to ask how poverty is understood and characterized and, briefly, how shame is construed. These topics are considered more fully in the companion volume (Chase and Bantebya-Kyomuhendo, 2014) and at the website <http://povertyshamedignity.spi.ox.ac.uk>.

UNDERSTANDINGS OF SHAME

The value of the arts as a lens through which to understand society is immediately evident in the congruence between the scientific characterization of the physiology of shame presented in Chapter 3 and its portrayal in the creative literature and film reviewed. Both point to marked similarities in the expression of shame across cultures and over time. In British fiction, words such as 'coloured', 'flamed', and 'sullen' are used to capture acute external and internal manifestations of shame that are subtly caught on film through demeanour, mannerisms, and body language that speak of embarrassment, self-deprecation, lack of confidence, withdrawal, anxiety, even depression, and sometimes anger (Chase and Walker, 2014a). In Urdu literature, shame is expressed as feelings of inadequacy, powerlessness, and inferiority with the idea that shame nourishes itself on a flaw in the individual (Choudhry, 2014a). Indian film and short stories reveal exactly the same characteristics of powerlessness, helplessness, and inferiority often indicated on film by the avoidance of eye contact, the head turned down and away, and self-conscious rhythmic hand movements and scratching of the face (Pellissery and Mathew, 2014a). In contemporary Chinese (Mandarin), one finds the concept of shame coupled with others including embarrassment, humiliation, pain, feeling wronged, and guilt, with physical manifestations including flushes, 'head down', 'do not want face', and 'shorter than others' (Yan, 2014a). In Uganda too, the face is a powerful window on the inner pain that is shame (Bantebya-Kyomuhendo and Mwiine, 2014a).

The notion that shame is relational, internally felt but externally imposed, is also reflected in literature and film with subtle differences apparent between more collectivist and more individualistic societies. The Urdu word for shame, *sharam*, has strong positive connotations to do with modesty and innocence and is used in this way in love poems spanning the last two centuries; negative attributes of shame are captured by two other words, *ruswaie* and *sharmindigi*, that respectively translate as 'degradation' and 'abashment'. In Chinese litera-ture, shame is seen as a strong motivator and hence inherently positive; shame, according to the Chinese philosopher Mencius, is the beginning of integrity (Wong and Tsai, 2007). By way of contrast, in the more individualist British and Norwegian societies, writers are prone to dwell on the negative conse-quences of shame: it dehumanizes, damages identity, results in depression and/or anger, and leads to self-destructive behaviour and even suicide. These differences in interpretation, although stark, are not mutually exclusive. Sui-cide associated with shame is a strong theme in Indian cinema and in the older Chinese literature, while the English word 'shameless', used to describe brazen, socially unacceptable behaviour, hints at the potentially positive role of shame in inhibiting undesirable behaviour. Had the protagonist felt shame and not been shameless, everything would have been better.

Interpreted in terms of scientific discourse, writers and film-makers from the collectivist societies reviewed tend to focus on the purposes of shame and those in more individualistic ones on its consequences. When the former deal with consequences, however, they are again negative, at least for those imme-diately affected. In Uganda, individual transgressions bring inevitable shame to family and community. The family is similarly prioritized in Urdu literature and Indian film with the collective honour attaching to it often being of paramount importance. Errant members may be shamed and coerced in the perceived interest of the extended family and in order to avoid the collective shame that would otherwise be experienced by all members of the family. Often this is seen to make women especially vulnerable to bringing and carrying shame, not least because of complicated rites attached to marriage and the dowry system. The caste system explicitly institutionalizes a collect-ivist interpretation of shame, with members of lower castes expected to feel shame, while dealings between members of different castes are closely regu-lated so as to avoid collective shame through association.

Shame is similarly institutionalized within the Confucian tradition. Society, built around the family, is held together by 'the five bonds', tightly prescribed mutual obligations that apply to different relationships and which are en-forced by the threat of losing face. The Confucian legacy is evidenced in both China and South Korea, although the competing influences of Daoism and Buddhism in China have further been overlaid by communism in both its state and market forms. The resultant complexity and subtlety is inherent in the construction of the two-character compound: *chiru*, 恥辱, usually used to signify shame. This includes elements of felt and imposed shame, humiliation, stain, and even injustice, but in combination usually alludes to damaged reputation and hence to a person's standing within a network of relationships. In Korea, film documents a rising individualism linked to economic growth and consumerism that is weakening Confucian obligations and sources of shame and replacing them with new social expectations based on individual success and consumption (Jo, 2014a). Similar expectations are evident in British literature dating back to the Victorian era when frequently self-made, industrial 'new money' began to challenge lineage as a source of status and respect. While family members might be negatively affected by an individual's transgressions, shame was already rendered largely an individual affair. Likewise, in Norway individuals in the modern city are portrayed in literature to be largely free of normative constraints. This is not to say that they do not feel shame, but rather that it is likely to be self-contained, based on introspection and a failure to fulfil personal aspirations, albeit ones that may reflect social expectations.

Shame, then, would appear to be recognizably the same emotion across these different cultures and settings. It is presented as something unpleasant and which, appertaining to the inner self, leads to concealment, retreat, avoidance, and ultimately to disintegration and even suicide. Authors and film-makers recognize that shame is felt internally by self, but with reference to external others and to the likelihood that they would wish to impose shame and might actually do so. While shame is varyingly depicted across cultures in terms of its reach, either being restricted to the individual or shared by the wider community, later works suggest that this distinction may be being eroded by time and economic development. Where differences remain, they attach to the extent to which individual hurt imposed by shame can be justified in terms of the presumed social benefits, be they enforced obligations or greater conformity.

CONCEPTIONS OF POVERTY

There is diversity in the conceptualization of poverty across cultures but with common themes of deprivation and hardship. Distinctions are apparent between absolute or subsistence poverty, portrayed as life lived on the edge of death, and more relativist interpretations. The latter entail comparisons of the degree of deprivation between one person or group and another or, especially in countries experiencing rapid economic change such as China and South Korea, comparisons between one time period and another, with personal memories of the past shaping perceptions of the present. Whenever the literatures surveyed reach back into the pre-modern period, poverty is presented as being endemic and severe. Life was and sometimes is shaped, first and foremost, by the need to eat in order to survive, with people eking out a precarious living from the land, labouring in the towns, and begging on the streets. Poverty is likened in Uganda to a painful illness, and in Pakistan to trauma—in the words of Meer Taqi Meer, the classical Urdu poet, to 'death in daily episodes'. Malnourished children serve as an ever-present reminder that life is harsh and cruelly indiscriminate.

A division between urban and rural environments is also evidenced that is linked both to economic development, and hence to history, and to agency. Except in times of natural disaster, the rural environment typically offers more means of sustenance than does the city. In urban settings, when employment is rare, crime and welfare benefits (if the latter exist) are often portrayed as the only means of alleviating the ravages of poverty. Life in the city also imposes new demands: the opportunities for material consumption; the often costly requirements of socializing, and the expectations of success shared by the protagonists themselves, by peers and by kin and friends at home in their villages. Such demands were perhaps heightened in modern China following the economic reforms, which opened up the possibility of self-advancement and promoted the prospect that 'getting rich is glorious'.

The concept of relative poverty is found in the British novel and Urdu literature long before the 1960s when it began to be adopted by social science. Owen, a character in the 1914 British novel *The Ragged Trousered Philanthropists*, provides a definition that has seldom been bettered: 'poverty consists not merely in being without money, but in being short of the necessaries and comforts of life'. Often the relativities were framed with respect to concepts of social class, status, and particularly 'respectability', which equated want of money with lack of breeding and lax morals. Chinese literature includes relativities defined with respect to: individual life trajectories; interethnic differences—for example, the relative decline of ethnic Manchurians; and immediate peers. It also recognizes divisions in contemporary experience between urban and rural, between the legacy of the former command economy and market driven production, and between the new economic classes being delineated by escalating inequality.

There are differences, too, in the narratives of causation that are evident both over time and between countries. In early literature, and more modern work adopting an historical perspective, poverty is presented as an inevitable part of the natural order of things. It is seen as the backcloth of life and a source of the trials and tribulations that demand the heroes and heroism that feature in myth and legend and provide hope to the merely mortal. In Ugandan literature poverty is still viewed as omnipresent, an untreatable cancer that protagonists attempt to live with by attributing cause to God or to malevolent curses. Elsewhere, early nationalist writings in India, for example, present 'the poor' as being downtrodden and oppressed (implicitly or explicitly) by the colonial power. More contemporary Indian literature, aspiring to be socially conscious, takes the reader into the lives of the oppressed revealing positive and negative agency, humour, and a common humanity. Indian cinema occasionally does likewise but explicitly turns life into popular entertainment, thereby inadvertently presenting poverty as the inevitable status quo. In China, during the Maoist period, the Confucian and Daoist acceptance of the status quo was challenged by novelists such as Zhou Erfu (*Morning in Shanghai*, 1981) who, consistent with Party doctrine at the time, portrayed poverty as a product of exploitation by the rich. However, in the present era when 'getting rich first' is official policy, this orthodoxy has now been overtaken by the idea that poverty is symptomatic of personal failure. The same idea has long been current in Britain—so much so that it has been deliberately challenged by directors making social realist films from the 1960s onwards. Twenty-first-century South Korean films also portray protagonists without wealth as losing out in life's race, while Norwegian literature struggles to explain the perpetuation of poverty in a universal welfare state, tending to focus instead on flaws in individual character.

Across the media and cultures considered, therefore, poverty describes the experience of extreme privation. Only in China, during the Maoist era, was poverty itself celebrated, a sacrifice made for the benefit of the nation. Elsewhere poverty has always been considered to be a scourge, an insidious evil. Those who show courage, dignity, steadfastness, and graft in the face of poverty take on the mantle of heroes, often in rags to riches stories that are common in fiction no doubt because they are rare in reality. Perhaps increasingly, though, with the power of the market and lure of consumerism, authors are looking not to God, fate, or nature for the causes and consequences of poverty, nor even to governments and systems, but to individuals and their vices of omission and commission. To the extent that this is so, either within fiction or the world that it reflects and possibly influences, it is likely to increase the chances of poverty being associated with shame.

POVERTY, SHAME, AND SHAMING

It is now possible to engage directly with the thesis that shame is everywhere associated with poverty. Through analysing literature, film, and proverbs the aim is to consider not 'what is' but 'what might be' and 'what ought to be'. The arts capture elements of reality, reflect social norms, and sometimes seek to change them. To the extent that artists locate shame with poverty by, for example, presenting protagonists as suffering shame on account of their poverty or engaging in shameful acts due to their poverty, it suggests that society would expect, and possibly might even desire, poverty to be a shaming experience. Whether in reality people find poverty shameful is the topic of Chapters 7 and 8.

Both science and the creative writing reviewed in this chapter suggest that shame is a relational phenomenon comprising both subjection to shame and the feeling of shame to varying degrees. In the context of shame attributable to poverty, Figure 5.1 sets out four simplified scenarios defined by the presence or absence of felt shame and the presence or absence of active shaming (Yan, 2014a). This elementary typology was used to analyse the core material from literature, film, and oral traditions and is employed here to structure the discussion. It should be noted, however, that the typology is very partial, focussing only on shame that might be attributable to poverty. Shame can obviously occur for many reasons other than poverty: appearance, physical or mental limitations, behaviour, social incompetence, bullying, etc. It may be associated with factors such as social class and education that may be directly or indirectly related to poverty, and to the determinants of any number of social hierarchies that are demarcated and reinforced by status differentials that are similarly policed, in part, by shame (Walker et al., 2013).

For reason of balance, this chapter addresses only the top-left quadrant in Figure 5.1 that symbolizes the coincidence of felt shame and active shaming by more affluent individuals and society as a whole. To oversimplify, this quadrant provides the strongest supportive evidence of Amartya Sen's assertion about the universality of shame and poverty. The other quadrants, including the lower-right one that would, in refutation of Sen, contain examples where poverty is not associated with any type of shame, are considered in Chapter 6.

Before considering the contents of the typology in detail, it is important to stress the coincidence and dovetailing of poverty and shame in all the material reviewed. The Urdu word *ruswaie*, meaing degradation, used as a synonym for

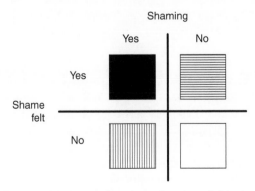

Fig. 5.1. Depiction of poverty, shame, and shaming
Adapted from Yan (2014a)

shame, sums up many of the accounts of poverty found in the literature and film. At the level of subsistence, the literatures portray people having to do whatever is needed to survive. From China, a woman in Liu Heng's 1986 novel *Gouride liangshi [Damned Grains]* washes mule dung to extract whole grains for the family meal, and in Lao She's 1935 work *Yuè Yár [Crescent Moon]* a daughter follows her mother into prostitution: 'I want to live. Shame is not what I caused.' From India, in the 1955 film *Pather Panjali* a young woman cries knowing that her family have insufficient money to provide for a dowry, and another widowed in the 1967 film *Thulabharam* kills the three children that she cannot afford to feed. The Urdu poet Nazeer Akbarabadi (1735–1830) aptly captures the inevitable deprivation that absolute poverty brings, concluding that: 'The poor know no politeness . . . fighting like dogs over every bone.'

Even relative poverty is widely portrayed in film and literature through manifestations of shame and dependency. A character in the 1945 novel *Krane's Café*, by the Norwegian author Cora Sandel, is warned off taking help from a potential employer because 'If you let her decide, there'll be nothing left of you. People like her can turn the lot of us into miserable beggars.' A protagonist in Walter Greenwood's novel *Love on the Dole*, published in Britain in 1933, reflects that there is no way that he can conceal his poverty: 'You know that your shabbiness betrayed you: It was apparent for all to see.' With film, the storylines are sometimes more extreme. Echoing the prostitution portrayed by Lao She in China, the 2006 British movie *London to Brighton* presents an 11-year-old homeless girl allowing herself to be pimped in order to earn enough for her to visit her grandmother in Devon. Poverty, then, is itself degrading, denying people the means to live up to expectations and forcing them to engage in survival strategies that may add to their degradation.

The frequency with which authors and film-makers present poverty as degrading means that the commonest depiction of the relationship between poverty and shame is one of being shamed and feeling ashamed—that is, 'the Sen quadrant' in the top-left in Figure 5.1. Depending on setting and vulnerability, the shaming is sometimes overt, as within the family or in a welfare benefits office; on other occasions it is more subdued.

Characteristics of Poverty-Related Shame

The depiction of shame falls between the commonplace and the extreme, with a multitude of variations in between that partly reflect the success with which people cope with or manage poverty-related shame (see Chapters 3 and 8). Examples of milder forms of shame frequently focus on rejection and the resultant sadness and unhappiness. Kishore Shantabai Kale, in his 1994 autobiographical story *Kolhathyachapor*, describes the emotional impact of lacking the new clothes necessary for him to attend the Indian Hindu festival of Diwali, while the Norwegian author Hansum, in his 1890 book *Hunger*, places the following thoughts in the mind of his main character: 'the hardships had got the better of me' and 'I, who walked there right besides these people . . . had already forgotten the very look of happiness' (Gubrium and Lødemel, 2014a). Sometimes people choose invisibility to avoid situations in which their circumstances could be revealed, while others become invisible as people ignore them like beggars in the street. At the other extreme, the shaming experience triggers processes of personal disintegration. Baqir, an unemployed father in Pakistan who appears in Ismat Chughtai's 1978 short story *Baikar*, when faced with the prospect of being unable to support his family, gradually becomes psychotic and dies. Many British social realist films, including *Secrets and Lies* (1996), *My Beautiful Laundrette* (1985), and *Train-spotting* (1996), portray alcohol abuse and the use of illicit drugs as mechanisms to dull the emotions, avoid reality, and to cope with exclusion and isolation. Suicide, as the final retreat from the shame of poverty, is a recurring theme in Indian film and Chinese literature. Characters resort to suicide in order to escape from the shame of being unable to live up to the obligation to feed their children (Subarna Rekha, 1965), to evade the pressures of indebtedness (Kathooriman, 2003), and to avoid the humiliation of having to prostitute principles in order to make ends meet. An example of the third kind is Xiaofuzi, in Lao She's 1936 novel *The Rickshaw Boy*, who hangs herself after being driven by her husband to sell her body for sex.

Another strategy that authors suggest people in poverty use to avoid shame is concealing their precarious circumstances. While concealment can lead to personal disaster, especially when people are found out, it is a strategy that is widely portrayed in literature and on film as one that is both commonplace and variably successful. In the Urdu short story *Chothi ka jora [The Wedding Shroud]* (1946), by Ismat Chughtai, an entire family conspires to spend beyond their means to impress a future son-in-law. From Chinese literature come tales of people covertly taking demeaning work to bolster income, of others seeking acceptable gifts to lubricate social advancement and putting them to alternative use if rejected (*Scattered Feathers*, Liu Zhenyunm, 1991), and of an entire ethnic group, the Manchurians, trying to live up to their past glories (*Nawu*, Deng Youmei, 1981). In British cinema and literature there are numerous illustrations of people keeping up appearances, for example, parents going without food to clothe their children (*The Woman Who Walked into Doors*, 1991). There are also examples of pretence, as when Beaver, in Waugh's 1934 novel *A Handful of Dust*, cannot afford to attend a party and feigns a prior engagement, and when Gerald, in the 1997 film *The Full Monty*, maintains the pretence of going to work each day despite being unemployed.

Women and Children

In fiction and film, as in reality (see Chapter 7), women and children bear the brunt of poverty-related shame. In the case of women, this reflects both their dominant role in domestic budgeting and their vulnerability in patriarchal societies. India serves as a good, if in some respects extreme, example. Women are shown skipping food to feed men in their family with consequential negative effects on their health and appearance; in Karoor Neelakanda Pillai's novel *Chekuthan [The devil]*, published in 1950 although written in the 1930s, the impact is made explicit: 'The hardship has made her old', 'Poverty has eaten up her body'. Indian women are nominally held in extremely high esteem and accorded great honour and respect, although the reality can be very different; an element in the plots of many films and stories is the disgrace that falls upon women who are forced to transgress social conventions. The dowry system reduces women, as the heroine in the Chattopadhyaya's 1928 Bengali short story *Deonapana* opines, to 'a bag of money' which, if empty, means that they are worthless. Indeed, the birth of a girl signals an expense as a result of which, in the 1997 film *Tamanna*, a daughter is disposed of as rubbish on the day of her birth. Kishore Shantabai Kale, in *Kolhathya-chapor* (1994), suggests that it is poverty that forces Marathi young women into situations where their chastity and honour is threatened. A woman is sexually abused because she is poor and helpless in the 1969 film *Kalli Chellamma*, and another is raped for similar reasons in the film *Vidheyan*, released in 1993. The ultimate disgrace falls on women forced into prostitution by poverty, a theme dealt with in a series of films, including *Aakaler Sandhane* (1980), *Salaam Bombay* (1988), and *Kaal* (2007). These depict women not only being ostracized by their family and society but also carrying the shame of their inadequate menfolk.

The above sequence of illustrations highlights another recurring theme, namely that poverty often triggers a cumulative sequence of shame-inducing scenarios. The shame begins with the sense of personal failure experienced when a lack of resources prevents the protagonist from adequately playing a role or fulfilling social expectations such as providing sustenance for their children or funding a dowry. It is then often compounded by the shame attached to subsequent social transgressions, for example indebtedness, theft, or prostitution. These might result directly from the initial impotence, or through attempts to rescue the situation or to prevent it from reoccurring. Often films and stories capture this process as a journey through time and space from poverty to social isolation and exclusion. An example is the 1966 British drama-documentary *Cathy Come Home*, which portrays a journey from respectability to destitution, homelessness, and the final insult, the removal of Cathy and Reg's children into care.

Children, like women, are presented as being especially vulnerable to poverty-induced shame; indeed, protecting them is one reason offered for why mothers go without things themselves and risk further shaming through engaging in theft and prostitution. School is an arena where adult and child normative values are forged, and poor children risk being shamed by peers and teachers. In *First Daughter*, written in 1996 by Ugandan novelist Goretti Kyomuhendo, Kasemiire unpacks her case on arriving at secondary school to be confronted by the matron with, to the mirth of her peers, the inquisition 'No toilet paper? She can use leaves'. The Norwegian novelist Jacobsen, in his 1991 book *Seierherrene [The Conquerors]*, portrays a woman teacher picking on disadvantaged children, and in so doing transforming shame into stigma: she 'doesn't try . . . to hide that some [children] are worse clothed than others but highlights the point, almost, as evidence of her own ability and culture'. Children also fear the ostracism that can be meted out by peers when they cannot afford to buy or do the things that other children do. Subho, in the 1970 Indian film *Ekhane Pinjar*, rejects school for this reason. Similarly, in the opening scene of the British film 2002 *All or Nothing*, the director, Mike Leigh, invites the audience to interpret the violence engaged in by children on the way home from school as resulting from an endemic sense of inadequacy and failure engendered by life in a poverty-stricken community.

Children also risk being on the receiving end of their parents' shame and inability to cope. Zhao, in the 1961 book *Chuangyeshi [Violent Storm]* by Chinese novelist Liu Qing, hits his five-year-old out of frustration knowing that he cannot afford to feed him, a vignette which is echoed in a scene in the 1967 Hindi film *Upkaar*, in which the mother beats her son when he asks for food having been fed the day before. In *Jude the Obscure*, the 1895 Victorian novel by British author Thomas Hardy, an eldest son takes on the shame of his parents, kills his siblings, and hangs himself explaining his actions with a note: 'Done because we are too menny'. Expected to work so as to help their family make ends meet, children are depicted doing jobs too demeaning for their parents: picking coal in the 1972 British film, *My Childhood*; and living off the streets in the red-light district of Bombay in the 1988 Hindi film *Salaam Bombay*.

Arenas of Shaming

School as a setting for shame and shaming emerges as a microcosm of the adult arenas in which shame is imposed. From the literature and film analysed, there might be more such arenas in collectivist societies than in individualistic ones, with possibly greater salience attached to them. Certainly within India, but also in China and Pakistan, rituals associated with family and religion are evidenced more in the film and literature reviewed. Dowries, weddings, and the administration of the final rites are the currency of family life in India and provide fertile ground for poverty-induced shame. The 1950 novel *Chekuthan [Devil]* revolves around the shame that a mother experiences from denying her daughter the possibility of marriage given that there is no money for a dowry, while in the film *Mother India* (1957) the shame of not being able to meet the costs of a forthcoming wedding is exacerbated by the need to borrow funds, concealing this fact, and then finding it revealed.

Similar motifs are evident, if less often, in British literature, especially that from the Victorian era when class-based mores were conspicuous, but also in modern films: a case in point is Stevie in the 1991 film *Riff Raff* who, temporarily homeless, is caught attending his mother's funeral in an ill-fitting, and presumably borrowed, suit. But while the family imposes obligations, sometimes the familiarity of the family protects and conceals. In *Wrinkled Faces*, a play written in 2010 by the Ugandan playwright Connie Ssebunga Masembe, the central characters Nabirye, Babirye, and Kaudha are dependent on their neighbours for basics like salt and it is in the community that they find themselves most exposed to shaming. The cruelty of the community is also exposed in the language applied to those in poverty; in *Black Mamba*, a 1973 play by another Ugandan author John Ruganda, they are described as 'leaches' and as being as 'dirty as pigs' and as 'poor as beggar's dogs'.

Authors explore class interaction both as a setting in which shame occurs but also as the vector of its transmission. While the contempt, abhorrence, and hatred of the lower classes revealed in the British novels of the Victorian period have dissipated, the shame felt by Chanu, trapped in the menial job portrayed in Monica Ali's 2003 *Brick Lane*, remains as palpable as that which Grossmith ascribes to Pooter in *The Diary of a Nobody* working in his clerical job, c.1890. However, disentangling class and status and the shame associated with poverty as revealed in literature and film is perhaps impossible. In China, this quandary is neatly represented by the poor literati. Fan Jin, in Wu Jingzi's classic 1750 work *Rulinwaishi [The Scholar]*, passed the civil service examinations and, although poverty stricken, finally won the respect of his father-in-law who was a butcher. However, the central character in Lu Xun's 1919 short story *Kongyiji* never secured the respect that he sought through scholarship and continued to live a life subject to ridicule.

Caste is a setting for shame that is unique to South Asia but which has affinities with class (see Chapter 1). The Vedic tradition confines lower-caste Dalits to the most menial of occupations and hence also to poverty, adding a third layer of shame by explaining membership of a low caste in terms of personal failings in previous lives. Relationships between castes are defined by rules couched in terms of shame but can, ironically, lead to persons of higher caste being shamed by the behaviour of persons from lower ones. This phenomenon is portrayed in Premchand's 1931 story *Sadgathy [Deliverance]* when a Dalit inappropriately asks a Brahmin priest to fix an auspicious date for his daughter's marriage and both protagonists feel ashamed (the Dalit on an ongoing basis on account of the Brahmin's insistence that he works for him as a servant). The gradual breakdown of the caste-based system of occupations, and the possible dissociation of poverty from caste, complicates understanding of the true locus of poverty and caste-related shame.

The employment market and the welfare institutions that lie adjacent provide settings for shame, shaming, and indeed stigma that are perhaps as acute as any revealed in the material reviewed. Low-status jobs can be shaming in themselves but also because they demonstrate that the persons doing them are so poor that they have to take them. In *The Burdens*, a play by the Ugandan John Ruganda, fourteen-year-old Kaija is prepared 'to sell groundnuts and carry pailfuls of excrement' to support the family but it is his mother who objects: 'No. How can I bear the derisive laughter of the slum women? . . . Don't put your mother's pride at stake.'

Unemployment, though, is generally thought to be worse than low-paid work. Dasan, in the 1987 Indian film *Nadodokaattu*, is unemployed, poor, and consequently unable to perform the duties required of a 'proper son'. In patriarchal societies generally, unemployment that challenges men's masculinity as providers is a repeated didactic motif. This emasculation is dealt with subtly in British director Mike Leigh's 2002 film *All or Nothing*, in which Phil, not unemployed but earning very little, tearfully tells his wife: 'I ain't got no skills. I don't earn enough money. I know I am a disappointment to you.' In Phil's case, his wife is employed which further saps his masculinity. In traditional societies, of course, women depended on men to provide for them and where men did not or could not support them, women's extreme vulnerability was exposed. In Deng Youmei's 1981 novella *Na Wu*, Chinese women lacking financial support from their husbands are forced by circumstance to become servants and subsequently the concubines of older men.

The dole queue, awaiting work and or benefits, is a powerful metaphor for public shaming and blatant stigmatization. As the Norwegian author Jacobsen observes in his 1991 novel *Seierherrene [The Conquerors]*: full-grown men have 'to stand in line with notes and beg and lower themselves'. The self-same image of degradation is found in the 1993 novel *Love on the Dole* by the British author Greenwood: 'a long queue of shabby men, hands in pockets, staring fixedly and unseeingly at the ground', and is a recurring image in many British social realist films including *The Full Monty* (1997) and *Raining Stones* (1993). Inside the office, the stigmatization, the diminution of the soul, continues for each day is a judgement day when officials separate the deserving from the undeserving. For Elling, in Ingvar Ambjørnsen's 1986 Norwegian novel *Hvite Niggere [White Niggers]*, 'The whole thing was a disgusting affair that had definitely reduced my self-esteem significantly, even if it hadn't been so damn high before.' There was no form of redress: 'We had come to beg, we had unfortunately no money to build a revolution.' In the Indian context, the

stigma of applying for public assistance is further complicated by the requirement in many situations to bribe officials in order to receive payment, a
subplot in the 2007 Malayalam film *Katha Parayumbol*. Welfare recipients
are shamed for using bribes and officials are shamed for exploiting the very
poorest.

Borrowing and lending are often similarly portrayed on film and in novels
as leading to both debtor and moneylender being shamed in a relationship
comprised of exploitation and dependency. In the British film *All or Nothing*
(2002), Phil has to borrow from his teenage daughter and does so with head
bowed. In Liu Heng's 1986 novel *Gouride liangshi [Damned Grains]* (1986),
complex dynamics of shame and dependency are established when the female
protagonist refuses to let her husband lend potatoes to her brother-in-law, but
is subsequently obliged by the brother-in-law personally to ask for a loan when
her husband gets into financial difficulty. Many Indian films take debt as a
central theme or significant subplot. They often reveal the vulnerabilities that
indebtedness creates and, as in the 2010 film *Peepli Live*, the susceptibility of
the borrower to being cheated. *Kasthooriman*, released in 2003, highlights how
moneylenders can deliberately exploit the shame that their clients experience
by using the threat of public exposure as a means of ensuring repayment. In
societies characterized by high levels of illiteracy, necessarily based on oral
traditions of trust and mutuality, the inability to keep one's word is itself a
major cause of shame. Shaming in such societies corresponds to the legal
sanctions that attach to written contracts. Thus when the moneylender in the
film *Kasthooriman* responds to the request 'Please do not shame me' with the
deliberately humiliating response 'So, do you have shame?' it might be interpreted as just this kind of sanction.

So while the film and literature reviewed suggests that the arenas in which
poverty is experienced as shame are culturally nuanced, shame does emerge as
an ingredient in much of the poverty depicted, with women and children
being particularly affected. However, as will be further elucidated in Chapter 6,
writers and film-makers do not portray every person in poverty as experiencing shame.

SOCIAL CONCEPTIONS OF THE POVERTY–SHAME NEXUS

Taking literature, film, and proverb as windows on social meaning, shame
seems to be portrayed very similarly across the seven national cultures; it is an
unpleasant emotion appertaining to the inner self that leads to concealment,
retreat, avoidance, and ultimately to disintegration and even suicide. Its

internal and external components, as identified in scientific writings, are echoed in creative literature and film. There is also the hint in materials drawn mainly from more collectivist cultures that the individual pain imposed through shame might sometimes be offset by social benefits accruing from enforcing obligations to ensure conformity.

There is greater variation in the conceptualization of poverty both over time and between countries. This is not surprising given the vast differences in living standards and rates of growth over the last one-hundred or so years to which the materials examined relate. Nevertheless, poverty is universally related to deprivation and hardship, be it measured in absolute or subsistence terms. It is also considered to be degrading, most noticeably so in urban areas. Except at times of natural disaster, the rural environment is generally benign, offering many ways of getting by. In the city, in contrast, when unemployment is high, welfare benefits and crime are all that there is and poverty necessarily means dependency on others.

In each of the diverse national cultures considered, poverty is presented as engendering feelings of shame that exacerbate the harshness of life's experience. Sometimes people are described being driven by poverty to take actions that are demeaning, irrational, subject to social disapproval, or even illegal, and that these add to the sense of shame, sometimes pushing people to the point where they appear to be acting 'shamelessly'. Women and children are identified to be particularly vulnerable to shame experienced as a result of poverty and, for the individual if not always the wider society, the consequences of the shame are portrayed as being corrosive. Shame leads to social withdrawal, concealment, and fantasy; it saps morale and can precipitate a loss of control resulting in mixes of anger, depression, and despair. Only occasionally is personal good magicked out of the shaming process as when people strive to keep up appearances despite the risks entailed, and feel a sense of achievement out of doing so. Sometimes, as reported in Chapter 6, shame is presented as provoking resistance, either by individuals in their interpersonal relations, or collectively with people coming together to organize against oppression. The sense of optimism conveyed by such episodes may itself hint at the improbability of such positive outcomes in real life.

The settings in which shame is described vary between cultures, as do the vectors of shame. In India and Pakistan, shame is institutionalized in the caste system. Ritual, religious festivals, and family events are all arenas in which shaming is reported to occur and in which the shame of poverty can be experienced. The clan, tribe, and village historically were important in determining and policing social codes and still create networks of allegiances in modern cultures as divergent as China, Uganda, and Norway. They are sources of support but also provide markers against which individuals judge their behaviour and progress, and mirrors that can reflect the shame of poverty. The family is similarly important as a source of mutual support, but also as a setting in which poverty-related shame is manifest through the inability to provide for dependants or to participate in financial exchanges based on reciprocity. In societies based on the nuclear family, shame may be experienced in private, behind closed doors, but within the extended family the shaming is semi-public can, through association, attach to the family as a whole. The workplace, the welfare benefits office, and perhaps especially the school are other venues where people can be made to feel the shame of their poverty—public evidence of economic and personal failure.

Studying creative media indicates that there is social appreciation that the experience of poverty is not just lack of income; it is also the inability to live up to personal goals and social expectations, a lack of social recognition and the shame that results from both. But is this always the case? Chapter 6 examines the three remaining quadrants defined in Figure 5.1, the content of which may qualify or even refute any notion of the universality of poverty–shame nexus, at least as represented in the realm of the collective imagination.

6

Conceiving of Poverty Without Shame[1]

While the mainstream academic and policy debate has focussed on lack of income as the defining feature of poverty, the literature and film reviewed in Chapter 5 reveal that creative writers and film-makers appreciate that, for many individuals, the hardships engendered by poverty are as much social and emotional as they are material. People in poverty feel themselves to be despised by others and come to despise themselves. They seek ways to avoid or deflect the shame and stigma heaped upon them by supposedly helping bureaucracies, by potential and ex-ploitative employers, and even by members of their own families. To the extent that the media surveyed reflect dominant values in the societies considered, they suggest that poverty is viewed as degrading and that people in poverty are seen as being disreputable and despicable if also vulnerable and needy.

If this is the dominant perspective warranting a chapter in its own right, other themes are represented by the remaining three quadrants in Figure 5.1. The first theme though, denoted by the top-right quadrant, serves to underline the importance of shame in the experience of poverty. It portrays people in poverty feeling ashamed even in the absence of explicit shaming. Hence, it demonstrates the power of social expectations in shaping behaviour and represents shame operating as an automatic regulator in the way that Scheff envisaged it to work. It is considered first before addressing the other two quadrants that challenge the universality of the poverty–shame nexus.

SHAME WITHOUT SHAMING

The Chinese novel *Yidi jimao [Scattered Feathers]*, written by Liu Zhenyun in 1991, includes two archetypal characters who are not subjected to shaming but who nevertheless feel shame (Yan, 2014a). The Lins lived during the early stages

---

[1] This chapter draws heavily on the following publications: Bantebya-Kyomuhendo and Mwiine (2014a); Chase and Walker (2014a); Choudhry (2014a); Gubrium and Lødemel (2014a); Jo (2014a); Pellissery and Mathew (2014a); and Yan (2014a).

of marketization. Short of money, the man is forced to take a job selling ducks in the market. He is depicted with his head down, dreading being seen by friends. In another incident, the couple are approached by neighbours with the offer of a voucher to get their daughter into a better day-care centre. They initially take this as evidence that they are held in high regard, but subsequently deduce that the offer was made purely so that the neighbours' daughter would have a friend to accompany her. The Lins feel ashamed in that they themselves do not have the networks to secure their daughter a place in day care and because they believe, rightly or wrongly, that they have been used.

In neither of the above illustrations is there any evidence that the Lins have been explicitly shamed. Instead, they internalize values about what is expected of people in their position in Chinese society; they should be socially well connected and should not need to engage in manual work. To the extent that the Lins are correctly reading these social expectations, their behaviour illustrates the power of social norms, society working on autopilot without recourse to explicit shaming. Zhenyun's portrayal accords well with the scientific literature reviewed in Chapter 3. Equally, it should be noted that the shame that was experienced as 'self-inflicted' pain did not, in itself, succeed in inducing behaviour that remedied the poverty that was the root cause of the shame. Indeed, Mr Lin might have been deterred from earning by imagining the shame associated with the type of job that necessity forced him to take. This insight into the futility of the pain, caused by society implicitly or explicitly shaming people who do not have the wherewithal to address the causes of their poverty, foreshadows a major disfigurement in the lives of people experiencing poverty that will be discussed in Chapters 7, 8, and 11.

Reference to the power of silent shaming is not restricted to collectivist cultures. It is evident, for example, in some British and recent Korean films that portray virtue with reference to economic success and the consumerism and work ethic that underpin modern capitalism. Sometimes the references are quite subtle, as in the 2000 British film *Billy Elliot*; the comfort and security of a teacher's house is contrasted with the want and insecurity of life in a mining community and points to the journey that the young protagonist is about to make through the application of honest hard work (Chase and Walker, 2014a). On occasion, the messages are more stark and brutal. *Riff Raff*, a British film released in 1991, creates a dog-eat-dog world of mutual exploitation based on a London building site that is peopled by more or less unsuccessful 'blokes'. In one scene, the foreman, observing his workers having a break, remarks: 'Look at those lazy bastards . . . the working class don't want work you know. Ask 'em to sit on their arses all day and they're as happy as pigs in shit.' The director, Ken Loach, is known to take a structuralist view of social issues (Lay, 2002), and here he seeks to expose both classism and the adherence to the work ethic that personalizes responsibility for success and failure and, correspondingly, for affluence and poverty. In so doing, depending on the receptivity of the audience, he risks inadvertently reinforcing the values he seeks to challenge.

Directors in the British tradition of social realism have tried to expose the divisive values of capitalism. In South Korea, they have typically embraced them in recent times. Whereas until the early 1980s Korean films would have portrayed the rich as being immoral, greedy, and exploitative, coincident with burgeoning economic growth and a new middle class, they have subsequently been depicted as heroic (Jo, 2014a). *Gippeun wuri jeolmeun-nal [In Our Joyful Young Day]*, produced in 1987, serves as an example, in that Hye-Rin chooses between two suitors, Oh Seong-wu and Young-Min, purely on the basis of their respective wealth.

Despite the perhaps different intentions of British and South Korean filmmakers, both create and reveal a world that applauds financial success and castigates economic failure. With such stark subliminal messaging, explicit shaming may be unnecessary; whether or not society intends to shame people in poverty, they are likely to feel ashamed. Korean film documents a change that parallels economic development, while Chinese literature reflects the transition to a socialist market economy. In Uganda, too, the contrast between oral tradition that embraces the existence of poverty and modern writing that despises it is marked (Bantebya-Kyomuhendo and Mwiine, 2014a). The suggestion, then, from this reading of the material under review that falls into the 'without shaming quadrant', is that the shame attaching to poverty may have increased with the ascendency of the global market and consumerism. Rather than shaming needing to be overt, the social pressures have become more pervasive and invidious, creating shame through osmosis.

SHAMING WITHOUT SHAME

The lower-left quadrant in Figure 5.1 represents the conjunction of society imposing shame and individuals in poverty neither feeling nor showing it. This might be characterized as the 'shameless quadrant', although such a label obscures instances in which shaming provokes positive resistance. As is already clear, the characteristic manifestations of the shame of poverty revealed by the materials studied are sadness, sullenness, retreat, avoidance, concealment, and sometimes despair, depression, disintegration, and ultimately suicide. However, certain people in poverty are portrayed in novels and film who exhibit none of these characteristics and who, in the presence of shaming by society, appear to fit into the shameless quadrant. Unfortunately, even with careful reading, it is often difficult to determine whether authors and filmmakers mean their protagonists to feel no shame or whether their markedly different behaviours serve to hide or counteract the shame that they truly feel. Sometimes the behaviour turns out to benefit the individual or society; more often the effects are presented as being negative.

ANGER AND SHAMELESSNESS

The anger and aggression which is exhibited by protagonists in film and on the page who are trapped by poverty and feeling desperately ashamed contrasts markedly with the conformist, downtrodden dole queue that epitomizes passive manifestations of poverty-related shame. This behaviour is, though, perfectly compatible with the scientific psychological and sociological literature on shame as reviewed in Chapter 3 (e.g. Scheff and Retzinger, 1991; Stuewig and Tangney, 2007). The anger seems to well up uncontrollably from the sense of shame itself, sometimes from the frustration of being unable to stem the source of the shame, and sometimes from the apparent inability to do anything at all. It perhaps features less in the literature of the more collectivist countries studied, but there is the suggestion in scholarship (Xu et al., 2005) that domestic violence was particularly prevalent in pre-communist China. Certainly hungry, miserable men who take out their frustrations on their wives feature in Lao She's 1936 novel Luòtuo Xiángzi *[Rickshaw Boy]*, while Xiao Hong recounts violence between mother and daughter-in-laws that is triggered by squabbles over limited resources in *Hulanhezhuan [Memoirs of River Hulan]*, written in 1941. Also the anger and violence portrayed in Korean films that deal with poverty and have been made since the 1997 Asian Financial Crisis is stark and vicious. *Crying Fist* (2005) is but one example in which a bankrupt ex-national champion boxer, Tae-Shik, returns to the ring in order to win back the pride, family, and life denied him by poverty.

The violence borne of shame and frustration portrayed in British social realist films is often generalized and undirected. The notion of angry young men with no money, nothing to do, and nowhere to go, depicted in the 1960 film *Saturday Night Sunday Morning*, has passed into folk law and is still a recurring motif in films such as *This is England* (2006) and *Kidulthood* (2006). In British literature, the anger and resentment of people suffering from poverty is perhaps more directed, if only in a generalized way, towards the rich who they hold to be responsible for their circumstances. But while the anger shown by those in poverty towards the rich sometimes erupts in individual confrontation, as in Elisabeth Gaskell's 1848 novel *Mary Barton*, the prevailing view conveyed by most novelists from Gaskell onwards is the lack of a constructive collective response.

In contrast Norwegian authors, who similarly describe deep anger felt in response to the shame of poverty, portray it more positively as a form of resistance. Jacobsen, in his 1991 novel *Seierherrene [The Conquerors]*, notes that while Marta can do little in the city to better himself, people like him 'don't lie down and sigh... They instead become angry, their laughter is hard and meaningless... and they don't ever listen to what is said to them' (Gubrium and Lødemel, 2014a). Hamsun's protagonist in *Hunger*, a book written a century earlier in 1890, 'gave a long spit over the sidewalk, without bothering whether it might hit someone, angry with and full of contempt for these people': 'I lifted my head and felt deep down how blessed I was to be able to follow the straight and narrow.' Not dissimilarly, Sandel, in her 1985 *Collected Short Stories*, presents women in situations where they might be portrayed as victims, but instead suggests that they use their anger and despair over the situations that they encounter to emphasize their independence and agency.

A theme more pervasive even than anger is the poor person who behaves shamelessly. Sometimes such people appear as likeable rogues and occasionally their behaviour is justified by force of circumstance, but often they are presented as selfish, exploitative, and loathsome, a characterization that is consistent with a social norm that such deviants are to be made to feel ashamed. Indeed, shameless behaviour, viewed by the non-poor, is considered as deviancy, as a threat to the established order that is potentially socially destructive, whereas viewed through the eyes of a person in poverty it may be a necessary survival strategy. Yan's wife in the 1986 novel *Gouride liangshi [Damned Grains]*, by Chinese author Liu Heng, steals to feed her starving children, shameless behaviour with good intent. If this rationale is accepted by readers it hints at the possibility of poverty without shame, as discussed in the penultimate section of this chapter.

However, a wide spectrum of views is evident as to the nature of the culpability that attaches to shameless behaviour. It is sometimes portrayed as an aspect of growing immunity to the degradation of poverty, as when the masseuse in Oasmi's Urdu story *Raees Khana* ceases to object to being taken for a prostitute (Choudhry, 2014a). Other authors take shamelessness to illustrate the depths of moral turpitude to which people in poverty can sink or, indeed, point to deficiencies in character that might help to explain poverty rather than being a consequence of it. In Liu Qing's 1961 novel *Chuangyeshi [Violent Storm]*, Long-Neck Han is seen to assist the wealthy in their abuse of poor villagers—in effect, to betray his class. In portraying poverty in terms of individual failings, novelists and film-makers may themselves be contributing to, as well as reflecting, the process through which society heaps shame on those in poverty. This is evident, for example, in Ambjørnsen's depiction of Norwegian benefit recipients as 'speed freaks' and 'women from the streets...dragging on filter cigarettes' in his 1986 novel *White Niggers*. Similarly, while many British novelists, from Charlotte Brontë in *Jane Eyre* (1847) to William Morris in *News from Nowhere* (1890) and Andrea Levy in *The Small Island* (2004), allude to the structural causes of poverty through narrators and commentary, the vast majority of the wealthy characters that populate their novels attribute their own success to hard work and poverty to inactivity and fecklessness. More contemporary, though not part of the British material formally analysed, it would be inappropriate not to mention Paul

Abbott's long-running television comedy drama series *Shameless*, which aired on Channel 4 in Britain for a decade until 2013 and has been remade for US television. Ostensibly based on working class life, the plot revolves around the Gallagher family, led by the feckless Frank who is forever fiddling his benefits to spend his ill-gotten gains on drugs and alcohol. The series reinforces the tendency, already mentioned in Chapter 4, for the British public to fuse poverty, benefit receipt, and 'scrounging'. Moreover, the unfortunate metaphor that Abbot chose when describing his ambition to write something that 'smelled like it smelled on the inside' is particularly apposite given the series' particular portrayal of modern poverty (Lawrence, 2013).

RESISTING SHAMING

The strategies of concealment and pretence adopted by protagonists to avoid the glare of shame that were discussed in Chapter 5 could be seen as passive forms of resistance. More active forms are also explored in film and literature. Some strategies, discussed first, are open to individuals; others require collective action.

Instead of living the double life inherent in keeping up appearances, a motif—common across the different cultures—is of the destitute person who finds dignity in being poor or who attains respect through other aspects of their lives. Many of the most uplifting episodes show protagonists realizing that they can overcome adversity through hard work, combining forces, or simply by living a good life, prioritizing personal morality, family, and other people. This is evident in genres as different as Dickens' *Great Expectations* (1861) and the hit films *Billy Elliot* (2000) and *Brassed Off* (1996) in the UK, the Urdu poetry of Nazeer and Iqbal in the eighteenth and twentieth centuries respectively, and in the literature of post-revolutionary China. To the extent that this response to shame entails a change in behaviour that could be contributing to a person's poverty, one might categorize it as restoration rather than resistance. It may be, therefore, that in these instances the vision of the writer or film-maker is somewhat reactionary, demonstrating that the social function of shame, to promote adherence to social norms, has proved effective. Equally, if this is indeed their goal, it further conveys the message that personal behaviour is the cause of poverty rather than structural factors. The fact that these stories are uplifting may equally reflect a reality in which such experiences are rare and primarily serve to give the reader or viewer belief that change is possible in their own lives, especially if they live in accordance with socially approved principles.

Other ways in which films and novels suggest that shame is resisted is through humour, logical reasoning, and behaviour, each used to deflect shame back on the protagonists who are engaged in shaming. In many films, typified by the 1987 Malayalam film *Nadodikkattu* which deals with issues of unemployment, disaffected youth, and exploitation, victims take control of a situation by cracking a joke rather than themselves being the butt of jokes (Pellissery and Mathew, 2014a). Radha, in the 1957 film *Mother India*, turns the tables of shame by holding to the highest principles of morality and refusing sexual favours to her moneylender. Likewise, Priya, in the 2003 film *Kasthooriman*, is successful in counteracting shame by explaining how multiple low-status jobs are helping her to fund her studies and thereby to build a career for herself and a good life for her family. In the same way that stories of individual achievement can be uplifting, so incidents in which tables are turned have a dramatic effect on readers and viewers, a phenomenon that is well appreciated by good novelists and film-makers. It is therefore important not to confuse dramatic licence with reality. How often individuals in poverty can and do defend themselves with humour and wit is an empirical question. What the depictions perhaps hint at, however, is a degree of social discomfort when people in poverty are seen to be abused and comforting reassurance that they, and potentially the reader or viewer if they were ever in similar circumstances, have the means to defend themselves.

The possibilities for a collective defence, formal and informal, are also explored by authors and film-makers. At the most spectacular level, the communist revolution and its aftermath in China can be interpreted, as it is by authors such as Zhou Erfu, Lui Qing, and Liu Heng, as a collective response to the degradation of poverty caused by class exploitation. The revolution and the Chinese Communist Party are credited with awaking people in poverty, causing them to shed the fatalism instilled in them by Daoism and Confucianism and to challenge their domination by the wealthy. In India, Dalit literature is itself a collective response to the shame inflicted by caste and the associated poverty and degradation. Formalized in 1958 through holding the first conference of the Maharashtra Dalit Literature Society (*Maharashtra Dalit Sahitya Sangha*) at Mumbai, the movement is epitomized by self-narratives, typically exploiting the literary forms of autobiography, poetry, and short stories to denounce romanticized views of caste and to expose the daily humiliation of untouchability (Beth, 2007; Dharwadker, 1994; Kothari, 2001).

In the Norwegian literature reviewed, the tendency is to look for evidence of collective action at the time of the development of the class solidarity that helped to deliver the current welfare state. Jacobsen, for example, locates his 1991 novel *The Conquerors* in rural Norway where workers, inspired by references to Jesus Christ and Stalin among others, believe that 'we the poor will inherit the farm'. But despite the successes of the welfare state, Jacobsen nevertheless conveys a deep pessimism in that the strike collapses and the strikers then turn on their leaders. This generalized pessimism is also evident in much modern British literature and film, but it means that modest achievements warrant celebration as unanticipated successes. Collective resistance is generally low-key and informal, and the welfare institutions that are the historic products of former class solidarity, notably benefit offices and job centres, are often presented as instruments of oppression and targets for resistance. In the 1997 comedy *The Full Monty*, a group of unemployed men come together successfully to pursue a common cause. In the process they are shown to recapture some of the self-esteem that unemployment and poverty has stolen from them and, in a memorable scene that forsakes realism to critique one of the most powerful icons of humiliation in Britain, they are seen dancing in line in a 'dole' queue while awaiting the payment of their unemployment benefit.

The Full Monty, through humour, and Dalit literature, by the sharing of personal experience, both illustrate that film and creative writing can themselves actively resist the social institutions that serve to bring shame to people in poverty. They also hold out the prospect that individuals in poverty can, either alone or together with others, challenge the people and institutions that shame them. Shame is presumed, but provides the psychic energy to fuel resistance. In contrast, other works introduce protagonists experiencing poverty who wilfully act shamelessly because they feel that they have no choice, do not care, or are straightforwardly amoral. What these competing perspectives within the 'shameless quadrant' share is the ability to drive a powerful story based on either righteousness or evil. As such, they are arguably dramatic devices rather than commonplace phenomena. Certainly, examples of collective action or rampant abuse are rare in the actual experience of people in poverty (to be reported in Chapters 7 and 8), but were powerful in shaping the beliefs of the relatively affluent about the nature and causes of poverty.

POVERTY WITHOUT SHAME

The bottom-right quadrant in Figure 5.1 suggests the possibility of poverty without shame, a powerful challenge to the universality of a poverty–shame nexus. The materials reviewed do in fact provide some evidence of poverty portrayed in this way, but it comes from particular societies at specific points in history.

Literature relating to pre-communist China and traditional India contains examples suggestive of poverty with only limited shaming. In China, the historical influence of Buddhism and Daoism is apparent in emphasizing acceptance of the inevitability of life. In his 1961 novel *Chuangyeshi [The Violent Storm]*, Liu Qing seeks to capture the essence of traditional China and with it the notion that life is a gamble and that some people receive a 'bitter lot' that 'attracts poverty'. Life is brutal and dignity a luxury. Lu Xun, in his 1919 novel, suggests that theft might be excused, certainly among the poor literati: 'To pilfer is not the same as stealing . . . It's the business of scholars.' Moreover, in this harsh world people take joy from simple things, such as the arrival of a son for Feng in Xiao Hong's 1941 novel *Hulanhezhuan [Memoirs of River Hulan]*.

A similar focus on the happiness that can attach to the simple things in life is evident in some Indian films dealing with poverty, including *Do Bigma Zamin* (1953) and *Tamanna* (1998). India shares with China the influence of Buddhism and the tradition of karma and of acceptance, while the caste structure associated with Hinduism gives moral force to the social inequalities that help to create and sustain poverty. Additionally, as explained in Chapter 1, Hinduism has established social institutions that partially accommodate the needs of beggars by creating a role and justification for them; giving to beggars is considered to be a means of pleasing God and of keeping bad luck at bay. There is the suggestion, though, that while people may inevitably be forced by poverty into acts of degradation that are legitimated by the need to survive, they are also required to accommodate the underlying sense of shame. A Malayalam proverb, for example, roughly translates as 'the wealth that one acquires shamelessly can rescue one from shame'.

From analysis of traditional Lugandan and Runyakitaran proverbs in Uganda, it is possible to glimpse the views and lived experiences of past generations of indigenous people alive at a time when poverty was more or less universal. Poverty was hard, like 'scorching sun' or 'torrential rain', sometimes 'worse than death'. It was attributed to multiple factors including foolishness, laziness, and promiscuity, but also to divine providence and to exploitation by the few who were relatively wealthy. While cooperation was possible and necessary ('*omwana taba womu*'—a child does not only belong to the individual parents but to the entire community), the proverbs nevertheless emphasize resilience, self-reliance, and hard work. They suggest that the wealthy warranted respect while poverty was construed as an individual burden. Those who were poor were encouraged to resign themselves to their station in life and to recognize that friends would disappear with the onset of poverty. In effect, the proverbs present a social code protecting the status quo. Moreover, more than one in ten of the proverbs collected contain elements that could be interpreted as shaming. These included: *Nnabyewanga, ng'akaliga akaliira mu nte (oba mu nyana)* (the poor should keep within their social realm);[2] *Atawone bwaavu, agula bikadde* (the poor foolishly perpetuate their poverty);[3] *Lwabaaga, lwafuna munywanyi we* (a poor person has no friends, because he has nothing to offer);[4] and *Mazzi masabe, tegaloga nnyonta* (begged water does not quench thirst). If

---

[2] Literal translation: a person who forces himself on to a different group, like a lamb which grazes among cattle (or calves).

[3] Literal translation: one who will remain in perpetual poverty, shops from second-hand dealers.

[4] Literal translation: when a poor despised person kills an animal, is when he acquires friends.

shame attaching to poverty was not markedly evident in pre-colonial Uganda, it might have been because so many people were poor. But what the proverbs suggest is that a simple dichotomy of a time, unlike now, when poverty was totally free from shame is unlikely to have existed in Uganda.

On the other hand, the Chinese literature suggests that poverty was shame-free between the time of the Communist Revolution and the arrival of the economic reforms of the 1980s. As already noted, communist orthodoxy during this era situated poverty within the dialectic of class struggle: people were poor due to their exploitation by the rich. Zhou Erfu's 1958 novel *Shanghai de zaochen [Shanghai Morning]* records how the populace were encouraged to attend meetings to share bitter experiences of the pre-existing era. Writers in this era celebrate basic survival strategies and even assign their characters names that resonate with the hope that people were expected to have, illustrated by Fa (getting rich) and You (have) in Liu Qing's 1961 novel *Chuangyeshi [The Builders]*. Rather than being shamed by those in authority, people in poverty were encouraged not to be ashamed but to take pride in their circumstances. If the novelists whose works have been reviewed are to be believed, and they were, of course, writing in circumstances when they were likely to benefit from official approval, this seems to be what poor people did.

However, that era is now passed. In China, in the bid for economic growth in which increased economic disparities are viewed as a necessary by-product of creating the financial incentives to achieve, poverty is something to be despised rather than celebrated. 'Getting rich is glorious', 'being poor is being a bear (an idiot)'. In India, too, economic and social change is associated with new values. Beggars, for example, once linked to the divine through Bhiksha-tana, the incarnation of the Hindu god Shiva as a beggar, are now increasingly singled out for disapproval, epitomized by the two words 'Get lost!' in Sastry's 1957 Telugu short story *Aakali [Hunger]*. Likewise, with modernization, advanced capitalism, and the growth of consumerism and individualism, poverty may increasingly have come to be seen as a personal failing, even indicative of socially and economically dysfunctional behaviour, and personally shameful because everyone is expected to be an economic success.

SELDOM SHAME-FREE AND OFTEN SHAMELESS

Tapping into societies' dominant values through the windows provided by literature, film, and oral tradition reveals that poverty is something to be despised. It is often thought to be caused by individual failures and to place people in situations where they have little choice but to abandon any good intentions and prior morality in order merely to survive. Some writers and film-makers explicitly use their art to challenge these values, to shame those who behave shamefully towards people in poverty, which indicates that such beliefs are neither universal nor immutable. Nevertheless, the evidence to be assembled in Chapters 7–11 indicates that the negative portrayals of poverty found in literature and film accurately reflect values that are widespread in the countries under consideration. Moreover, they are held not only by the affluent and powerful but also by many people in poverty, and add significantly to the poverty-related shame that they experience.

The representation of individuals in poverty as being concerned about what others might think and chastising themselves for their own economic failure is entirely consistent with scientific understanding of the role of shame as a mechanism through which society seeks to control behaviour. Shame 'works' to the extent that it never has to be applied, with individuals instead policing their own thoughts and behaviour. The adherence to shared values illustrates, too, the cultural attachment to the individual work ethic that is so vital in societies wedded to economic development and to commercially fuelled prosperity. As is demonstrated in Chapters 9 and 10, belief in the work ethic encourages the public, including not infrequently those experiencing financial hardship, to equate poverty with social and moral failings, most notably with laziness. The depiction of shared values between rich and poor is somewhat at odds with the stigmatizing distinctions between 'them' and 'us' discussed in Chapter 4 that are sometimes found in political discourse and in sociological writings associated with the ideological right. The latter present people in poverty as constituting an underclass separated from mainstream society by different interests, ideals, and morals (Lewis, 1969; Mead, 1986). However, conversations with people experiencing poverty reported in Chapters 7 and 8 suggest that authors and playwrights may be accurate in their depiction of shared values and common aspirations.

That certain distinctions—such as those between 'us' and 'them' and between mainstream society and 'the great unwashed' (Bulwer-Lytton, 1830; Wright, 1868)—are not more evident in the materials reviewed requires comment. They are distinctions that often dominate in political discourse and public opinion (see especially Chapters 9 and 10). But, while people in poverty were sometimes presented in film and literature as being despicable and disgusting, and occasionally as threatening and frightening, more often they are depicted as characters warranting pity rather than contempt. Their shamelessness is generally portrayed as a product of force of circumstance rather than proactive choice, and anger as an understandable response to their situation. As heroes and heroines, they fight against the odds and sometimes succeed. Given the inherently political nature of poverty (see Chapter 1) and the small numbers of texts and films reviewed, it is possible that the authors and film-makers studied were keen to build support for reform by presenting their protagonists in a good light. Moreover, because the literature was deliberately identified from educational syllabi, it reflects establishment perspectives that may be liberal or, in the case of China until recently, explicitly pro-poor. In terms of storytelling too, it is easier to build audience engagement with likeable characters while uplifting narratives that celebrate human achievement typically engage the empathy of the reader directly, exploiting people's propensity to see the best in themselves. All these reasons may help to explain the importance of the 'Sen quadrant' in Figure 5.1, representing both shame and shaming, relative to the 'shameless quadrant'.

However, the same factors cannot explain the limited salience of the lower-right quadrant in Figure 5.1 that represents occasions when poverty is not shameful and people in poverty are not subject to shaming. There is no denying that both film and literature allude to such occasions, but for the most part they are situated in the past. An exception is China. This perhaps reflects the legacy of revolutionary rhetoric that praised people experiencing poverty for their role in resisting and overthrowing capitalism. It may also be a product of the rapid transition from mass endemic poverty, characterized at its worst by unimaginable famine, to a vast improvement in economic circumstances for most people that has occurred within a lifetime. The irony of this finding, juxtaposed against recognition that China is the archetypal culture bonded by shame rather than guilt, is inescapable. Perhaps the ubiquity of shame in Chinese culture serves to submerge that which is attributable to poverty.

It may also be that Chinese literature will soon begin to reflect the shift in official rhetoric that increasingly lauds individual economic success and follow modern South Korean film in castigating people in poverty for being total failures. Undoubtedly, the material reviewed gives cause to believe that the advance of the market and consumerism has meant people are increasingly accorded status in terms of what they own and are correspondingly held personally responsible for economic failure. Best seen in South Korean film, plots now assume wealth and despise failure, whereas in the past praise was heaped on those with the fortitude merely to survive. But if the shaming of poverty has increased alongside rising living standards, this does not necessarily mean that poverty was shame-free in traditional, agrarian economies characterized by endemic poverty. Certainly, Lugandan and Runyakitaran proverbs point to a past reality in which being poor could have been just as shaming as it is today.

Read alongside Chapter 5, it is clear that creative writing, film, and proverbs point to the ubiquity of poverty-related shame. But important though this material is in demonstrating the feasibility of discussing such complex phenomena as poverty and shame and the associations between them across very different cultures, it relates directly only to worlds of imagination. Chapters 7–11 address the reality of poverty-related shame beginning, in Chapter 7, with the life experiences of people currently living in poverty.

7

Shame in the Everyday Experience of Poverty[1]

With a few important exceptions, poverty is depicted in the literature and films reviewed in Chapters 5 and 6 as being degrading, causing people to debase themselves in their battle to survive. People in poverty are seen to be shamed in their families and communities when unable to fulfil the roles expected of them or to reciprocate gifts of exchange, and shamed in their dealings with official-dom that expose them to public ridicule. Sometimes persons experiencing poverty are depicted as shameless, resisting the humiliation heaped on them, occasionally in ways that demonstrate moral strength and resilience but more often through the adoption of antisocial behaviour that turns out to bring them no benefits and often to make matters worse. Shame felt on the inside is portrayed as destructive, with people in poverty engaging in fantasy and self-deception, retreating into themselves and into a spiral of despair, depression, and failure that sometimes ends in violence or suicide.

These accounts, told as stories through literature, film, and proverbs, can be interpreted in at least three ways. Firstly, the stories have entertainment value: they are designed to appeal to their respective audiences and have largely been successful in this, standing the test of time and being selected as important by experts in their respective fields. Secondly, they often have didactic intent. This is explicit in works that were chosen for study in school syllabi on account of the salience of the issues covered, their exemplary literary techniques, or usually both. It is true too of proverbs that survive due to their aptness and utility as vectors conveying cultural understandings and norms. Film-makers, notably those who work within the social realist tradition, seek to change attitudes and opinion by presenting aspects of the real world as it is to those presumed to be unaware of them. In these regards, the films' narratives are conveyors of social expectations and meanings, sometimes challenging the status quo, more often

---

[1] This chapter draws heavily on the following publications: Bantebya-Kyomuhendo and Mwiine (2014b); Chase and Walker (2014b); Choudhry (2014b); Gubrium and Lødemel (2014b); Jo (2014b); Pellissery and Mathew (2014b); and Yan (2014b).

supporting it. Finally, all films, not just those of the social realist genre, provide necessarily filtered accounts of real life appertaining to beliefs and behaviour.

Both poverty and shame are sufficiently similar in the way that they are represented in these different story formats, and across the diverse cultural settings observed, to warrant the next step in exploring the existence and nature of a poverty–shame nexus in real life and real time. This next step is to investigate how far the stories carried in oral traditions and in works of imagination resonate with lived experience today. In this chapter and Chapter 8, the focus is on the experiences of adults and children who encounter poverty. Do they feel shamed by others? Do they themselves feel ashamed of their poverty, and if so with what consequences for themselves and others? Social expectations and processes of shaming those experiencing poverty in social and public discourse are considered in Chapters 9 and 10.

For the most part, the evidence is drawn from new research employing a mix of in-depth interviews and other ethnographic methods (see Chase and Bantebya-Kyomuhendo, 2014 for details of samples and methods). As mentioned in Chapter 5, this was conducted in 2011 and 2012 in rural areas of Gujarat and Kerala in India, in urban and rural parts of Norway and Pakistan, and in urban China (Beijing), Korea (Seoul), and Britain (two areas of high deprivation in the South Midlands). In selecting people for interview, about thirty adults in each setting, a judicious balance was sought between the need to facilitate some comparison across countries without doing damage to the veracity of lives lived within particular cultures (Table 7.1). For the most part, the adults interviewed had dependent children, although in Beijing respondents belonged to a new class of poverty: former workers of now dissolved state owned enterprises who tended to be older than persons interviewed elsewhere. Poverty was defined with respect to local norms. In Uganda, India, and China, people were identified though local agents: village elders in the first case, key informants combined with direct observation in the second, and neighbourhood committees in the third. In Norway and Korea,

Table 7.1 People in poverty: respondents' characteristics

| | Number of respondents | | | |
| | Adults | | Children | |
	Men	Women	Boys	Girls
China	20	13		
India	12	17	14	14
Korea	8	23		
Norway	11	17		
Pakistan	15	14	7	8
Uganda	13	17	17	13
UK	11	31	18	4

respondents were recipients of social assistance, and in Pakistan, where about half of respondents were receiving social assistance, they were all identified from administrative records. Respondents in Britain lived in severely deprived neighbourhoods and were recruited via community organizations; all had, at some point, received social assistance benefits. It additionally proved possible to talk with children variously aged between 8 and 18 in the same localities as adults in India, Uganda, Pakistan, and Britain. Conversations with children were typically conducted either individually or in small groups. Children were not interviewed in Norway, Korea, or China.

Given the different cultures and the enormous variations in living standards that characterize the seven countries, one might expect marked disparities in the lived experiences of economic hardship. Figure 7.1 compares the countries according to: the Human Development Index (Norway has the highest score of 0.955, the highest in the world, while Uganda records a low score of 0.456); the Gender Inequality Index (India, Pakistan, and Uganda exhibit high inequality); and the OPHI Multiple Poverty Index or, for Norway, the UK, and South Korea, the OECD relative poverty standard. It is evident that Norway, South Korea, and the UK have similar profiles that contrast markedly with those of India, Pakistan, and Uganda which share common features, while China has a distinct profile falling between the other two clusters. Yet despite these differences, the thrust of Chapter 4, largely supported by the creative writing and film analysed in Chapters 5 and 6, is that shame is everywhere associated with poverty and that this has similar consequences for individual well-being and social competence. Certainly, with instructive qualifications, this is true of the people in poverty who

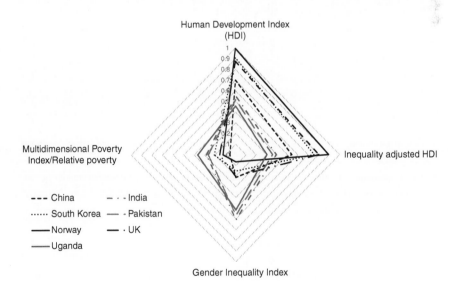

Fig. 7.1. The seven countries compared, 2012
UNDP (2013)

were interviewed in each of the seven countries, as is demonstrated in the remainder of this chapter and in Chapter 8.

POVERTY ITSELF

In material terms the poverty suffered by landless farmers in India, Pakistan, and Uganda is, of course, radically different from that experienced in urban Beijing or Britain, and different again from that faced by an Iraqi immigrant in outwardly prosperous western Oslo or an ethnic Norwegian living in a small coastal town.

All respondents in Uganda were subsistence farmers growing foodstuffs for family consumption, some supplementing incomes through casual labour (Bantebya-Kyomuhendo and Mwiine, 2014b). At best, they occupied single-storey housing that was rarely weatherproof, comprising a couple of rooms and built of sun-dried bricks with corrugated iron roofs. Many, however, lived in makeshift grass-thatched single-room dwellings without internal facilities for cooking and sanitation. A third of the households interviewed lacked access to clean water. In India, respondents were mostly daily labourers, but some families had a cow to supplement their income (Pellissery and Mathew, 2014b). Unlike in Uganda, where homesteads were dispersed, the single-storey houses were located cheek by jowl in village clusters. Generally comprising one or two rooms with cooking space outside, they were usually constructed from locally sourced timber and thatch with soil floors except when state funding allowed for concrete floors and walls and corrugated roofs. Water was generally supplied from communal taps, soil and water closets were rare, and access to electricity variable. In Pakistan, interviewing took place in both rural and urban locations (Choudhry, 2014b). Families in the former typically lived in small one- or two-room homes that they had built largely from mud (*katcha* houses) without sanitation or running water. In urban areas people often incurred the additional cost of renting. Even the best urban housing was located in *Katchi Abadis* (squatter camps), often three- or four-room houses were subdivided, with a family or many migrant workers sharing a single room, cooker, and sanitary facilities. Respondents in rural areas mostly worked the land, either for themselves or as peasants, while those in urban areas typically worked as day labourers, paid on a daily basis in cash. Most of the children interviewed worked, the majority full-time without attending school.

The persons interviewed in China all lived in Beijing in an area dominated by large factories that once housed state owned enterprises that have now been upgraded and taken over by private sector companies and international corporations (Yan, 2014b). Overshadowed by modern high-rise developments, respondents mostly lived in one-room apartments in dilapidated five- or six-storey concrete blocks dating from the era of Soviet influence but supplied with electricity and communal piped water. Most respondents had previously worked for state owned enterprises, but over a third were now unemployed and most of the remainder were working in low-skilled contract jobs.

In Britain, respondents mostly rented local authority properties, either brick-built, three-bedroom terraced housing or two- or three-bedroom apartments in concrete high-rise properties, both located on the outskirts of town (Chase and Walker, 2014b). The properties had piped water, electricity, and heating but several suffered from health-affecting dampness. All the respondents had at one time or another received out-of-work benefits and only about 12 per cent currently had a job, mostly in low-skilled or service sector occupations, with a similar number undertaking unpaid voluntary work.

Reflecting the uptake of social assistance in South Korea, twenty-three out of the thirty-one respondents interviewed were woman and seventeen, in total, were lone parents (Jo, 2014b). All resided in medium-rise apartment buildings in Seoul that dated back to the 1970s and were equipped with electricity and running water. Some occupied 'half underground' dwellings or basements that suffered from damp, while heating was often inadequate in winter. About half of the respondents were working, although mostly in part-time and temporary positions, many of them employed in menial jobs in the public sector. When respondents had children of school age, the children all seemed to be attending school regularly.

The respondents interviewed in Norway lived in three different locations: a small fishing town on the west coast, an industrial suburb in Oslo, and a wealthier district on the other side of the city (Gubrium and Lødemel, 2014b). Most lived in apartments that were generally weather proof and well-equipped, although they were often somewhat smaller than the Norwegian norm. Unusually for Norway, most respondents rented their homes often with financial assistance from the welfare office. All the respondents were unemployed, with approximately half engaged in an activation programme providing training and work experience, and half in receipt of social assistance.

Judged by material standards, respondents across the seven national sites lived in different worlds. The financial pressures on them were similarly different in degree and conceivably also in kind; decisions such as going without a meal that may result in hunger are not commensurate with the choice to eat poor-quality rather than nutritious food for reasons of cost. But measured against local expectations, the pressures on parents to provide the best that they could for their children, their families, and themselves may be much more comparable. As will become increasingly apparent, the failure to live up to those different expectations takes a markedly similar toll on the personal well-being and social functioning of people in each of the research settings. The argument is that the shame resulting from poverty is an important catalyst in shaping a relatively uniform response to different degrees of material hardship.

THE EFFECTS OF POVERTY

The effect of poverty, where poverty is taken to be the absence of resources necessary to match needs, is to restrict the ability of people to achieve the things expected of them and which they expect of themselves. These expectations equate closely with the capabilities that Sen argues enable individuals to fulfil their potential to lead rewarding and engaging lives, although he declines ever to list them (Sen, 2005). Nussbaum (2000) has advocated a set of capabilities derived from Aristotelian writings that are weighted heavily to the aesthetic, while Clark (2006) has found that low-income people living in both urban and rural parts of South Africa tend to conceptualize the good life in terms of more practical considerations relating to the availability of jobs, housing, education, income, family and friends, religion, health, food, good clothes, recreation and relaxation, safety, and economic security. Respondents in all seven countries talked of their frustrations about being unable to achieve the kinds of material aspirations identified by Clark, and the challenges of making hard decisions between competing demands. Equally, many had aspirations other than material ones, often quite modest in scope, to do with esteem and a sense of worth. However, failure to achieve these latter aspirations was often part of the personal and social costs associated with being unable to fulfil material ones. Sometimes people were also forced explicitly to sacrifice their sense of inner worth in order to attain material goods.

Basic Necessities

Food and housing were issues of concern to many respondents almost regardless of context. Both are matters of subsistence but each is also rich in symbolism. Both suggest security, but with limited resources they can instil a sense of insecurity and real fear for the future. Both provide statements of social position, indicating success or demonstrating failure and, especially when a person is economically successful, both can serve as means of self-expression. However, there is no more telling symbol of failure than the inability to provide appropriate food and shelter for oneself and one's family;

for respondents this was the epitome of shame and demonstrable evidence of having succumbed to poverty.

Accommodation for respondents in rural India, Pakistan, and Uganda typically meant upwards of six adults and children living in one or two rooms. They spoke of the overcrowding, disturbed nights, lack of privacy and the indignity and dangers, particularly for women, of having to urinate and defecate in fields and open spaces. Child respondents in Uganda talked of their embarrassment at living in a mud and thatched hut and of their unwillingness to invite friends home from school, a response echoed elsewhere. In Britain, particular streets had reputations that meant that friends did not want to be invited home. Even in Norway, a parent confessed to not wanting his daughter to bring friends to their 'simple' apartment for fear that she would be marked out 'as different'.

But housing is as much about security as it is about facilities. Hence, although food may be a family's first concern, housing was often their first priority especially for those renting. Whereas the amount of food eaten could be varied, rent generally had to be paid in full with the sanction of eviction. One in six respondents in Korea was in imminent threat of homelessness, bailiffs being called in Britain was seen to have traumatic effects on families and children, while land theft was instanced in Uganda. Even for those not at immediate risk of losing their home, the landowner or landlord was often a figure of fear who had to be appeased. For others, it was inclement weather that washed away the sense of security.

Living Up to Expectations

Social conventions and institutions that bind society together—family, community, education, and other public services—proved to have even greater potential for shaming than the need to secure basic necessities. To participate actively in any of these requires a basic level of resources and respondents believed themselves to be placed at a clear disadvantage. In India especially, but also in Pakistan, China, and Uganda, the demands of the family and ritual were paramount, imposing significant and sometimes precisely defined costs that were often in excess of what could be afforded. In Uganda not to be invited to village community events was often interpreted as a humiliating consequence of poverty.

Equally, there were additional expectations imposed by society, such as school attendance and preventative healthcare, that carried with them real costs since they were less often free at the point of use than in Norway and Britain. Living up to social expectations is a challenge for anyone and can become a personal nightmare for those suffering poverty, as the accounts of the people interviewed testify.

Debt and Financial Control

Work and employment, the keys to the resources that open the door to active social participation, were generally in short supply, many respondents having limited skills and education. People with low incomes saw themselves as potentially trapped in a vicious life—an intergenerational cycle in which limited human and social resources constrained the acquisition of the financial means necessary to invest in their children's futures. Needing to ensure that inadequate resources could be stretched to meet immediate demands, many respondents found themselves caught in the continuing short-term, dealing with today's needs at the expense of tomorrow's.

For those on a low income, even to succeed in meeting basic needs required exceptional budgeting skills. Women often carried the burden of responsibility and the risk of shame. Such juggling frequently entailed respondents borrowing in cash and/or in kind and, when in debt, a miscalculation or misfortune could spiral into financial disaster. People typically intensely disliked borrowing and were afraid of its repercussions; added to fear of the landlord was the anger of the moneylender, the scorn of the relative, and the threat of formal sanction, legitimate or criminal. In debt, people lost control of their lives and forfeited their reputations and their respectability. In Uganda, for example, respondents coupled borrowing with begging as something decent people did not do. Even so, many, perhaps most, respondents in Uganda and elsewhere were in debt and were worried about being so.

Given these pressures it might go without saying that respondents did not much like living in poverty. Indeed, they despised poverty and often despised themselves, and children sometimes their parents, for being poor. All this hardship did not deny respondents happiness. Both Islam and Christianity encourage their followers to compare their socio-economic condition with that of others, leading some respondents paradoxically to mention their thankfulness while almost concurrently expressing their unhappiness with life. In Uganda, adults talked of the happiness they found in being able to share food and give gifts at harvest time and to help those worse off than themselves. Similarly in Britain, mention was made of the helpfulness of friends, the sense of loyalty, the idea of 'all being in the same boat', and of the notion that everybody was willing to help out in the way that 'moneyed people' would never do because they did not understand the pressures.

Respondents lived with these pressures and some took pleasure from the fact that overall, in broad terms and for most of the time, they were coping adequately with them. They sometimes felt, too, that they were successfully bringing their children up to cope with financial pressure, to live frugally in expensive Oslo for example, making birthday presents rather than buying them. But it was the combined pressure of having to cope with limited resources while knowing that one was poor and unable to live up to one's own expectations, or those demanded by the community, that shaped lives to the detriment of sustained happiness.

THE EXPERIENCE OF SHAME

At no time in any of the interviews conducted did interviewers introduce the concept of shame or anything like it. Instead, respondents were encouraged to talk about their lives, their material circumstances, the things that made life relatively easy, and those that made matters difficult. However, it became evident quickly and in most cases, from what respondents said and the way that they said it, that their lives were not only hard but that they knew them to be hard. Knowing that they were poor was as difficult, if not more difficult, than simply being poor.

INTERNAL SHAME: TO FEEL ASHAMED

In Chapters 5 and 6 it proved helpful to organize the material in terms of whether people in poverty were shamed or not by society and whether or not they actually felt ashamed (see Figure 5.1). From the interviews it was very clear that the vast majority of respondents in every cultural setting had felt ashamed on account of their poverty; for many the shame lingered and was often there all the time should they stop to think about it. In addition to this internal shame, respondents described how they were at risk of being shamed in a variety of arenas that differed in importance, and to some extent in kind, between the various cultural settings. The conjunction of feeling ashamed and being shamed because one was poor, the top-left 'Sen quadrant' in Figure 5.1, was an inevitable and defining characteristic of life; much of what people did they did partly to push this reality into the background, but the ever-present risk and recurring reality was that circumstances would force feelings of shame to the forefront of their lives. Correspondingly few respondents said that they had never been shamed nor felt shame as a result of their poverty. Indeed, in the setting where this might have been thought most likely to occur, among the traditional rural subsistence farmers of Uganda, the sense of shame among respondents was palpable. Likewise, there were precious few examples where people felt no shame despite shaming by others, although there were many accounts of people trying to hide their shame, a phenomenon explored further in Chapter 8.

The dual points of reference that social psychologists identify as generating internal shame (see Chapter 3), the self and the other, were clearly apparent in accounts of respondents' own lives just as they had been evident in the creative writing reviewed in Chapter 5. Firstly, there was the sense of failure in not living up to their own expectations due to limited resources, and secondly there was the belief that as a consequence of this failure they were not valued by other people. Ugandan respondents wanted land, a permanent house, cattle, a business or gainful employment, food security for their families, possessions such as a motorbike and solar panels, and private education for their children. Most had few or any of these things, and the vast majority of adults interviewed believed that as a consequence of this material deprivation they were not regarded as persons of worth in their society—people who would be allowed to speak in community meetings, people whose opinion counted for something. They spoke of shame, humiliation, and stigma and expressed feelings of worthlessness, low self-esteem, self-pity, disillusionment, and hopelessness.

The strength of the words and of the feelings underpinning them were echoed by respondents in the other countries. In India, words equivalent to 'sadness', 'small', 'hurt', 'worthless', 'dejection', and 'rejection' were commonly used along with words that were closer to 'shame' and 'embarrassment' and also, more occasionally, to 'anger' and 'rage'. But the shame attributable to poverty was often merged and sometimes not clearly distinguishable from that linked to other sources of shame that in turn reflected, or indeed contributed to, poverty: desertion; widowhood; the lack of a son; and, of course, caste. In Britain, in the context of needing to 'struggle', 'scrimp and save', 'borrow, beg, and steal' to keep their 'heads above water', respondents similarly felt 'small', 'awkward', 'embarrassed', 'uncomfortable', 'guilty', 'rotten', 'degraded', 'crap', 'useless', 'dirty', 'worthless', 'a failure', and 'acutely inadequate'. In Pakistan, most respondents considered money to be the basis of social respect and that, without it, they were denied the possibility of living a respectable social life. Furthermore, people employed as domestic workers in affluent households and therefore confronted directly by visible inequalities in wealth experienced a heightened sense of 'social exploitation', 'inferiority', and 'shame'.

Things were perhaps a little different in China. As elsewhere, poverty meant tightening belts, with a focus on securing sufficient food and adequate (usually second-hand) clothing. Paying for health insurance and educational costs were worrisome burdens and people tried to get by without the humiliation of borrowing money. But fewer admitted to feeling ashamed, instead stressing their endurance and the support that they received from family and friends. Given their characteristics as former workers of state owned enterprises, considered to represent the 'new poverty' in China, respondents not surprisingly saw economic restructuring as a root cause of their circumstances to which they were prone to add fate and ill-luck. This reasoning—which pushed responsibility away from themselves—may partially explain the lower salience of poverty-related shame among the Chinese respondents. Other comparable research, similarly conducted in Beijing a year earlier (2009) but among slightly older residents experiencing poverty (aged 60 plus), identified shame as one of four key causes of stress (the others being low income, disease and ageing, and the inability to care for relatives, Chen et al., 2013). These respondents explicitly compared themselves negatively to senior cadres 'who lived in heaven' rather than 'under the ground', and spoke of themselves in degrading terms such as 'beggars' and 'inferior'.

These latter reactions are directly comparable to those of respondents in South Korea (Jo, 2014b). There, the sense of personal failure, constructed within a legacy of Confucian familial expectations and obligations, was added to by social and political aspirations. Economically transformed over 60 years—initially by nationalist, authoritarian governments intent on promoting and exploiting 'a strong hard-working mind-set'—everybody in South Korea is expected to have both benefited from and contributed to its economic growth (Jo and Walker, 2013). Moreover, the economic growth and associated urbanization and changes in family structure have undermined the ability of the traditional family to deliver the financial support that continues to be expected from it. Korean respondents therefore often felt ashamed with respect to self, family, community, and state.

In Norway, being poor, jobless, and receiving social assistance were closely intertwined, separating some respondents socially and even ideologically from the wider society. These feelings are illustrated by the following statements from three lone parents receiving social assistance (NAV, or *Ny Arbeids- og velferdsforvaltning*):

> It's shame . . . one has to experience it to say it . . . I'm a burden on other people . . . Can anyone be proud of going to the social assistance office and asking for money? I don't think so'
>
> . . . you start asking the sort of questions like 'Aren't I good enough?' You start to have doubts.
>
> . . . I don't really see myself as worthy enough . . . it has to do with self-confidence or self-image maybe. What is it that [people] talk about?

These respondents were not only failing in relation to their own aspirations, they were also dependent on social assistance and hence on society as a whole—they described themselves as 'parasites'. The fact that they did not have the jobs that they wanted and were expected to have was inextricably linked with self-image. The same was often true to an exaggerated extent for migrants, many of whom had often had higher-status jobs in their countries of origin. From joblessness stemmed frustration, a sense of hopelessness, and, perhaps among a number of the Norwegian respondents, a growing alienation from the norms of mainstream society. It was not that they did not feel shame or that they sought to lessen their sense of shame by rejecting the norms that framed it; they simply could not live up to those norms without a job, without sufficient income.

In sum, the ubiquitous sense of personal shame associated with poverty captured in creative writing and film seems to be replicated in real life, as does the nuanced relationship between poverty and shame found in China which is further discussed in this chapter.

EXTERNAL SHAME: TO BE SHAMED

The common belief of respondents that, being people in poverty, they were not fully or adequately valued as humans by others, was justified by reference to their own experience of being treated with disdain and contempt as well as their subjection to negative public discourses. According to respondents in Uganda, for example, other people said that poverty was associated with laziness, dishonesty, lack of focus, and unreliability. The media in Britain, respondents believed, similarly promulgated the view that poverty was linked with indolence and criminality but also with drug use, promiscuity, and benefit dependency. In Norway, poverty was equated with social assistance, joblessness, drug users, and immigrants. While these views seldom accorded with respondents' understanding of themselves, in their dealings with others they kept being presented with a distorted image that they were unworthy and no doubt guilty of laziness, or worse.

While respondents wanted the better life denied to them by lack of money, and to be able to play the roles expected of them as worker, parent, and good citizen, they frequently saw the odds of achieving these goals to be irrevocably stacked against them. Moreover, they had also often internalized the belief that they were responsible for, and somehow therefore the cause of, the predicament in which they found themselves. This latter understanding was frequently reinforced by persons and institutions with whom they interacted on a daily basis in a variety of arenas. These arenas varied in importance between the different cultural settings shaped by varying normative expectations, but almost invariably exposed people in poverty to shaming or to the fear of being made to feel ashamed.

The Family

The importance of the family to respondents in India meant that it placed demands on them that seemed often to rank next to food among life's basic necessities. Children come first but obligations attached to the roles of son, daughter, brother, and sister are sometimes equally immutable. And, while the family was perhaps more salient as an arena of shame among respondents in the more collectivist societies of the global South, respondents living in Norway and Britain were not immune from the pressures of family.

Biology and society insist that parents care for their children. If they cannot do so financially, their sense of economic failure and personal inadequacy is repeatedly reinforced in dealings with their children. In the Ugandan context, for example, children were often ashamed of their homes and of their parents, blaming their parents' illiteracy and lack of skills for the poverty that the family experienced. It is difficult, both emotionally and practically, for parents to cope with children who repeatedly ask for things that cannot be afforded; it underlines parents' inability adequately to provide for their family and creates fault lines of tension within the family. Adult respondents in Pakistan commonly said that they attempted to keep the parlous state of family finances from their children for as long as possible, not involving them in knowledge of household circumstances until they were older. However, possibly for this reason, and because of limited acumen, younger children were reported to be more tenacious in their demands such that older children and parents had to make sacrifices on their behalf.

Later in life, children were more likely to appreciate that parents could not give them food if they had none themselves and therefore learned to temper their own demands. In China, where it proved to be impossible to interview children themselves, parents tended to note how 'mature' their children were in that they did not demand things that were unaffordable. Several children in the British sample spontaneously explained that they too did not press their parents for things, not least because they recognized that parents felt 'a bit ashamed' that they could not buy everything that they needed. This process has been described before and characterized as 'learning to be poor' (Shropshire and Middleton, 1999; Ridge, 2002). In adopting this behaviour, though, children were aware that a likely consequence was opprobrium at school because they lacked the currently fashionable acquisitions that were the totem of group acceptance. Moreover, other work with younger children in Britain (aged 10 and under) suggests that they knowingly, strategically, build up pressure on their parents, escalating demands at times when money is least scarce and the chances of successfully breaking parents' resistance are greatest (Middleton et al., 1994). That said, one British respondent, a lone mother with a 4-year-old son, explained how he, on overhearing her complaining about the difficulty of making ends meet, offered up his birthday present, a Nintendo DS, which they subsequently sold to help pay off outstanding debts.

Parents often have to negotiate and reconcile the demands and expectations of their children with those of the wider family. While responsibilities of parenthood—the need to do right by one's children—tend to ultimately trump all others, the sanctions available to the wider family can be severe. There are finely tuned expectations in the more collectivist cultures that govern familial relationships stipulating who, for example, should provide care for which elders and in what way. Failure to provide and to reciprocate appropriately is to offend wide sections of the family and to risk ostracism and indeed disinheritance. In India, respondents reported disputes over unpaid dowries, non-repaid loans, and unrequited gifts that had left them excluded from family events or explicitly ignored if they attended. There were even examples of exploitation of poorer family members. In Uganda, relatives attempted to evict a lone parent, aware that the victim would not have the financial resources to resist. Similarly, a widow in Gujarat explained how her ration card had been taken by her brother-in-law such that she was left wanting.

Even positive support from family—in the form of cash, gifts, and loans for example, 'the difference between keeping your head above water or sinking'— can reinforce the sense of shame since, as one British lone mother explained, 'it is all to do with admitting the fact that you cannot cope'. Other respondents agreed that it was 'horrible', 'embarrassing', and 'dreadful' to have to accept help from other people. This sense of dependency can also be aggravated by pressure for reciprocity.

Gender distinctions were real. Women in Pakistan were especially prone to shaming within the family. Polygamy was perceived to create second-class wives who tended to receive less attention and less income and therefore were more vulnerable to exploitation, while widows were particularly susceptible to poverty, having unclear rights and obligations within the family. Women forced by circumstance, rather than choice, to take up paid work were not excused from the intricate sets of family responsibilities and obligations, which became additional burdens that could not be avoided because of the fear of being shamed. Likewise, for complex cultural reasons women in India and Uganda were more likely to describe excluding themselves or being excluded from family gatherings that their husbands continued to attend.

For men, everywhere, the failure to provide and the need to rely on others or on welfare benefits was perceived as a challenge to their sense of masculinity: a British father to two children admitted that he felt 'like shit . . . I'm the man in this relationship. I am meant to be the man . . . to take care of the missus and my kids. And I don't'. The sense of personal shame was likely to be magnified by the opprobrium exerted by the community. Indeed, in Uganda classic shame (*okuhemuka*) arising from the failure to provide basic necessities can only be suffered by husbands—the de facto household heads and breadwin-ners. Hence, some Ugandan women intimated that issues of social worth were not their concern, but those of their husbands, male relatives, or of menfolk generally. Others, though, felt ashamed of their husbands and yet others took on the same shame that their spouses felt. This was further complicated in India—where women are traditionally held responsible for household affairs—if men wasted income on alcohol and tobacco or denied women access to, or information about, household income. A British mother even asked her unemployed husband to leave because he was no longer contribut-ing to family income despite 'loving him to bits'.

In sum, while the family is the first defence against poverty, when resources are scarce familial obligations are a constant threat and reminder of personal failure and inadequacy. Like the house that leaks, there is often not the sense of comfort or security that makes it a perfect home.

School

Part of the security that home and family can provide is familiarity and sameness. At home, the experience of extreme poverty can seem normal; a child may be unaware that life for others is different. School, however, broadens horizons, shatters illusions, and removes the child from the security of sameness to create an arena in which severe shaming is prevalent.

This was true even in Uganda where, despite policy intentions for an inclusive education system, universal primary and secondary schools essen-tially serve the children of low-income parents. Children recognized this reality. Most felt that even attending a state school marked them out as being poor, vulnerable, and needy (key eligibility criteria for entry) and that the education was less good than in private schools. This generally both 'annoyed' children and made them feel 'worthless'; one 15-year-old girl summed up this perspective succinctly: 'I know I am poor, but it is not my choice. It is not my identity!' Some, though, recognized that a state school was the only way that they could get any education at all. Within schools, children were involved in an ongoing process of comparison and were faced by stark differences: smartly dressed or not, more than one set of uniform or not, hungry or not, pocket money or not, calculator or not, the list was endless.

In Uganda, children did not repeatedly mention being picked on and bullied. They did though in Britain, where possessions were a source of acceptance, dividing in-groups from out-groups, and where life in the play-ground was constructed as 'a competition with everyone else'. One explained how 'the next day somebody else brings something even bigger and better' and that the intention of such protagonists is 'to show you up'. The same was reportedly true in Norway, with the sense of relative deprivation increasing as children got older and the sense of anxiety being passed from children to parents who were unable to respond to their children's financial expectations. In India—where differentials are starkly apparent through payment and non-payment of fees, free school meals, and personal equipment supplied by charities—child respondents reported being segregated at school by children from better-off homes who refused to talk and play with them.

Only in Pakistan was there evidence to counter the possibility that the school is always a cockpit of comparison and shaming. There, very few of the children interviewed attended school at all. Those that did, did not dwell on the divisiveness of income. Indeed, even allowing for differences in family incomes children attending school seemed to have more friends, more opportunities to engage in social occasions such as visits to festivals and other cultural events, and were more likely to express life satisfaction, happiness, and greater hope for the future.

Children were generally very optimistic and ambitious. They wanted to be pilots, teachers, doctors, and business people, and like many of their parents, especially those who had been unable to attend school, they often believed that education provided the best route out of their poverty. But nevertheless in the playground they had to battle against the consequences of being 'poor'.

The Workplace

For many adult respondents, those who worked as daily labourers or were unemployed, the labour market was, like school, an arena of constant comparison where those who were poorest felt that they came off worst. Standing in the job queue served to mark a person out as being different and inferior to others who had jobs. In India and Pakistan daily labouring was the norm, and yet respondents still felt the inferiority of rejection, believing that the better jobs went to other people who were perhaps fitter, younger, or who could afford the necessary bribes. The constant rejection—which in Britain and Norway often meant repeated unanswered job applications, standardized rejection slips, and failure at interview—took a considerable toll on people's self-confidence. To work was what one was expected to do, what one wanted to do, and without a job people lost their positive identity; one Norwegian lone mother mused with dejection that 'jobless' would be engraved on her gravestone.

However, the kind of work one did also mattered. In Pakistan and India the structural addition of caste in regulating the labour market meant that those of lowest caste, or who were outside the caste system (Catholics in parts of Pakistan for example), were systematically relegated to the most unpleasant occupations. Respondents in China, who as employees of state owned enterprises had once been part of the vanguard of worker class enjoying high status as 'masters of the state', now had largely to be content with low-paying, insecure occupations because they lacked the entrepreneurial skills demanded by the reformed Chinese economy. The loss of esteem was palpable, as indeed it was for the aforementioned migrants into Norway who found that the professional qualifications that they had acquired in their home countries were not accepted, or that their language skills did not match the kind of jobs to which they aspired. In Britain, many respondents felt the only jobs open to them were 'shit jobs', ones lacking in status, paying low wages, and without security or prospects. People needed to work and worked in the jobs they could get, but they were constantly reminded of their lowly status and seeming powerlessness to do anything about it.

The workplace could also be a site of exploitation and abuse. Consistent with the theoretical discussion in Chapter 4, begging was universally considered to be socially unacceptable and was, therefore, in itself humiliating and shameful. Moreover, it exposed people to verbal and sometimes to physical abuse on the one hand, and to being ignored and thereby being made to feel invisible and inconsequential on the other. Casual daily labour in India, Pakistan, and Uganda meant a process of daily negotiation, akin to begging for work, in which the employer had the power to employ or not employ and the instant sanction of dismissal or non-re-employment. This sanction carried the immediate prospect of no money and perhaps even hunger, and the longer-term consequence of having once been labelled unreliable or a troublemaker. Chinese workers making the transition from employment in state owned industries to insecure work, often via long spells of unemployment, had to adapt to a subservient role where they were no longer able to challenge management as they felt they had previously been able to do.

Explicit accounts of ill-treatment at work were mainly related by women and children and often concerned domestic service work. Specific examples were cited by respondents in Pakistan, Uganda, and Norway. In the last case, a respondent described how sexual overtures had been made in a job interview that had created for her a fear concerning the legitimacy of all subsequent interviews. In Pakistan, domestic work is minimally regulated if at all, and relations between householders and servants revolve round complex relationships of mutual dependency. Many respondents spoke of the kindnesses of their employers, which they variously attributed to simple generosity, the Islamic principle of Zakat requiring that a fixed portion of one's wealth is given away, and to understanding that charity that begins at home can bring advantages in terms of staff loyalty. More sinister were reports of unpaid wages underpinned by threats of calling in police on the pretence of theft or other dire consequences. Similar reports came from children interviewed in Pakistan, who spoke of irregular payments to cover food and transport in lieu of wages while, on average, the sums paid by employers to the children interviewed were just 37 per cent of the Pakistani minimum wage. Some

Pakistani children also reported that the training promised to them was never delivered, thereby tying them to their current employer; yet others reported physical beatings.

Some adult respondents in Norway, Britain, and South Korea who had been placed on employment or work experience schemes as a condition of receiving welfare benefit similarly spoke of exploitation. They believed that they were doing real work for the benefit of employers but not being paid real wages. Moreover, they felt further aggrieved when their hopes of being taken on as permanent employees were dashed. Whether this kind of exploitation is in any way equivalent to that experienced by child workers in Pakistan is questionable, but it nevertheless emphasized to respondents their vulnerability and powerlessness. They needed income to survive more than they had means to resist abuse.

The experiences that many respondents recount from the workplace smack of stigma. While they were shamed by their public exposure and felt ashamed because their income and earnings were insufficient to make ends meet, they also reported discrimination and exploitation on account of their weak financial position. The sceptic might suggest that these findings are likely to be biased because it was to the benefit of respondents to blame others rather than to admit their own inadequacies. However, as will become apparent in Chapter 9, these accounts are largely corroborated by members of the very groups that they accused of subjecting them to discrimination and stigma.

Officialdom and Community

For the most part, respondents' contact with officialdom and their engagement (such that it was) with the wider community served to reinforce their sense of shame. As in other arenas, this resulted from subtle interactions between internal shame and reactions to external shaming that cumulatively shaped respondents' sense of self over time. Sometimes this happened because they were required to admit to their poverty and the personal failure that this instilled in order to access the services or support that they needed. Sometimes it occurred vicariously because of how they were treated by officials among others, or perhaps simply because of how they felt they had been treated or stigmatized. Sometimes, even, their own insecurities may have triggered the response that they feared, or merely reinforced their beliefs about the negative light in which other people saw them.

The almost universal sense of failure associated with poverty was possibly most strongly evident among the Ugandan respondents, who considered the label of poverty to be dehumanizing, the epitome of indignity. It was something that they resisted internalizing because it smacked not only of failure but also of social rejection that served to erode their sense of self as human beings.

Resistance to accepting the label of poverty extended to boycotting antipoverty programmes since, as one respondent speaking for many explained, the benefits would not outweigh the feeling of shame, even if they were able to buy everything they wanted as a result: family essentials, livestock, and personal development. This made state schooling, which in Uganda is primarily reserved for needy children, very problematic. It generally put a premium on private schooling, which only one of the families in the study could manage to afford, and meant that children were constantly reminded of their status as poor, something that they tended to blame on their parents.

Respondents in Norway, a country epitomized by universal welfare provision, were of financial necessity forced to rely on means-tested social assistance (NAV). This they considered to be demeaning, not least because they felt that it was assumed by society and bureaucracy caseworkers alike that recipients were especially needy, lazy, or dependent. The system meant that they were ranked into a six-step trajectory towards normal paid work that felt like a hierarchy of shame, in which one started close to the bottom alongside people facing difficult times as drug users, lone parents, and immigrants. Recipients acknowledged the 'joy' that they had initially felt at reaching the penultimate step in the hierarchy, the Qualification Programme (QP) of work experience. They contrasted the fact that they received a wage and that they were 'contributing' to society with their previous experience as social assistance clients, which one respondent described as having had 'everything stolen from you; you're not a participant in society, you're only a burden'. However, the imposition of the NAV hierarchy was made invidious by the fact that progress through it often appeared to be random and arbitrary. Many respondents spoke of the systematic lack of expectation, concern, and follow up that seemed to be endemic in the system, which meant that their fate appeared to depend on the discretionary decisions of caseworkers, creating a sense of great uncertainty and powerlessness. Also, people felt both exploited and disillusioned when work experience secured on the QP programme did not translate into permanent employment.

In the British benefit system respondents found the rules and regulations to be sometimes petty, often dehumanizing, and increasingly punitive: 'you're not allowed to wear "a hoodie"'.[2] They felt themselves to be treated as a group—part of the 'crackdown' on supposed exploitation of the benefit system—or as 'just a number'. They were 'made to feel small', constantly completing forms rather than being related to as fellow human beings. Recipients of the Chinese Minimum Standard of Living Scheme (MSLS, often termed Dibao) frequently found their dealings with officialdom equally stressful. Applications needed to be renewed every six months, forms completed again, and evidence supplied usually requiring travel back to their towns of origin in order to demonstrate that they had no assets such as land or housing. Applicants also needed to prove that they

---

[2] A 'hoodie' is a garment with a hood associated in the public mind with youthful troublemakers.

had failed job applications, and one respondent described the humiliation that she had experienced in seeking documentary evidence as to why an employer did not consider her fit for a position. In China, names of MSLS recipients are publically posted in the neighbourhood in order to solicit any information that could suggest that they should not be eligible for benefit; however, only one respondent considered this to be an infringement of privacy.

A number of South Korean respondents similarly reported the humiliation that they incurred as a consequence of needing to demonstrate that they were unemployable in order to receive social assistance (NBLSS, National Basic Livelihood Security Law). Moreover, as a legacy of the Confucian reliance on the family, the means test for social assistance extends to the applicant's direct kin and their spouses and, in the case of co-residence, to siblings, grandparents, and grandchildren. Applicants are obliged to personally request the agreement of all relevant family members to means testing, thereby exposing their own precarious circumstances and committing kin to a reduced income, or else to publicly disown them in order to release them from their financial obligation. This provision necessarily imposes stigma, not only on the applicant but also on the larger family, resulting in low take-up of NBLSS, considerable financial hardship, and significant familial strife (Yeo, 2004).

In India, stigma attaching to benefit receipt ironically seemed to be trumped by the prevalence of corruption. Every five years a 'below the poverty line' (BPL) list is compiled which gives people access to various government schemes. However, such is the abuse of the list that inclusion has become a matter of esteem rather than contempt. To succeed in having one's name listed alongside those of large landowners indicates that one must have influence with the village leaders who are the gatekeepers to the BPL.

The stigma of poverty and benefit receipt was not necessarily restricted to agencies dealing with social problems. Many respondents in Uganda cited examples of when they were slighted by their local community, such as being excluded from the community meetings and events that are of central importance in rural areas, simply on account of their poverty. Indeed, at a community meeting held to hear the results of the research, some of the respondents interviewed had to listen to the discussion while sitting on the floor outside. Ugandan respondents also spoke of: land and possessions being stolen in the knowledge that, as people living poverty, they would not be protected by the law; being left alone when desperately ill rather than being taken to hospital; and being accused of sorcery and witchcraft. A respondent in Pakistan encapsulated the impotence and vulnerability felt by many of the people interviewed across all seven countries when he explained that:

> It is not that the rich always treat the poor badly. It is just that they always have the power to treat them badly. It's their choice to decide how to behave at a particular moment.

Respondents might have added that the rich can behave against people in poverty with impunity.

In Britain, a number of respondents reported feeling that they were always being judged, be it by professionals, the media, or the public. More than anywhere else negative images taken from television and especially the press were cited as evidence of the stigma attaching to poverty:

> There's a stigma isn't there, there's a stigma attached to it. You know ... living on a council estate, being on benefits, ra, ra, ra ... it's like the image portrayed in the media and stuff—you're this kind of ASBO-hoodie.[3]

The view was that such negative images were ubiquitous, with the result that they were continually being judged wanting. One respondent described how, from the viewpoint of the headmistress of her son's school, she 'ticked all the boxes'. Putting thoughts into the headmistress's mind, she envisaged her thinking:

> She lives on [Road Name], that ticks her off as a bad parent; she's a single mother ... doesn't have a job ... emotional problems ... she's struggling ... son's got behavioural problems' and reasoning: 'Oh my God, it's just another one of those mothers.

The conclusion that the respondent drew, rightly or wrongly, was that the headmistress 'couldn't give two monkeys' about anything that she said.

While the central role of the media in fuelling the dynamics of community stigma, apparent in Britain, was less marked in the other national settings (see also Chapter 10), the perceived negativity of community attitudes was not (although Chinese respondents were less vocal about it). When it came to applying to antipoverty programmes, however, the internal shame reinforced by perceptions of stigma inherent in the system and manifest in the behaviour of officials was apparent everywhere.

THE CENTRALITY OF SHAME

The adults and children interviewed in the seven countries lived very different lives. Culture, climate, religion, environment, politics, and economic development all varied massively. The only thing known in advance that they had in common was that they were considered to be poor by the standards of their societies, often as judged by people living locally. This was deliberate to provide a preliminary although not definitive test of the universality of shame associated with poverty. And like the evidence from literature and film, the conclusions point to shame being an important constituent in the

---

[3] An ASBO is an Anti-Social Behaviour Order that can be issued against an offender in an attempt to prevent them from engaging in antisocial behaviour.

experience of poverty in each of the different national settings, albeit with subtle differences in the triggers of shame and the relative importance of the arenas in which it occurred.

There is other material from around the world that tells a similar story. The *Voices of the Poor* study undertaken for the World Bank (Narayan et al., 2000a, 2000b) revealed children in Bangladesh, India, and Moldova feeling 'marked' by shabby clothing; an unemployed father in Guinea-Bissau who felt ashamed at being unable adequately to feed his children; poor people in Armenia feeling a lack of self-worth and loss of status at being unable to maintain basic hygiene; and poverty in Madagascar being equated with the inability to adhere to local customs and norms. Earlier research in Britain has shown that the word poverty itself is stigmatizing and shunned, people in poverty instead describing their everyday experiences as 'mundane, limited, constrained, full of drudgery or struggle' (Castell and Thompson, 2007). Elsewhere in Europe and North America there is similar evidence that poverty is experienced as personal failure with social success being measured in terms of conspicuous consumption (Beresford et al., 1999; Clasen et al., 1998; Edin et al., 2000; Schwarz, 1997).

While resources for food, shelter, and clothing are necessary to ensure health and survival they are also laden with symbolic significance, as are the relationships, social conventions, and institutions that constitute culture and frame individual lives. Poverty, by definition, makes it almost impossible to meet even basic needs without the exceptional budgeting skills that respondents explained and typically demonstrated. Such juggling often entails borrowing in cash and kind, and when in debt the smallest miscalculation or misfortune can spiral into financial disaster. Poverty makes it very hard to succeed in living up to the expectations of being a good parent, offspring, relative, friend, or citizen. Despite respondents generally believing that they had done their best against all the odds, they mostly considered that they had both failed themselves by being poor and that others saw them as failures.

As anticipated by the socio-psychological literature, this internal shame was further reinforced by external shame manifest in the talk and actions of others. This occurred within the family, neighbourhood, and wider community. It was also reported happening in the workplace and during contacts with officialdom where reports of discrimination, exploitation, and stigmatization were most in evidence. Even children could not escape this external shame because school, except possibly in Pakistan, was an engine of social grading, a place of humiliation for those without the possessions that guaranteed acceptance.

No parent could escape the shame of failing to provide for their children. The other obligations imposed by the family varied between cultures in the detail of their specification, while the balance between positive support and demanding expectations also differed across societies and between families. In China, a culture that makes fine distinctions between different kinds of shame, overt complaint was less marked than elsewhere. Generally, women were perhaps more frequently exposed to shaming than men because they were more often responsible for domestic budgeting and childcare, and were subject to greater demands with respect to hygiene, personal presentation, and familial obligations. Men, though, more often carried responsibility for financial provision and fielded criticism of the family as a whole. They often shouldered the shame of unemployment and exploitation at work although women and children, particularly those in domestic service in developing countries, reported more abuse—physical and psychological—as well as being exposed more directly to differences in comparative wealth and status.

The novels and film reviewed in Chapter 5 and 6 perceptively foretold the real-life experiences of people in poverty in all but one respect, namely that few of the sample warranted the adjective 'shameless'. The overwhelming majority of respondents reported experiencing shame because of their poverty. Even in China, where some respondents did not admit to feeling ashamed, they did not fit the fictional archetype of a rogue, loveable or otherwise; they simply saw themselves making the best of a bad lot. The reason for this difference between the worlds of imagination and experience could be selectivity; why should someone who is shameless wish to participate in research or admit to ever feeling ashamed? Equally, shamelessness might be a way of dealing with shame, to be brazen about shame rather than about poverty itself. Chapter 8 goes on to discusse people's responses to shame, and the extent to which poverty-related shame is as debilitating as much as the psychological research reviewed in Chapter 3 would suggest.

8

Responses to Poverty-Related Shame[1]

The evidence in Chapter 7 suggests that shame is very often central to the experience of poverty. It arose, as both Amartya Sen (1983) and Peter Townsend (1979) anticipated, from the inability of people to afford fully to participate in the communities and societies of which they were ostensibly part. However, what neither Sen nor Townsend emphasize, but which is consistent with psychological and sociological theory (see Chapter 3), is that respondents were not only ashamed of their poverty but often felt that they were explicitly shamed by other people and in public discourse. This observation is genuinely important, especially in light of the confirmatory evidence to be presented in Chapter 9 that overt shaming of people in poverty is not a figment of the imagination but a common occurrence. It demonstrates that poverty is not only relative and multidimensional with a psychosocial component—be it lack of self-efficacy or capability—but also relational in the sense that the experience of poverty is determined by others as well as by self (Siegrist, 2003; Taylor, 2011). Poverty is made, socially constructed day by day; it is not simply what is. The inability to fulfil social expectations that makes people feel ashamed also carries the social sanction of being shamed, a further risk to psychic well-being that has to be coped with and, insofar as possible, managed by people living in poverty.

The theorizing reviewed in Chapter 3 suggested that, to the extent that shaming has positive social consequences, these are most likely to occur when shame is merely threatened rather than when it is actually imposed. Furthermore, shame has largely negative effects on the persons targeted especially when, as in the case of poverty, most individuals are unable directly to address the source of their shame. From a sociological perspective, Scheff (1997) saw people in these circumstance either feeling ashamed and hiding their pain, or else repressing the shame that led to pent-up anger while simultaneously prompting accusations of shamelessness from the community. Psychologically the results are predicted to be severe in terms of low self-esteem, depression, anxiety, and even suicide (Furukawa et al., 2012; Tangney and Dearing, 2003).

[1] This chapter draws heavily on the following publications: Bantebya-Kyomuhendo and Mwiine (2014b); Chase and Walker (2014b); Choudhry (2014b); Gubrium and Lødemel (2014b); Jo (2014b); Pellissery and Mathew (2014b); and Yan (2014b).

However, little of this previous work has considered the consequences of the shame associated with poverty. The creative literature, film, and oral traditions reviewed in Chapters 5 and 6 suggest that poverty-related shame might have a wide spectrum of consequences ranging from the mild to the personally and socially destructive, partly dependent on how people sought to manage the experience.

In this chapter, the predictions of serious personal consequences arising from shame are explored, with reference to the life experiences of people living in poverty drawn from the same interviews as in Chapter 7 (Chase and Bantebya-Kyomuhendo, 2014). The evidence points to a range of outcomes, few if any positive, most deleterious, and some quite extreme. It also reveals that respondents used many of the same techniques for managing the shame as did protagonists in novels and film. It should be stressed, however, that the concept of managing shame is not without its problems. Conceptually the boundaries between the emotion and its consequences are not always clear. Moreover, empirically the existence of shame is necessarily presumed on the basis of behavioural manifestations such as covering one's face or from hormone levels, which can variously be considered either a cause or a consequence. Furthermore, managing implies a degree of conscious control and also the resources, psychic or otherwise, to carry through on a particular strategy which may not be the case, or may not be recognized as such by the individual concerned. In the interviews shame was spoken about, behaviour was explained, and feelings were described as a single entity that shaped and constrained life; this entity denied emotional sunshine and curtailed thoughts of the future such that respondents' attention was generally focussed on the now and the possible.

BEING NORMAL

People generally have no option but to do the best that they can in the circumstances in which they find themselves. As explained in Chapter 7, respondents first made sure, insofar as they could, that they and their families had sufficient food to eat, somewhere to live, and adequate clothing. Beyond these acts of survival, a great motivation was to avoid the glare of shame by appearing to be normal, to be part of the majority, and not to be seen as being poor or the poorest of the poor. Strategies typically began with practical attempts to alleviate the causes and consequences of poverty, ending with pretence and deceit when such attempts failed.

Instrumental Responses

Whenever possible, people did what they could to change their circumstances for the better. Such an instrumental or problem-orientated approach to avoiding the shame induced by poverty meant people seeking to minimize the impact of poverty, maximizing resources and minimizing expenditure in the short-term, and working towards more sustained income in the future.

For the most part, respondents were reasonably successful in achieving short-term goals over which they had some degree of control, but they had more difficulty in negotiating the largely structural constraints that determined future outcomes. Nevertheless, there were often limits to even what could be achieved in the here and now. Nutrition, for example, was often inadequate despite the best efforts of respondents. In India and Pakistan children were noticeably underweight and their growth stunted (Choudhry, 2014b; Pellissery and Mathew, 2014b), while obesity was common among British respondents (both adults and children), a fact that was attributed by respondents to 'cheap junk food' and 'comfort eating' (Chase and Walker, 2014b). Strategic challenges were also being addressed by some respondents and, of course, the most successful might no longer have been poor and so would not have been included in the samples interviewed.[2] A family in India hit by crop failures and indebtedness put everybody to work including, against local norms, unmarried daughters, thereby foregoing the avoidance of shame for the sake of the financial security to which they aspired. Certain respondents in Britain and Norway were undertaking job training and remedial education classes, and parents generally prioritized their children's education, except perhaps in Pakistan were the demands of survival were at their greatest.

There were also examples of people turning their lives around or, at least, trying to do so. A number of Norwegian respondents receiving social assistance had a history of drug abuse and were in the recovery phase (Gubrium and Lødemel, 2014b). They were prepared to accept the stigma associated with assistance because it not only provided hope and reassurance but also discipline and potentially skills. A Filipino migrant whose life had fallen apart with a failed marriage, unemployment, and a bout of depression felt that all he needed was 'a little push' to be able to manage again. A lone mother who had survived an abusive relationship felt that she had now made the choice to be a success in life, something that she 'would not have dared to do' six months earlier. Another said that pride had not prevented him from seeking help, but the reality of this was that he found dealing with a public agency 'a little bit more anonymous . . . less pitiful' than relying on friends.

This last quotation illustrates that people seeking to make a break from the past, or even to cope with current circumstances, often have mentally to negotiate the tension between personal pride, feeling good about oneself, and its antithesis 'loss of pride', which may sometimes equate to feeling ashamed. British respondents stressed how important it was to be coping and to be seen to be coping; thus being in work, even if poorly paid, gave people a sense

---

[2] A number of relatively prosperous people who had had poor beginnings were interviewed in the third stage of the project.

of pride and made them feel better about themselves. Equally, respondents spoke a lot about the need to swallow or to bury their pride in seeking help and assistance. Thus, on occasion, the spur to avoid the shame of being poor, to cope financially and to advance, came headlong up against the desire to be proud of oneself by living up to expectations of self-reliance and self-sufficiency and the aspiration to be seen to be coping well.

Keeping Up Appearances

As well as striving to make ends meet, respondents therefore also felt the need to keep up appearances. In Uganda, parents sought to ensure that clothes were washed, the family was turned out looking tidy, and (if possible) children had a change of clothes for school (Bantebya-Kyomuhendo and Mwiine, 2014b). In a small Norwegian fishing town respondents felt that it was crucial to appear 'normal' and 'respectable', while in the prosperous Oslo suburb it was thought to be essential to ensure that one's children looked and behaved no differently from anyone else's. In Britain, polish for the house and a haircut sometimes symbolized the difference between dignity and overt dependency. If appearances could be maintained by making do, handing on clothes, buying from charity shops, and economizing on eating, then the approach might prove to be sustainable; it was, after all, the majority strategy in all the national settings. However, the strategy proved vulnerable to impulse purchases, to social pressure to join in, and to miscalculation. Moreover, if it could only be sustained through borrowing, it often proved to be a disaster. For example, one respondent in Uganda admitted that he had felt compelled by the need not to be ashamed to pledge a sum that he could not afford in a community fundraising function; another made sure that he was seen spending what he had so that he would not be thought of as poor, a concept he felt people associated with thieves and beggars; and a third, aged 81 and truly destitute, considered himself wealthy, spending whatever he had recklessly without caring for the morrow.

Keeping up appearances could and frequently did lead respondents into a charade in which they concealed problems, pretended that things were fine and avoided situations in which their circumstances and their shame could be exposed. While they sustained the pretence and 'held things together', major problems could be avoided or at least postponed, but there was always the constant fear of being 'outed'. It will be recalled from Chapter 6 that Gerald, in the 1997 film *The Full Monty*, maintained the pretence of going to work each day despite being unemployed. Not dissimilarly, a male respondent in Norway was pretending to his wife that the work experience that he was attending was a proper job. Likewise, a British respondent made out that her volunteering was paid work and that she was not on benefits, while another always said that he worked as a labourer rather than admitting that he was actually in receipt of disability benefits. Concealment and pretence were not restricted to employment status. A paid support worker who was employed in a children's centre, interviewed in Britain, was unable to admit that she was having difficulty making ends meet for fear that her higher paid, professional colleagues would count her as 'no better' than the clients with whom they were dealing.

Sometimes respondents seemed to be concealing things from themselves as well as from others. A migrant Russian respondent living in Norway explained how she and her husband kept their economic difficulties from their children, telling them that a job was just around the corner when experience suggested otherwise. One Ugandan respondent so loathed her poverty, understanding that others associated it with laziness and lax morals, that she sought to conceal this loathing by pretending that she was content with her lot, enduring the hardship lightly and above all by conveniently blaming curses on the family and supernatural forces beyond her control. Another respondent in Uganda admitted that, in denying the shame that she felt, she was seeking to convince herself and others that she was 'doing something about her situation' and that her impoverishment was only temporary. In Britain, respondents spoke of trying to convince themselves that money was not the most important thing, that it could not buy happiness and that they did not mind what people said about them and about others like them.

Keeping up appearances was very often a conscious strategy viewed as necessary in order to maintain morale and self-respect. The ever-present danger was that the pressures could become excessive, engendering the need for pretence with the further danger that people could begin believing in their own pretence. For many, there was only so long that they could perpetuate the myth that they were fully in control.

AVOIDING THE NORMAL

A very common practice was to circumvent the possibility of shame. Mostly this was achieved by physically avoiding situations in which shaming could occur. Sometimes the avoidance was more psychological than practical with occasionally the very deleterious consequences predicted by social psychology (see Chapter 3).

Withdrawal

Respondents in all seven national settings sought to avoid the possibilities of shaming by stopping going out with friends or inviting people home to eat.

Likewise, many began declining invitations to weddings, community receptions, and similar events, although others had never been able to afford to participate in such activities. The change was usually justified as a measure to reduce cost, but it also meant that they were less likely to be placed in a position in which they would subsequently need to reciprocate in ways that they could not afford. Some excuses smacked of self-pity, but in so doing revealed the corrosive effects of poverty-related shame. In Britain, a lone mother explained that there was no point in going out when 'there's nothing to talk about except that you feel a bit depressed, you haven't got enough money to pay that bill or eat that day'. A respondent who was a lone father similarly said that he 'shut the curtains and hid away', not wanting 'to be the victim'. Many respondents in Uganda also spoke of withdrawing into their home, keeping themselves to themselves, and 'keeping quiet'. Likewise, a study of older people experiencing poverty in Beijing found them to be isolated, because as one respondent explained: 'I dare not meet the neighbours. When I see them far away, I hide myself' (Chen et al., 2013). Avoiding social life meant avoiding shame, but also resulted in a decline in the numbers of people that would be available to assist in the event of a crisis, thereby adding to the vulnerability of life in poverty.

Equally, withdrawal was not entirely of the respondents' own making since it was sometimes enforced by, or was conditional on, the behaviour of others. Very often social events are closed unless one has been invited, which means that others need to initiate contact. A female respondent in Pakistan explained how she longed to visit her daughter but lacked the wherewithal necessary to buy the customary gift; she was only released from her isolation by her daughter and son-in-law visiting her. Sometimes, social isolation is both a product and a cause of depression that reinforced a sense of hopelessness, a phenomenon that was perhaps most notable in South Korea (Jo, 2014b).

Sometimes the hiding was specific, concealing themselves from the money-lender in India and the bailiff in Britain. Sometimes it was more generalized, as illustrated by respondents in Uganda not participating in village meetings because they felt that they were not given a voice but were instead actively 'looked down on' and 'humiliated'. Likewise, British respondents felt disenfranchized, pilloried by the media as workshy and scroungers, and targeted by politicians and government—'them' with welfare cuts and 'beat the benefit cheats' campaigns. They saw themselves as governed by people with power who had 'no clue', 'no idea' how much they were struggling and who would have had 'no chance' of surviving on the limited resources that respondents had to live on. In Norway, respondents found security among people who did understand, those who were also social assistance clients who knew the cost of things and not to ask too much of each other.

Avoidance and Disintegration

Sometimes the tendency to hide that was observed might be what psychologists call avoidance behaviour. Certainly two female respondents in India linked heavy drinking by their husbands to the lasting effects of crop failure and land change and their inability to recover economically. In Uganda, children spoke quite freely about their fathers' excessive drinking (one claimed that 'all adults were drunkards') and associated violence at home as did certain female respondents, although it was not fully clear whether they attributed drinking to poverty or poverty to drinking. In Norway and Britain there was more mention of drug than alcohol abuse, but again there was little reflection on cause and effect.

A number of respondents in Britain and Norway mentioned suffering from depression which in Britain they tended to link directly to poverty. They variously reported lying awake worrying about bills and bailiffs and feeling that they 'were not managing' and, as a consequence, 'staying in bed all day'. One British woman, with no job and a disabled child to care for, could see no way in which her circumstances could change and said that she lived life with a cloud over her. In Norway, respondents mostly emphasized that their low self-esteem, depression, and loss of motivation were not due so much to a lack of money but to their joblessness, inactivity, and the lack of structure in their lives. Clinical depression was rarely if ever mentioned by respondents in the other countries, although the behaviour that some of them described—the aforementioned retreat inside, the social isolation and reluctance to interact with others, the alcohol abuse and negative resignation—could be indicative of similar conditions were the medical resources available for diagnosis and treatment.

Film and literature quite often present suicide as the ultimate retreat and escape from the shame of poverty and, lest one consider this to be either overstatement or dramatic licence, it is salutary to note that suicide among poor farmers in India has become so prevalent that benefit schemes have been introduced to support dependents of the deceased (Mathew, 2010). An Indian respondent who had been abandoned with her two children took them to a high reservoir dam intent on committing suicide when still a teenager, only to be persuaded from her attempt by passers-by. She explained that the combination of financial hardship, the need to return to live with her parents, and ostracism by her brother left life as 'a question mark'. A number of the British respondents had also contemplated suicide and two who had actually tried gave the reason as debt, which in the context of other things, including the demands of being a parent, made life 'all too much'. Another person explicitly linked the motivation for suicide directly to the effects of shame when she mused on how such feelings could emanate from not being able to keep up with social expectations.

RESISTING THE NORMAL

The strategies considered so far reflect Scheff's characterization of people hiding and perhaps repressing their shame when they are unable to address its cause. Psychologists also report anger sometimes being expressed rather than repressed, triggered by perceived lack of agency and the resultant frustration at not being able to live up to expectations (Stuewig and Tangney, 2007). This anger can in turn result in the incontrollable rage and violence that was depicted in some of the British social realist and modern Korean films reviewed in Chapter 6. Alternatively, various writers have located such anger as a trigger for collective resistance. The evidence from the research interviews is of a more muted resistance.

Anger and Resignation

Respondents frequently talked of frustration and about feeling angry but seldom referred to rage and violence. This is perhaps not surprising given the social taboo on violent behaviour. Nevertheless, as already noted, significant numbers of children in Uganda reported violence occurring at home, which they connected with heavy drinking. A mother in Pakistan was also prepared to overcome reticence about talking about violence, admitting to taking out her anger on her children. She also said that her husband, when asked by the children why he did not work, responded by beating them. A respondent in India confessed to directing his anger towards his sisters; he had lost his land and position but they were well settled and supported by their husbands. In this case, however, threats of violence were mediated by physical distance and hence amounted to verbal fantasy rather than actuality.

Indeed, most of the anger reported by adults was generalized and frequently directed at government and the 'system'. However, 'the rich' were also targeted. They were generally considered neither to understand people in poverty nor to care; indeed, they were thought to exploit 'the poor and weak' whenever the opportunity arose. Former employees of state owned industries in China, for example, were angry at the erosion in the status of workers vis-à-vis entrepreneurs, and also about the growing economic disparity within the country (Yan, 2014b). In Norway, anger was very often directed at the social assistance system with which all respondents had contact, while in Britain the government was frequently the target of such anger, often explicitly personified in terms of the Prime Minister, David Cameron.

Children also occasionally admitted to being angry. This could erupt when they were told that they could not have the things that they wanted, or might be repressed but fester inside and become directed against their parents and society at large. Children in Pakistan admitted this to be the case and, as described in Chapter 7, many of the children in Uganda were deeply ashamed of their circumstances and often cross about them, blaming their parents and yet feeling confused about how they should feel given how much their parents were struggling to put food in their mouths and clothes on their backs. The children and young people interviewed in Britain, notably teenage boys, also talked about anger, and at least two of them had been referred to counsellors for guidance on anger management. Clearly, behavioural problems have multiple causes and it would be inappropriate to claim that poverty and the associated shame was the sole cause. That said, one of the youths who had been referred for counselling spoke about how he had to control his anger 'when other people [had] stuff and [were] gloating about it'; this he did through pretence: 'trying to make up things' so that he did not 'look stupid'.

In films and literature there are examples of anger being channelled into collective action and, while there was very little evidence of this among the people interviewed, presumably the potential is there. There is considerable evidence suggesting links between poverty and social unrest (Muggah, 2012; Panic, 2005), while the activities and commitment of such representative groups as ATD Fourth World and the European Anti-Poverty Network are fuelled by responses of people in poverty to the injustice and 'violence' of poverty (ATD, 2013). However, a sense of resignation was much more common, with respondents feeling that the forces against them were too great to be meaningfully challenged and that mere survival, or the attainment of decency, required all the energy that they had at their disposal. Much more rarely people gave up trying to keep up a facade, knowingly (and sometimes possibly due to illness unknowingly) flouting social convention. There were hints of this in the profligate spending of a couple of respondents in Uganda and perhaps among the most disaffected social assistant recipients interviewed in Norway.

Chinese respondents generally saw themselves as victims of state policy, comforted themselves that others were worse off than they were, and looked forward to retirement age when they believed that pensions, 'the security sachet of retirement', would alleviate their economic hardship. In India, the tight structure of social obligation made exposure to shame almost unavoidable and, given the close association between poverty and caste, institutionalized; as a consequence, respondents tended to accept poverty and shame as inevitable features of their everyday lives. In Norway, the lives of social assistance recipients were regulated by the system against which they railed (not least because it assigned them to categories that they felt constituted a hierarchy of shame), but which they believed themselves to be powerless to change. In South Korea, the social assistance system led to humiliation in the office, at work, and within their families that they were unable to resist since only benefit saved them from destitution. Similarly, in Britain respondents felt themselves to be labelled as shameless within the social security system and by the media and politicians, and could only challenge this by seeking to lead respectable lives. In Uganda and Pakistan, as in India, obligations imposed by family, community, and culture meant that exposure to shame was a daily occurrence, but the powerful instinct for survival trumped thoughts of protest and rebellion.

Reflecting Blame and 'Othering'

While respondents sometimes pretended that they did not mind what others thought about them, in reality they mostly cared deeply and consequently they often felt hurt. In particular, they found it difficult to reconcile what society said about poverty, that it was due to personal inadequacy and immorality, with what they understood about their own lives and what they believed about themselves. Sometimes they sought to deflect the blame back to the protagonists, accusing politicians of being out of touch, the media of being political, and other people of being self-serving. Why, one Norwegian respondent asked, did people 'use all their energy being snobs?' wondering pointedly whether 'they were really that good'.

More often, though, respondents resolved the conflict between public belief and personal experience with the thought that it must be other people who were feckless and lazy and who abused the benefit system, since it was not them. In so doing, they engaged in a process of shaming that was very similar to that against which they were reacting, a process that Ruth Lister has termed 'othering' (Lister, 2004; Chase and Walker, 2013). Many of the respondents receiving social assistance in Norway contrasted their commitment to finding work, albeit in some cases recently precipitated by changes in their own lives such as breaking a drug habit or becoming a parent, with the casual attitudes of others. They complained, too, that the system favoured others: you needed 'to look the part . . . pitiful . . . [and] . . . play the part; . . . look mean and you'll get what you want'. Sometimes ethnicity was used as a label: 'immigrants . . . they think it [social assistance], it's some sort of party'.

In Britain, respondents also sought to distance themselves from dominant social constructions of the 'undeserving' which seemed to be arrayed in a hierarchy based on work, work history, benefit receipt, family size, and migration or 'citizen' status. People working or able to demonstrate a decent work record held the moral high ground; those on benefits distanced themselves from stereotypical benefit cheats, and most felt superior to migrants who it was claimed took 'all the jobs and housing'. Similarly in Uganda, house owners perceived themselves to be superior to squatters and to 'transients'.

Other Ugandan respondents sought to demonstrate that they were upstanding and coping by reference to behaviours of which they disapproved: begging, theft, not sending children to school or sending them to school unkempt, heavy drinking, promiscuity, etc. They emphasized, too, their acts of generosity to people worse off than themselves and, while these acts may have been motivated by altruism, there was sometimes a touch of self-righteousness in the enthusiasm with which the stories were told. For example, one reported that his neighbour had been in trouble: 'She had nothing to eat. When I realized her dilemma, I gave her some foodstuffs. I felt happy, fulfilled inside.' Other benefactors reported that they felt 'clean in [their] heart', 'so happy' and 'fulfilled . . . because the help offered' was 'voluntary and selfless'.

This process of looking to others who were thought to be less worthy than themselves may have been a way of deflecting the glare of shame that they themselves both felt and had heaped upon them. In part, too, it seems to have been a way of massaging their own self-esteem by identifying others as more blameworthy than they were, as well as reconciling the incongruity between their view of themselves and the opprobrium that they so often received. The phenomenon may also help to explain why there was so little evidence of collective anger and resistance; the shaming created divisions among people in poverty thereby making their common interests less clear.

SEPARATED BY SHAME

Respondents coped with the shame that they felt and that they said was poured upon them as a consequence of their poverty in various ways, many of which would have been expected from the academic literature addressing shame. The vast majority sought to make ends meet in the best way that they could and were perhaps spurred on in this endeavour by the fear of shame. In reality, however, most were trapped in poverty by limited skills and by a structural lack of opportunities. Unable to escape from poverty and the associated shame, they sought to keep up appearances and to pretend that things were fine. This strategy was pursued by almost everyone and generally worked while they could sustain the pretence and cope with the fear of being exposed. However, with limited resources the pretence could easily get out of hand: people would find out and the debt collectors close in, leading to anxiety, depression, and suicide attempts.

For many respondents resources did not allow for the maintenance of a social life. In addition, people often sought to avoid shame by withdrawing socially, thereby reducing the number of scenarios in which shame could occur but limiting the social capital that could be drawn upon at times of crisis. However, it was sometimes difficult to determine whether the social isolation that respondents described was truly intended, the result of being shunned by other people, a symptom of depression, or a combination of all three. The social and psychological costs of poverty and the associated sense of failure, real or perceived, can be severe.

A further response to shaming that academic scholarship predicts and is echoed in film and fiction is anger. There was some evidence of this, occasionally directed at specific family members but more often generalized as expressions of contempt for government and hatred of the system. What was not much in evidence was collective action arising from the anger and shame. Respondents were generally too focussed on survival and convinced that the system was too big to change; many also believed that other people, 'them', would never listen or understand.

The prospect of collective action was further impeded by the process of 'othering' and the strength of its ripple effect (Chase and Walker, 2013; Lister, 2004). People shamed for being poor seem to distance themselves from the shame by passing it to 'others' who they consider to be less worthy than themselves. For individuals this means that they need no longer consider themselves to be the poorest of the poor, at least not in moral terms. But the process is socially divisive, concealing the common interests of people in poverty and limiting the prospect of collective action. By participating in this process, respondents also fuelled the very belief that they knew in their own lives to be untrue, that poverty was largely about lack of trying rather than the absence of opportunity.

Scheff (1997) argued that the threat of shame was the glue holding society together, and that shame when actually imposed had the potential to blow society apart. Chapter 7 demonstrated that people in poverty not only often felt ashamed but also believed that shame was continually imposed upon them by other individuals and by social institutions, beliefs that seem very plausible in the light of evidence presented in Chapters 9 and 10. However, while social unrest can be provoked by poverty, and might in microcosm represent society being blown apart by the frustration and anger of people shamed for their poverty that they can do little about, acceptance and fortitude seem to be much more common. Based on the evidence presented in this chapter, one reason for this (apart from the need to expend energy on basic survival) is that the ripples of shame dividing people in poverty that result from the process of othering impede their political mobilization. This, in turn, limits the threat posed by poverty to the status quo and thereby leaves existing power structures intact.

9

Shaming People in Poverty

Attitudes and Actions[1]

Shame, it has been argued, is internally felt but also externally imposed. Chapters 7 and 8 have viewed poverty-related shame through the experience of people defined as living in poverty according to the disparate norms of their respective societies. They reported feeling ashamed as a result of the poverty that prevented them from fulfilling their expectations and responsibilities as a person, parent, relative, and community member. For many this was an ongoing experience that acted as a cancer on their lives while others, for a variety of reasons, were better able to manage or cope with the shame that they experienced.

While it was clear that people were personally frustrated by their inability to achieve their aspirations and to meet their own standards, life, they said, was made much harder by repeated reminders that they were social failures. Such reminders came from both social acquaintances and from officials with whom they had to deal. Often they were additionally told that their failure was due to moral shortcomings. However, as any detective will witness, hearsay evidence is generally insufficient for a conviction. It might be, for example, that people in poverty interpret the words and behaviour of other people through the lens of their own shame and mistake innocent actions for deliberate shaming or stigma. Therefore, in this chapter, poverty and shame are examined from the perspective of people who are relatively affluent so as to triangulate accounts of the interactions between people in poverty and those who are not.

For the most part, the evidence assembled is derived from conversations with groups of people living in the same localities as those selected for interview on account of their poverty (Chase and Bantebya-Kyomuhendo, 2014). In addition though, reference is made to survey data on attitudes derived mostly from the World Attitudes Survey and, in order to investigate

---

[1] This chapter draws heavily on the following publications: Bantebya-Kyomuhendo and Mwiine (2013, 2014c); Chase and Walker (2014c); Choudhry (2013, 2014c); Gubrium and Lødemel (2013a, 2014c); Jo and Walker (2013); Pellissery and Mathew (2013, 2014c); Walker and Chase (2013); and Yan (2013, 2014c).

the treatment of people in poverty by officialdom, to policy analyses conducted in each of the case-study countries (Gubrium et al., 2013).

The people involved in the research conversations were recruited somewhat differently in the various settings. In Britain, many tens of people were approached in two urban shopping districts following which thirteen women and eight men were interviewed in seven micro-groups each comprising of between two and four people. Additionally, four focus groups were conducted with thirty-eight children aged between 12 and 15 within state and private schools. In Norway, snowball sampling (that is respondents identifying other potential respondents) was used to identify and recruit twenty-two adults who participated in six micro-groups in two urban communities and one rural, coastal locality. Elsewhere, respondents were approached through elders and community councils. In India, two groups, one of men and one of women, and another group comprised of teachers were held in both Gujarat and Kerala, a total of six groups involving fifty-one adults. In addition, sixteen children aged 11 to 15 were engaged in activity groups. Five groups were held in China, respectively comprising recent college graduates, upper middle class entrepreneurs and professionals, working class industrial and service sector workers, migrant workers, and retired persons previously working in state owned enterprises. In Pakistan, a focus group of men, one of women, one with parliamentarians, one comprising civil servants and representatives of the media, civil society organizations, and social intellectuals, and one made up of children aged between 10 and 16 were conducted. Finally, eight groups were held in Uganda divided between the rural area in which in-depth interviews with people in poverty had previously been undertaken and an urban area nearby. Separate groups were organized for women and men. The discussions, which with prior permission were recorded, were transcribed and (except in the case of Norway) analysed in the vernacular to retain as long as possible the rhythms and nuances of the original conversation.

Briefly before reporting and reflecting on these discussions, it is appropriate to locate them within a global context since, while the case-study countries are not considered representative of all countries, it is relevant in drawing conclusions from them to know the extent to which they are in any way exceptional.

GLOBAL PERCEPTIONS OF POVERTY

The way that people respond to those in poverty is likely to reflect their understanding of the nature, and particularly the causes, of poverty. To the extent that they believe poverty to be disgusting and degrading, they may distance themselves from it both emotionally and physically. Moreover, if poverty is believed to be avoidable and the result of individual failings, they are likely to blame people for being poor. This may affect the tone and content of their discourse and, to the extent that they interact directly with people in poverty, they may engage in shaming behaviour; this could be unconscious, gratuitous, or designed with the best of intent to encourage people to change their ways. One would anticipate that people would be much less judgemental if they believed that poverty was the result of structural factors, luck, or possibly divine intervention.

Survey evidence on people's understanding of the causes of poverty shows marked global differences. In the mid-1990s, respondents to the World Values Survey were presented with a simple binary choice between 'laziness and lack of will power' and 'social unfairness' (see also Barrientos and Neff, 2010). Figure 9.1 summarizes the findings, showing that in some countries virtually everybody ascribes poverty to people's laziness while in others overwhelming majorities believe that poverty is the product of social unfairness. If ideas on causality were the only factor determining the shaming of poverty, this evidence would seem in itself to refute notions of universality. However, beliefs as to the causation of poverty are unlikely to be the sole influence on shaming behaviour. Moreover, the findings offer interesting insights linking back to the earlier discussion on the cultural conceptions of poverty and shame and the priority given to poverty in public policy (see Chapters 1 and 4). Very many respondents in Taiwan, China,

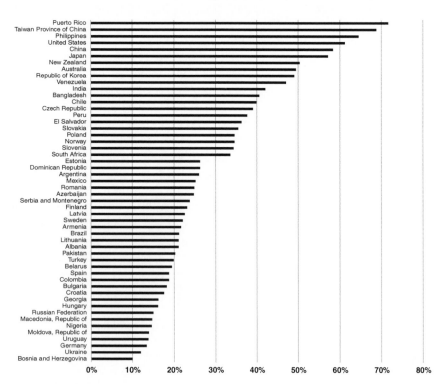

Fig. 9.1. Global perceptions of the causes of poverty: percentage citing 'laziness and lack of willpower'

World Values Survey 1981–2000 <http://www.worldvaluessurvey.org/>

Japan, and South Korea locate laziness as the principal cause of poverty. These are all countries with a Confucian legacy, a collectivist rather than an individualistic orientation, and cultures that emphasize shame rather than guilt. Equally, though, these societies have all also pursued developmentalist policies that place economic growth above individual social welfare as the prime goal of public policy, and in doing so have strongly promoted the work ethic.

Respondents in Anglo Saxon countries—Australia, New Zealand, and the US—societies that are fiercely individualistic and also known for their commitment to the work ethic, similarly prioritize laziness above unfairness as the principal cause of poverty. The same is true of two collectivist societies, Puerto Rico and the Philippines, which have been politically much influenced by the US. Anglo Saxon countries are also usually described as guilt-based societies, but the predominantly Catholic countries (ideal-type guilt-based societies) differ markedly among themselves, with substantial proportions of respondents in Venezuela, Chile, Peru, El Salvador, and Poland blaming poverty on laziness, and equally large majorities in Uruguay, Columbia, and Spain attributing poverty to social unfairness. The suggestion, focussing on extreme cases, is that a societal commitment to the work ethic may be more associated with beliefs about the causes of poverty than distinctions made according to the perceived degree of individualism in a country or the social and cultural attachment accorded to shame or guilt.

Neither Britain nor Uganda were included in the case-study countries of the World Values Survey. Among the five remaining countries that were included as case studies, only in China did a majority of respondents think that laziness was the main cause of poverty. Nevertheless, over 40 per cent of respondents in South Korea and India took the same view, as did about more than a third of those in Norway. Pakistan is the sole case-study country located in the lower half of Figure 9.1, with just 20 per cent of respondents citing laziness and 80 per unfairness as the underlying causes of poverty.

A similar question on the causes of poverty has been included many times in surveys in Britain. It includes laziness and lack of willpower as causes of poverty, but adds a number of other possibilities to the response set. The percentage citing laziness as the main cause of poverty when the question was asked in the mid-1990s, the same time as the World Values Survey, was just 15 per cent, placing it below Pakistan. However, it is impossible to determine whether this figure would have been higher had respondents been offered fewer alternatives. Moreover, the proportion of Britons citing laziness as the main cause of poverty had been much higher in earlier years (Figure 9.2). In 1976 the corresponding figure was as high as 43 per cent and it has increased markedly since the 1990s, reaching 28 per cent in 2003; in the latest survey in 2010, 24 per cent named laziness as the most important cause of poverty. There are unfortunately no equivalent data for Uganda. The best are from neighbouring Kenya, where a survey of television viewers conducted in 2013,

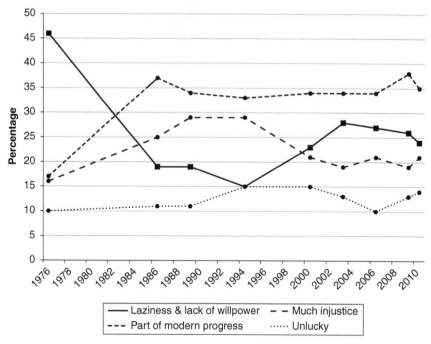

Fig. 9.2. Perceptions of the causes of poverty in Britain, 1976 to 2010
Adapted from Clery et al. (2013) and Walker et al. (1984)

and hence representative of only the most prosperous 58 per cent of Kenyans who own television sets, found that 26 per cent of respondents gave laziness and lack of willpower as the main reason for poverty and a further 22 per cent cited it as the second reason (Park et al., 2013b).

To recap, matched against global public opinion the case-study countries reflect more or less all shades of opinion on the causes of poverty, although respondents were perhaps somewhat more likely to believe that laziness was the most important cause of poverty than the 'average world citizen'. However, the only available comparative data are twenty years old and, as British surveys indicate, public opinion changes.

THE FRAMING OF POVERTY

The remainder of this chapter engages with the ideas and opinions of people who are not currently poor, drawn from the seven[2] case-study countries. It

---

[2] Focus groups were not held in South Korea, but later sections of this chapter draw on material from an analysis of national policies (Jo and Walker, 2013).

begins, in this section, with reflections on their understandings of poverty before examining, in the next, the use of stigmatizing language. Thereafter the accounts given by people in poverty—that they are repeatedly shamed in a range of social settings—are interrogated by juxtaposing them against the stories told by their supposed antagonists.

Poverty and its Causes

Group discussions are designed to provoke participants to talk, to express views, to listen, and to reflect. Perhaps inevitably in such contexts, people's expressed views change during the course of discussion and some make statements that entirely contradict remarks that they have offered earlier. This phenomenon of fluctuating views and opinions was much in evidence in most of the groups, although possibly to a lesser extent in China (Yan, 2014c).

Nevertheless, most people started in the discussions with a very similar conception of poverty almost irrespective of where they lived. They saw poverty in absolute terms relating to the lack of resources necessary for survival, and spoke about poor housing, lack of clothing, and a shortage of food. Possibly reflecting memories of famine, some groups in China settled on people having nothing to eat as the definition of poverty. Sometimes people moved beyond just lack of income, recognizing that poverty also meant a lack of opportunities; this was notably the case in Pakistan and Norway and perhaps to a lesser extent in Britain. In Britain, Norway, and China respondents often subsequently discussed whether poverty existed any longer in their country, poverty often being described in relation to famine and starvation that they knew of in Sub-Saharan Africa (Chase and Walker, 2014c; Gubrium and Lødemel, 2014c). In China, relaxing a definition of poverty based on hunger, there was generally recognition that poverty still existed in rural parts of the country and some urban migrants were also thought to be poor.

There was some appreciation in China of the concept of relative poverty, and it was this idea that enabled respondents in Norway and Britain to engage with the possibility of poverty still existing in their societies. In China, poverty in rural areas was thought to be different from that in cities and people related poverty to different times in their own lives. In Norway, relative poverty was seen as a problem largely confined to drug users, migrants, and possibly the Roma community. In Britain, relative poverty was believed to be much more widespread, although some people felt that it was wrong to use the term 'poverty' to describe mere 'hardship'. Moreover, a minority of British respondents only acknowledged that poverty existed after they had been introduced to vignettes based on the experiences of the people in poverty who had earlier been interviewed, at which point the conversation often turned to whether or not the poverty was real in the sense of being inescapable.

In India, Pakistan, and Uganda there was little debate over whether poverty existed; it self-evidently did in the rural areas in Kerala and Gujarat and in both the rural and urban districts in Uganda where respondents lived. In India, people in poverty were identified in terms of deficiencies in the basic essentials of food, clothing, and shelter and in relation to government housing schemes, caste, tribe, and attendance of children at school. In Uganda, the totemic distinguishing features also related to basic essentials in terms of food: 'less salt'; housing: 'grass-thatched houses', 'houses you can see into', 'no mattress or proper bedding'; and clothing: 'torn old clothes' and 'children running round naked' (Bantebya-Kyomuhendo and Mwiine, 2014c). Re-spondents in Uganda also quite often associated people living in poverty with negative behavioural traits including theft, drunkenness, and dirtiness. In Pakistan, there was a tendency to distinguish rural from urban poverty, the former romanticized as a simpler life that was more natural and contented ('in winter, they sleep inside and, in hot summers, they stay out in the open under the trees'), the latter more demanding and stressful with less support (Choudhry, 2014c).

The use of behaviour as a discriminating feature of poverty tended to reflect thoughts on the reasons why poverty existed. The reasons given, certainly in Uganda, India, and Britain, although to a lesser extent too in Pakistan, Norway, and China, were individualistic. In Uganda, three sets of factors were evident that were echoed elsewhere but with sometimes different illus-trative characteristics: lack of skills and general competency; behavioural characteristics (laziness, alcohol abuse, and polygamy); and family back-ground linked to similar behavioural traits and to educational deficiencies that resulted in the 'inheritance of poverty'. In India, respondents quite often additionally referred to tribal groups among whom the causes of poverty were believed to be cultural ('they will stay naked for ever') and the result of a failure by people to grasp the opportunities offered by industrialization and economic growth (Pellissery and Mathew, 2014c). British respondents couched much of their explanation in terms of people not working and on the reasons for this: 'a poverty of aspirations', poor life choices, a lack of work ethic, and an accept-ance of dependency on the state or on other people. Respondents in Norway similarly spoke much about bad decisions and poor choices that led people to fall into poverty, discussion sharpened in the context of a welfare state that was believed to be comprehensive and supportive. They also pointed to cultural factors with analyses that closely coincided with the Ugandan discussion on inheritance.

The focus groups of Chinese respondents, deliberately undertaken with people with different types of life history, tended to have varying explana-tions for poverty. Most groups placed considerable emphasis on economic restructuring and the decline of state owned enterprises, although migrants largely dismissed this idea saying that anyone could get jobs in the city. They argued instead that the real problem of poverty was in rural areas where people worked hard for subsistence incomes without access even to old-age pensions. To these structural reasons, some respondents added health issues and disability that prevented people from working, and also an absence of 'connections' necessary to access jobs and other resources within the Chinese context. Strikingly, given the evidence from the World Values Survey that many Chinese people blame poverty on laziness, moral weaknesses were seldom mentioned. This may be because their specific backgrounds caused them to focus on structural factors. It might equally be a consequence of strict codes of politeness expected in public discourse, and the legacy of the revolutionary era when poverty was seen as a personal virtue required for the greater good of collective economic progress. Certainly, as is revealed later, there were glimpses in the discussions of underlying views more consistent with those found in the World Values Survey.

In Pakistan, inflation, mass unemployment, lack of education, poor infrastructure, restricted access to Zakat (state social assistance run according to Islamic principles), and corruption were often cited first as structural causes, but respondents were often equally convinced that those who were poor were not trying hard enough and that only 'the idle and lazy' 'drowned in acute poverty'. Structural factors were also discussed in Norway, although less often than individualistic ones: a labour market that offered few openings for those without skills, discrimination against ethnic minorities, and a problematic welfare system. In Britain, discussion tended to flip between individualistic and structural reasons—including the global recession, unemployment, the rising cost of living, and an inept education system—but almost always returned to individual deficiencies as the principal cause of poverty. Structural reasons were little mentioned in either India or Uganda, with the exception of teachers in India who identified the failure by government satisfactorily to address the problem of poverty.

The fact that, with the possible exception of respondents in China, respondents typically held people responsible for their own poverty explains the context for the extensive blaming and shaming that people living in poverty described in their interviews.

Understanding the Responses

While there were strong similarities between respondents in countries as disparate as Britain, India, and Uganda, there were some differences within and between countries that warrant discussion. One possible factor is the degree of distance, financial and social, between poor and non-poor and, linked to this, the nature and sources of information that the more affluent had about people living in poverty.

In Britain and Norway respondents directly volunteered to participate in group discussions without mediation by neighbourhood councils or gatekeepers. This means that these respondents are likely to have been more interested in social matters and more sympathetic to the circumstances of families in poverty than affluent persons in general. A not insignificant number of people in the focus groups across all countries reported that they had been born into poor families, and a number drew on knowledge of acquaintances or members of their own families who had recently been made redundant or, for some other reason, had come to experience hardship. Those who had had direct experience of poverty typically claimed that, as a result of this experience, they well understood the difficulties faced by families experiencing poverty; but they were also prone to offer the example of their own success as evidence that anyone could escape poverty if they did well in school, worked hard, and made the right decisions. The implication, sometimes left unsaid but often stated, was that people in poverty had failed in each of these respects and were continuing to do so.

As previously noted, the various groups of respondents in China clearly reacted differently to poverty, reflecting their own life experiences that provided distinct reference points. Migrant workers consider the urban poor to be affluent compared to those in rural China who live in mud dwellings without facilities, and who need to work the land continuously in order to meet school and health costs and to fulfil social obligations in their village communities. Former employees of state owned enterprises saw unemployment as the major cause of poverty, whereas a number of recent graduates and persons currently employed in working class jobs considered themselves to be poor relative to other people in Beijing.

Respondents in Uganda, India, and Pakistan explained that they gained their knowledge of what it was like to be poor from direct engagement with people in poverty on a day-by-day basis. They lived among them, they saw them at community gatherings, they witnessed 'the squalor that they chose to live in', and they employed them in their homes and in their businesses. Ugandan respondents also noted that people in poverty always volunteered their help in times of crisis or celebration. However, non-poor respondents in all three countries also said that they knew from direct experience that 'the poor' were untrustworthy, thieves and drunkards, cynical and negative in their approach to life, easily prone to anger and frequently abusive, and dismissive of people with talent and success such as themselves. Their relationship with people in poverty, they explained, was one of mutual dependence. Such people needed work and income, and by supplying employment respondents enjoyed a better way of life and took pleasure from the fact that they were able to help tackle poverty. But they said that it was a fraught relationship bedevilled by the arrogance, unreliability, and laziness of people in poverty.

In Norway, but perhaps especially in Britain, respondents said that they gained much of their knowledge about poor people living in their country from the media. Some professionals in both countries gained insight into the problems of people in poverty through their dealings with clients. As with the teachers in India earlier in this chapter, they tended to offer more structural accounts of poverty, although these were frequently interspersed with 'unbelievable' instances of personal inadequacy and dreadful situations. In Norway, there was mention of parties on the populist, political right trying to stir up hatred—especially of migrants—from which respondents said that they wanted to distance themselves. They noted, too, that while the media did not 'bash the poor', they did praise the achievements of the rich and endorse their lifestyles through the flattery of extensive coverage. They also observed increasing scepticism in the media towards people living on state disability benefits and a negative attitude towards the Roma community.

Most respondents in Britain claimed that virtually all that they found in the media was scepticism and negativity towards people in poverty and living off benefits. Many respondents sought to distance themselves from such positions, dismissing the stories of scroungers and benefits abuse found in what was often referred to as the 'gutter press'; 'that kind of thing', they argued, was what sold newspapers in Britain. However, their conversation was replete with references to stories that they had read in newspapers and heard on radio that were frequently used as evidence that people were poor because they made the wrong choices, lived on 'sink estates', had children too early in life, and found life on benefits much easier than working. Radio and, to an extent, television (especially news programmes) were, in contrast to newspapers, believed to be a source of factual knowledge; they believed what they heard if not always what they read.

Some respondents in the British discussion groups, especially those who encountered people in poverty in a professional capacity through work, or who knew people in their family who were receiving benefits, tried hard to reconcile positive experiences with the negative accounts in the media, sometimes citing what they knew to be positive as possible exceptions to the negative rule. Those who themselves had claimed benefits as a result, for example, of unemployment, teenage pregnancy, or relationship breakdown were also prone to cite their experience as being exceptional; they did not choose 'to have kids when young in order to obtain council housing', they did not 'sleep around' or claim benefits in preference to working; they had faced real problems in their lives and managed to come through them. In so doing, they engaged in an activity akin to the 'othering' practiced by people in poverty that preserved intact the collective view that poverty was caused by individual failings while reconciling contradictory experience to the contrary.

Taken overall, therefore, discussions reveal a quite complex story of the multiple causes of poverty often coloured by respondents' own experiences. However, aside from in Pakistan and China, conversations homed in on individual limitations, unwise decisions, and questionable behaviour as the principal reasons for the continued existence of poverty. Be it the narrower range of personal backgrounds of the people interviewed in China or social convention, they were certainly less inclined to blame poverty on poor people than respondents in other countries or indeed their co-nationals who took part in the World Values Survey. Finally, while in Pakistan the overall state of the economy was seen as a major factor determining the extent of poverty, most of those who took part in the discussions considered that it was ability, aptitude, and individual graft that decided who was poor and who was not.

THE LANGUAGE OF SHAMING

The people in poverty whose voices were heard in Chapters 8 and 9 said that they felt shamed both by the things that other people said and the things that they did. This section addresses the first of these concerns—language—and explores whether or not the words used and the use to which they are put by more affluent individuals supports the contentions of people experiencing poverty.

Words and Labelling

While the language used by respondents in India, Pakistan, Britain, and Uganda when referring to people in poverty was robust and often derogatory, it was much more muted in China and, for the most part, in Norway.

Many of the adult respondents in India clearly held people in poverty in considerable contempt. They used abusive terms to describe people experiencing poverty and talked extensively about their drunkenness, their irresponsible spending on mobile phones and television sets, their refusal to work, and their immediate spending of earnings on alcohol such that the one day they worked was followed by several 'lazing around' recovering from the effects of alcohol. Being poor was often equated with being dishonest, and examples of not paying back loans were frequently cited as evidence of this. Similar language was heard among children who admitted that their peers from low-income homes were publicly taunted and ostracized, that their views were dismissed, and that they were frightened into playing separately for fear of assault. There are laws in India that prevent discriminatory language being used against people on the basis of caste and it was clear that people felt constrained by this. Equally, they admitted to using abusive language in private or when, as teachers, they were talking in the staff room.

Likewise, the focus groups in Uganda often generated a tirade of abuse. Men suffering from poverty were not only thought to be lazy, drunkards, and unwilling to work. They were described as being 'arrogant, unprepared to listen to good advice', 'breeding every other year like vermin', being either impotent or promiscuous and each way despised. Women were said to 'do nothing but roam about the village, gossip mongering': 'the poor man spends all the money drinking, the wife wakes up at 10 a.m. and doesn't even bother to go and dig for food'. One respondent offered the motto that 'you associate with a poor person at your own risk'. In Pakistan, such abusive language was largely reserved for people without work, especially men considered to be living off the income of their female relatives, Zakat and other benefits, and especially those engaged in 'professional begging'. Further distinctions were made between people working who nevertheless sought support from relatives or the state, accumulated debts, or pilfered from their employers and those that did not work; the former were seen to be opportunist or corrupt whereas the latter were accorded a degree of respect. As elsewhere, the tone of the language tended to change with the topic under discussion. Sympathy was evoked when talking about the structural causes of poverty but evaporated rapidly to be replaced by the language of strong criticism and contempt when the conversation moved on topics such as the behavioural characteristics of people in poverty and their attitudes to work.

Similar distinctions, between the merits of people working and those who were not, were apparent in the discussions in Britain. However, in Britain the difference between being poor and being on benefits was very often lost because respondents seldom considered that it was possible for anybody who was earning to be poor. Hence, respondents typically used terms like 'scroungers', 'benefit bums', and 'welfare dependants' interchangeably with the generic labels: 'poor people' or 'the poor'. Quite frequently respondents distanced themselves from the most derogatory terms saying that they were ones used by the media. They nevertheless adopted expressions such as: 'a social burden' (attached to benefits recipients, particularly those with children); 'sink estates' (places 'where the desire to do better is crushed out of you as an individual'); and 'working the system' and 'being happy being on benefits' to describe people purported to participate in a 'culture of dependency'.

In Norway, pejorative language was used sparingly, being largely reserved for Roma people. Respondents did distinguish 'us' from 'them' when referring to people in poverty, and used terms such as 'awful' and 'terrible' to describe their circumstances, typically with a mix of sympathy and despair. However, Roma people were quite often characterized as 'sitting around', smoking or begging, and being bound to 'their cultural traditions'. In China, the language was much less derogatory with opprobrium being reserved for professional beggars, former prisoners receiving social assistance, and able-bodied persons 'too lazy to work'. However, it is perhaps revealing that the Chinese respondents felt that children from poor families might get bullied at school since children do not hide their prejudices. The adults opined that such children might defend themselves from such attacks by working hard and performing well in class. Two teachers reported that, in their experience, children from poor backgrounds would try very hard to conceal their financial circumstances unless they were so desperate that they needed to seek financial assistance from the schools. This discussion among Chinese adults raises the issue of where children from more affluent homes acquired their prejudices and one might assume that this would be, at least to some extent, from their parents. It could be, therefore, that these comments about the views of children offer a glimpse of the true views held by the Chinese adults that were concealed in the social setting of a focus group.

Deserving and Undeserving

Respondents in all the societies were apt to make distinctions that parallel the discourse between the 'deserving' and 'undeserving' poor that was present in the development of Western welfare provision from the sixteenth century (see Chapter 1). This was apparent even in China with the three aforementioned groups, beggars, former prisoners, and the indolent, failing to attract much sympathy. There were other groups of people in poverty that the Chinese respondents considered undeserving that differed by focus group, reflecting their own particular circumstances. The retirees held little affection for adult children who were dependent on their parents, while migrants who are generally prohibited from claiming social assistance in Beijing had little sympathy for those who received it. What these Chinese discussions illustrate, however, is that distinctions can be made without specific reference to the availability of benefits, but that they necessarily take a different form.

In Norway, it was possible to detect a hierarchy of 'the undeserving' or at least a set of more or less deserving groups that was defined according to varying criteria. One set of criteria concerned the acceptance or otherwise of responsibility: persons who worried about their circumstances or who appeared to feel ashamed were held in higher esteem than those who did not, such as persons who behaved shamelessly, who had given up trying, or who simply did not care. Similarly, those who explicitly refused to shoulder blame or responsibility for their circumstances, blaming others or an absence of jobs, were not looked upon favourably and nor were the 'fake' poor. Often Roma people were offered as examples who were considered to be far less deserving than the 'real' poor which, in marked contrast to the views expressed in other countries, included heroin addicts. Finally, Norwegian respondents distinguished between those whom they thought had 'chosen' poverty from those for whom it seemed unavoidable. In the context of the generous welfare provision, 'deservedness' appertained to whether or not the state should continue to provide funding to particular groups of people, at what level, and subject to what conditions.

The discourse between deserving and undeserving was particularly marked in the British groups and closely linked with belief in the importance of the work ethic, contrasting with views about the prevalence of the abuse of benefits and general irresponsibility. There was a strong theme that the benefits system was too generous and provided an attractive lifestyle for those who were 'workshy' and those who chose to have too many children, too young. Echoing current discourse at a political level and reflected in the media, there were repeated references to people who wanted 'rights without responsibilities' (Chase and Walker, 2013). Several respondents argued that 'the large numbers' receiving benefits 'at enormous cost to the tax payer' was demonstrable evidence that a 'benefits culture' situation already existed in Britain. Equally, when vignettes taken from the earlier fieldwork with people living in poverty were shared with the groups, such strong views often softened only to re-emerge as people challenged the reasons why people had found themselves in such precarious circumstances. Had they not borrowed too much? Could they not really cut down on their expenditure? Why did they have so many children? A subtext underlying much of the discussion between deserving and undeserving was that society was meeting the cost of supporting people in poverty; this meant people paying higher taxes at a time when financial stringency was lowering the incomes of everybody except the very rich who could afford accountants or could transfer their assets beyond the reach of taxation.

The distinction between deserving and undeserving took rather different forms in India, Pakistan, and Uganda, and at first glance was less marked than that seen in Britain, Norway, or even China. It perhaps appeared less obvious in India and Uganda due to the vehement contempt in which all people living in poverty were held by the non-poor. In essence, everybody in poverty was considered to be pretty much the same with very few exceptions made due to extenuating circumstances. A second factor, however, was the lower salience of state support for people with low incomes. In both countries, state schooling served as a potent symbol that distinguished children from poor families but, equally, it was widely considered that the education provided by state schools was noticeably inferior to that provided by private schools. In contrast with the belief in Britain that benefits were too high, in India and Uganda it was recognized that benefits received through the education system were limited. Furthermore, in Uganda many of the antipoverty programmes, especially those directed at agricultural improvement, did not directly benefit the poorest families but were taken up by people who had land and therefore were in a position to gain from state subsidies and investment; some non-poor respondents in the focus groups may have in fact been benefitting from this form of government support.

In the case of India, state support in the form of an employment guarantee and, in Gujarat, subsidies in the aftermath of the 2001 earthquake, were disliked by many of the non-poor respondents. The dominant view, voiced loudly, was that the payments encouraged laziness and reduced the willingness of people to take the work on offer. Respondents considered themselves directly affected by this since they were dependent on domestic workers and on daily labourers to work their land. The state support had made labour more difficult to acquire since people nowadays had an alternative, and this had eroded the hierarchy of respect because it was now necessary for them to persuade low-status people to work for them.

Limited state provision in Pakistan, and in the case of Zakat with access restricted by religion, meant the distinctions on the basis of deservedness scarcely applied in the British sense of the term. Because there was so little available to deserve, discussion took on a distinctly moral flavour unconnected with practical provision. Some argued that cutbacks in the free provision of religious schools meant that people in poverty increasingly lacked the necessary training to know right from wrong. The abstract notion of morality also allowed the discussion to shift focus to a consideration of immorality—less of the rich than of politicians and the corruption that slowed economic progress and meant that even access to the meagre benefits available was dependent on political patronage.

Uganda and India have both experienced increases in employment and entrepreneurial opportunities created by economic growth and, in the case of Uganda, specifically by the discovery and exploitation of oil. In this context, respondents pointed out that many people in poverty were not taking up these new opportunities and were therefore likely to remain poor. Not too much attention was paid to the possibility that people living in poverty had neither the financial or human capital at their disposal to exploit the new opportunities that were becoming available. Both the process of economic development and the existence of antipoverty programmes fed the negative attitudes held by respondents who were not themselves poor. However, the attitudes were generalized and did not seem to create the cleavage between the deserving and undeserving apparent in the other countries.

To conclude, while the claim made by people in poverty that they are repeatedly shamed verbally cannot be proved simply by reference to the tenor of discussions undertaken, the transcripts certainly provide supportive prima facie evidence.

SOCIAL EXCLUSION AND THE PRACTICE OF SHAMING

The final task in this chapter is to reflect on the claims made by people in poverty reported in Chapters 7 and 8 that they are shamed by the more affluent in numerous different social arenas and in their dealings with officialdom. Priority is given to material relating to the delivery of antipoverty programmes in each of the case-study countries drawn from comprehensive policy analyses (Gubrium et al. 2013). But first it is appropriate briefly to summarize the responses to the accusations made by people in poverty that were put to respondents in the groups comprising of their more affluent counterparts.

Social Settings

Chapter 7 described how important it is to people experiencing poverty that they are able to keep up appearances, to fulfil their obligations to family and community, and to ensure, insofar as they can, that they appear 'normal' and that their children do not stand out as being 'different'. From the perspective of respondents in the group discussions, with the possible exception of those in China, this behaviour by people in poverty tended to reinforce the general belief that they were profligate, wasting money on unnecessary show, and prioritizing short-term needs rather than saving and investing for their futures.

In Uganda, community is strong with public meetings and events such as funerals providing occasions in which all members of the community are expected to participate and often to contribute in cash or in kind. In the in-depth interviews with persons in poverty, respondents reported that they were often not invited to such events because they were poor and sometimes they excluded themselves because they could not afford to go. When they did go, they reported that they were often shunned, and in public meetings their views were not listened to on account, they believed, of their poverty. These perceptions were confirmed in the discussions with their more affluent peers who argued quite openly that they sought to avoid conversations with people in poverty. They variously suggested that people in poverty: 'felt uncomfortable mingling with rich neighbours' being 'used to their station in life'; that alternatively, they did not know their level and were prone to remind you 'that it was the same God who blessed you with riches as deprived them'; that they rejected advice and were as likely as not to 'insult you in response'; and that 'when they are with the rich, their smiles are a mockery, their laughter sarcastic, dirty and damaging'.

In India, people in poverty spoke about the importance of ritual and reciprocity and the efforts that they went to in order to avoid the shame of failing to fulfil obligations. Such efforts were broadly dismissed in the group discussions as being wasteful and as evidence of people seeking to live above their station that was likely to cause them to go into debt. Likewise, people were criticized, for example, for buying lights at the festival of Diwali. So, whereas rich and poor in Uganda gave similar accounts of their interaction, if not the underlying rationale, in India rich and poor apparently had entirely different understandings of the importance of fulfilling social obligations. However, it is not necessarily the case that the more affluent would translate these generalized opinions into their own lives; certainly the Indian respondents complained loudly that people in poverty could not be relied on to pay off their debts.

In Britain, the formality of community demands are probably less than in either Uganda or India, although the burden of reciprocity in terms of, for example, birthday presents remains. Moreover, the dynamic of consumption, which means that yesterday's luxury becomes today's necessity, imposed considerable demands on low-income families who wished to avoid standing out as different and deprived. Certainly, respondents in the focus groups criticized individuals in poverty for conspicuous consumption and cited televisions, mobile phones, and branded trainers as demonstrable evidence that poverty was the result of profligacy. This position was even taken by some Norwegian respondents, although they tended to refer explicitly to the social pressures created by a consumption-orientated society, exacerbated by growing inequalities.

The reality of the situation in all the countries was that rich and poor seldom meet informally. Residential segregation was apparent everywhere, existing on a micro-scale in rural India and Uganda, where proximity made some contact inevitable, while in Norway and Britain they generally lived separately in different parts of the town. Mixing even within the family is often thwarted by difficulties. Respondents in Pakistan, India, and Uganda admitted to deliberate attempts to avoid demands for assistance from poorer kin.

While persons experiencing poverty seek social engagement and social acceptance, they often cannot afford the former and are not afforded the latter. Indeed, their attempts at engagement are often rejected and even used as evidence to justify the differentials: 'the poor' are poor because 'they' try to be like 'us'. It might be pushing the evidence too far to suggest that the affluent wish to maintain differentials in consumption and participation in order to reinforce their own position and to retain the overt evidence of economic success. However, the explicit statement by respondents in India and Uganda that poor people seem increasingly to be forgetting their rightful position is at least consistent with this interpretation.

The lack of contact reduces the scope for overt shaming in informal settings. It occurs, though, in domestic settings when staff are employed. Having servants was common among those interviewed in Uganda, India, and Pakistan. Many of the rules of employment were inherently stigmatizing, underpinned by discriminatory assumptions: restricted entry to parts of the home, separate dining, no use of family utensils, etc. The justifications offered by respondents often revealed the prejudicial lens through which they viewed people in poverty, even those that they had employed: 'If you asked them to wash their hands before eating, they'd lie to you and say they'd already done so'. The same prejudice is evident in public policies as is explained in the final section of this chapter.

Stigma and Officialdom

It will be recalled from Chapter 7 that people in poverty most often reported overt stigmatization and associated discrimination and stereotyping in their dealings with officialdom. People felt that they often had publicly to expose their poverty and to admit to their personal failure; that failings were presumed and hence that they were treated with suspicion; that they were often discriminated against in terms of quality of provision; and indeed that they were even exploited because they were powerless to resist. These accounts find support in many studies of institutional stigma, some of which were discussed in Chapter 4, and also in policy analyses undertaken in the seven countries that serve as case studies in this volume (Gubrium et al., 2013). Elements of stigma are evident in the framing, structure, and delivery of policies in each of the countries. This section focusses on delivery, that is on the immediate interface between bureaucracy and the person in poverty receiving a service or benefit or, indeed, not receiving one to which they would have been entitled.

The multiplicity of elements implicated in the institutionalized shaming of people in poverty are for simplicity grouped into those encountered in accessing services, those relating to the lack of respect accorded to service users, and those appertaining to the poor quality of services that are generally provided. It is important to register that not every service is poor nor is every person receiving a service badly treated. The opposite of each negative attribute is a positive one that amounts to treating people with dignity rather than disrespect; such positives characteristics could constitute the basis of model provision or serve as performance indicators that might be used to hold providers to account (see Chapter 11). However, the reality is that the generality of provision across all seven countries is heavily stigmatizing either as the product of intent or the result of apathy or passive contempt. An important reason is probably the powerlessness of people in poverty both as individuals and as a class, unable to mobilize through lack of resources and possibly constrained in doing so by the othering arising from the imposition of shame (see Chapter 7). In Uganda, people in poverty have no choice but to send their children to free but overcrowded and under-resourced UPE (universal primary education) schools (Bantebya-Kyomuhendo and Mwiine, 2013), while in Britain they generally cannot afford housing in the catchment areas of the best state schools (Walker and Chase, 2013). In China, people are forced by necessity to overcome their reluctance to apply for Dibao (social assistance) and appear pitifully grateful for the help received (Yan, 2013; Zhu and Lin, 2010), while in India people in poverty reliant on the Public Distribution Service (PDS) have no choice but to buy grain that they believe has been adulterated (Pellissery and Mathew, 2013).

Access

Much research has focussed on the take-up of welfare benefits and provision for people in poverty (Brewer et al., 2006; Robles, 2013). This points to lack of information, the mismatch between eligibility criteria and perceptions of need, compliance costs including overcoming felt stigma, and the hassle associated with institutional arrangements that are often extremely burdensome and sometimes discriminatory.

Policies that are not universally accessible but targeted on people in poverty are necessarily divisive, but they are often accompanied by the negative stereotyping and discrimination that transform shame into stigma. The well-intentioned Norwegian system of staged support for getting unemployed benefit recipients back into employment has, as noted in Chapter 7, inadvertently created a highly nuanced status hierarchy with intense shaming made worse by unclear criteria for movement between each stage. In Britain, each generation of schemes—'poor relief', 'the dole', 'the social', and 'welfare'—has become tainted with the label of 'undeserving', whereas in India *Thozilurappu Paddhathi* (the 'work guarantee scheme'; National Rural Employment Guarantee Act (NREGA)) is often referred to as *Thozhiluzhappu Paddhathi* (the 'lazy work scheme'), while in Uganda the 'education for all' policy, *Bonabasome*, is widely known as *Bonabakone* ('illiteracy for all'; 'food you cannot eat').

Problems of access—and stigma—can be intensified when allocation decisions are based on discretion. Discretion enables officials to fine-tune provision to individual need, the application of what the British academic Richard Titmuss (1971) termed 'creative justice', but equally it can disempower applicants who, without clearly ascribed rights, are at the mercy of officials who may not always be scrupulous. In South Korea, discretion under NBLSS operates within an institutional culture that prioritizes reduction of abuse, presumes deceit, and gives applicants little benefit of the doubt. In Pakistan, discretion is practised in administrative settings imbued with religious ideals that deem abuse of the Zakat system to be a major sin; given that the rules of the scheme are opaque and open to interpretation, officials assume almost divine authority (Choudhry, 2013). In China, access to Dibao is policed by neighbourhood committees that, while intensely knowledgeable, can be intrusive and even discriminatory (Solinger, 2010; Zhou, 2012). In both India and Pakistan, where access to benefits often entails mediation between applicants and local politicians, discrimination is often overt. In India, recipients need to be registered on the BPL ('below poverty line') list, and require considerable social and even financial resources to get their names added (Pellissery, 2007). Likewise, in Pakistan there is evidence of intensive lobbying to be included in a poverty survey that forms the basis for administration of the BISP (Benazir Income Support Programme). In Uganda, too, access to support through the National Agricultural Advisory Services (NAADS) seems to exclude the most vulnerable who do not have sufficient influence over the gatekeepers to the system. In these settings, the prevalence of patronage and bribery forces applicants to add the shame of corruption to that of poverty.

Lack of Respect

The prevailing view among people in poverty accessing public services was that rather than being accorded respect, they were generally treated with contempt. There were occasions when this was not the case, and these were often remembered long after the event with individual staff being identified and praised. However, the institutional logic, particularly within social assistance systems that make cash and other allocations conditional on need, is to target resources through procedures of exclusion. Moreover, of course, institutions are staffed by people from the local community that share, or are likely to be influenced by, the same negative perceptions of poverty described previously in this chapter.

Given limited resources, procedures for the determining eligibility and entitlements are often detailed, driven by accountancy principles that sums should add up and be supported by evidenced documentation. In systems based on discretion, either formal or more illicit, the limited funds available increase the power of gatekeepers and the prevalence of corruption. Either way, the message conveyed to applicants is less that 'you are welcome and these are your rights' and more that 'you have to justify your right to be here and to be claiming benefits'. In seeking to identify the eligible, applicants feel that they are all under suspicion, a perception that often accurately reflects the administrative logic of targeting as it is interpreted by staff and management. The net result is often complex systems of evidence gathering and checking undertaken by staff who are frequently stressed by high workloads and sometimes low wages, and yet whose work has profound implications for the lives of often vulnerable applicants. The direct result is commonly that applicants are necessarily engaged in hassle and feel themselves to be hassled, often unnecessarily.

The Chinese Dibou system is locally administered, with benefit levels and eligibility criteria also determined locally (Li and Yang, 2009). Very often, though, fraud prevention is a driving impetus influenced in part by the *huji* residence registration system that excludes many local residents from eligibility even though their need is palpable (Zhou, 2012). Detailed information is required for biannual reviews that can entail applicants needing to revisit their place of origin, home visits by officials, and interviews conducted with a range of people knowing the applicant (Duoji, 2001). In South Korea, the presumption is that able-bodied people of working age should be self-sufficient or supported by their extended family (Lee, 2010). Hence, applicants need to demonstrate their incompetence or the inability or unwillingness of their kin to support them, a process that is both humiliating and, given the extensive discretionary powers of officials, perilous (Huh, 2009). In Pakistan, the state takeover of the Muslim system of Zakat has created conflict between the heavy state emphasis on documentation and security and the religious tradition of discreteness, making public and open support that was once private and unobtrusive. In Britain, the complex system, currently undergoing reform, has meant applicants claiming multiple benefits administered by different organizations and needing repeatedly to supply similar information, requiring applicants frequently to admit their failure publicly. The enormous scale of the enterprise leads, as in Norway, to accusations of dehumanizing systems that treat people as numbers rather than as individuals.

In addition to collecting information necessary to establish eligibility, systems often impose behavioural conditions on applicants. The administrative logic behind such conditions varies greatly but is generally of two kinds: conditions that are thought likely to add to a person's well-being or promote their financial self-sufficiency; and ones that provide further checks that applicants truly are in need. Specific conditions are often designed to reflect both motivations. Recipients of unemployment benefits in Norway and Britain are required actively to seek work and not to have left their previous employment voluntarily. Working-age recipients of Dibao and NBLSS, in China and South Korea respectively, are, to the extent that they can access benefit at all, generally obliged to work for their benefit, while in Norway and Britain, as in most OECD countries, activation policies are increasingly making benefits conditional on engagement in specified work-related activity. Social assistance in India is generally provided in kind as employment, through the NREGA, or as food and provisions through the PDS. Increasingly, too, there is a move globally, following reports of the success of conditional cash transfer schemes such as Oportunidades in Mexico and Bolsa Familia in Brazil, towards conditioning receipt on participation in education and health care.

To the extent that the conditions are reasonable, they can be taken to confirm applicants' perceptions that authority assumes people in poverty are incapable of making rational decisions about work or spending on basic essentials without coercion. To the extent that they are unreasonable, for example through obligations to undertake demeaning work with no training and little scope for progression, they may add further humiliation to the stigma of benefit receipt. Certainly, this was so among many respondents in South Korea, Britain, Norway, and some in China—case-study countries with work-based conditionality. In Norway, respondents were inclined to see the conditionality as an infringement of their civil rights, as evidence of governmental paternalism, and as a form of exploitation: real work for substandard wages. This last interpretation was also common in Britain, while the public humiliation of undertaking menial work and the sense of powerlessness dominated conversation in South Korea and has been reported in other studies: 'dolphins fed fish by a keeper' (Jo and Walker, 2013; Lee-Gong, 2011). Even in China, where surveys of Dibao recipients record high levels of satisfaction, minorities still report loss of face (21 per cent; Ma and Zhao, 2006) or embarrassment (16 per cent; Zhu and Lin, 2010) as a consequence of claiming benefit.

Poor Provision

Finally, adding to the shame of poverty and the stigma of claiming social assistance, there is the poor quality of provision, the delays, the paperwork, the dilapidated or shabby accommodation, and the low level of benefits. In part, this reflects the dictum that 'services reserved for the poor rapidly become poor services'. However, policies designed for people experiencing poverty are often explicitly designed to be poor. This can be to avoid attracting abuse (claims from ineligible persons), for reasons of fairness of treatment vis-à-vis people who are not poor, or to keep costs for the taxpayer to a minimum. The fact that millions in China, India, Pakistan, and Uganda live in extreme poverty that has been globally accepted to be a breach of human rights is demonstrable evidence of inadequate programmes of too limited scope. Correspondingly, in Britain, South Korea, and even Norway concern about work incentives ensures that benefits are kept low so as (generally) not to exceed minimum wages. While low benefits may succeed in ameliorating the worst excesses of poverty, they perpetuate the shame of inadequate incomes. Moreover, the imposition of sanctions for non-compliance with conditionality may forcibly reduce incomes while adding an additional and deliberate tier of shame.

The under-resourcing of provision with insufficient staff who are often inadequately trained is an endemic problem that, historically, has been most prevalent in the global South, but which could increasingly become important in countries of the North as they continue to grapple with enforced austerity. Queues, delays, errors, ill-treatment, and hassle were seen to be the norm by respondents in receipt of social assistance and are generally confirmed by other studies (Jung, 2007). Inadequate investment in education and healthcare additionally reinforces processes that perpetuate poverty caused by limited skills and poor health.

It was often difficult for respondents to determine whether the hassle that they encountered with officialdom was the product of limited investment or deliberate attempts to deter or humiliate them. Either way, it added to the stigma of benefit receipt; lacking privacy and on display in queues, it made even more public their confession of failure while demonstrating that society did not care enough to meet their needs adequately.

POVERTY-RELATED SHAME IS RELATIONAL

The literature on shame reviewed in Chapters 3 and 4 asserts that shame is relational, being both internally felt and externally imposed. That people in poverty repeatedly feel ashamed on account of their poverty was clearly demonstrated in Chapter 7, although the evidence base is limited in numbers if rich in detail. Moreover, it seemed that people frequently felt that they were humiliated by the actions of others and in their dealings with institutions. They therefore took such precautions as they could to avoid being shamed which sometimes created problems of their own (see Chapter 8). In effect, their words and experiences corroborated the notion that shame is a relational phenomenon, not something that is self-imposed.

This chapter has sought further supportive evidence of the existence of this external shame. By its very nature this is difficult to demonstrate without observational data. However, through listening to the discussion of people who are not poor, and through collating information on the delivery of policies, much confirmatory evidence has been assembled. Taken together, it establishes at least a prima facie case supporting the contention that persons in poverty are humiliated and despised by their more affluent counterparts.

An additional argument that has been developed is that whatever the true reason for participating in shaming behaviour, be it sincere attempts to coerce people better to help themselves or a self-justifying defence of the status quo, individuals justify their actions by reference to the notion that people are responsible for their own poverty. The evidence presented suggests that such a belief is widespread but with subtle differences apparent across different countries. Many times in the analysis it seemed appropriate to group together respondents from Uganda, India, and Britain in terms of their views and to contrast them with those from China, Norway, and Pakistan. Respondents from the first three countries often used robust negative language, dismissing people in poverty as being lazy, inadequate, and untrustworthy. Accounts of the causes of poverty were predominantly individualistic, and often prioritized bad behaviour and weak character. These views were present in the groups in China, Norway, and Pakistan, but were muted and juxtaposed against structural accounts of the causes of poverty and the possibility of individual misfortune. The groups were not, of course, statistically representative and no claims are made as to national differences. Indeed, there is a suspicion that the particular characteristics of participants in the Chinese groups masked individualistic assumptions as to the causes of poverty, while the Pakistani and Norwegian respondents readily slipped into individualistic arguments when considering the circumstances and behaviour of particular individuals. Moreover, the divisions by country became less marked as respondents struggled with the concepts of deserving and undeserving poor. These emerged spontaneously in Norway, China, and Britain, typically in relation to the provision of welfare payments to individuals, but were less evident in India, Pakistan, and Uganda where provisions were less developed and more tarnished by corruption. There was, though, in India and Uganda, a corresponding debate that distinguished between those people in poverty who took up the new opportunities offered by economic growth and those who did not.

The claim that people in poverty are actively shamed by the non-poor and by bureaucracy has likewise been investigated with a similar conclusion, namely that they very probably are. The scope for interaction between poor and non-poor varied markedly between different settings. It was sometimes difficult to avoid within the family, which did not stop the more affluent from trying to avoid meeting with their poorest kin. Interaction occurred almost daily in rural areas and when the affluent employed domestic staff, but informal or social contact rarely took place at all in urban areas. When it did occur, so did the shaming. Respondents confirmed that they behaved just as people in poverty said that they did. Moreover, they added that attempts made by people in poverty to engage, to reciprocate in kind, or to appear 'normal' were frequently interpreted as feckless wastes of money or as evidence of 'them' trying to live above their station. Likewise, sensitized by the experience of the respondents reported in previous chapters, it is immediately evident that antipoverty programmes in all seven countries frequently inflict shame in the way that they control access to benefits and treat beneficiaries. Designed and often funded by taxpayers who are not poor, they are underpinned by shared beliefs about the individualistic causes of poverty. The institutional logic to restrict expenditure and target resources efficiently imposes heavy compliance costs on applicants who are forced repeatedly, and often very publicly, to admit their failings and to place their lives in the hands of officials who are often too busy to treat them properly. They are made to perform, to repeat the words of a recipient of NBLSS in South Korea, 'like a dolphin fed fish by a keeper' often in return for mere subsistence (Lee-Gong, 2011, p. 16).

So the evidence assembled in Chapters 7–9 is highly consistent with the associational logic captured in Figure 4.1, namely that poverty causes people both to feel ashamed and to be shamed by society through their social relationships and in their dealings with policy institutions. Chapter 10 goes on to explore the processes through which social attitudes both shape and are shaped by policy logics, and the role of the media in mediating these processes.

10

Shaming People in Poverty

Media and Policy[1]

There are now strong empirical grounds for believing from the accounts of people in poverty that they are repeatedly shamed in their dealings with others and with officialdom. Respondents cited in Chapter 9 'admitted' shaming people in poverty while the policy analyses indicated great scope for shaming in the implementation of policy. Such behaviour was often not considered inappropriate, reprehensible, or unusual, although direct personal contact with people in poverty was comparatively rare, especially in social settings, and was frequently deliberately avoided by people where possible. In certain countries, mindful of social convention and legal restrictions, the language used in public when referring to those in poverty was respectful whereas in others there was no such restraint. Moreover, the indications are that in private, and when discussing certain subgroups experiencing poverty, disrespectful language was in common usage everywhere.

The aim in this penultimate chapter is to explore further the coincidence between individual behaviour and public discourse. The associational model presented in Figure 4.1 differentiated between shaming occurring in informal interpersonal interactions and the stigma associated with policy. This analytic distinction has the merit of simplicity but now requires further elaboration. In Chapter 4, stigma was defined as institutional shame, but it was also distinguished from shame in terms of intent. Whereas shaming may be instigated to foster social cohesion, stigma is necessarily divisive with the divisions often being reinforced through stereotyping and discrimination. Individuals may engage in stigmatizing as opposed to shaming behaviour if the intent is malicious. Indeed, it may even be possible for the cohesion-building goals of shame to be achieved through stigmatizing behaviour, although the research drawn on in Chapter 3 suggests that shame is invariably counterproductive if it is actually imposed as opposed to merely being threatened.

---

[1] This chapter draws heavily on the following publications: Bantebya-Kyomuhendo and Mwiine (2014c); Chase and Walker (2014c); Choudhry (2014c); Gubrium and Lødemel (2014c); Pellissery and Mathew (2014c); and Yan (2014c).

The distinction between individual shaming and institutional stigma may not therefore be hard and fast. Indeed, a particularly interesting question is whether the negative attitudes towards people in poverty that lead to shaming and the stigma inherent in much policy delivery are related and, if so, how. Advocates of democracy, dating back to at least Edmund Burke, would argue that the two are related in that politicians take their cue from the will of the people (Burke and Stanlis, 2000). However, not all the seven case-study countries are equally democratic. Moreover, political scientists have drawn attention to the many actors and processes at play that might mediate or moderate the influence of public opinion, or more accurately people's views, on policy formation (Kingdom, 2011; Manza and Brooks, 2012). Possible actors include ministers, other politicians and elected officials, bureaucrats, academic advisers, lobbyists, and journalists variously empowered or constrained by institutions such as political parties, employers, trade unions and other interest and lobbying groups, the media, the constitution and law making conventions, and of course the electorate. Rather than attempt a thorough political analysis, the focus here is restricted to the role that the media, explicitly print journalism, may play in mediating social values, public opinion and policy intent, and subsequently in influencing policy structures.

As in almost everything else in social science, the role of the media in shaping policy is contested. Some argue that it is vitally important (DellaVigna and Kaplan, 2008; Manza and Brooks, 2012), others that its influence is much exaggerated (Kingdom, 2011). What is clear is that the processes involved are complex, often issue specific, and typically include a mix of direct and indirect effects. Occasionally media campaigns put items on the policy agenda by simultaneously building support among the general public and policymakers (Manza and Brooks, 2012). More often the media follow policy issues that are already under discussion by politicians or being promoted by social movements, sometimes magnifying their significance and building a momentum for reform, and on other occasions acting as a block on policy change (Kingdom, 2011). At times the media is used by government and interest groups to initiate discussion or to exert pressure on recalcitrant policy actors, while in other instances the media successfully targets key policy entrepreneurs or effects change through mobilizing public opinion (Manza and Brooks, 2012). While such activity might reflect the importance of the 'fourth estate' as a vital check on the power of vested interests, there is also concern that the media may, in its ownership and influential readership, represent powerful vested interests. It has even been accused of biasing the democratic process by deliberately framing issues through its selection and presentation of information (DellaVigna and Kaplan, 2008). Equally, though, for much of the time the media appears to have no discernible effect on policy agendas because matters are too mundane or technical to be of interest to the general public, or because the policy dynamic is firmly controlled by other policy actors sometimes deliberately working out of the media spotlight (Kingdom, 2011; Knoepfel et al., 2007).

While much of the research has sought to explore the impact of the media on individual attitudes and specific policy decisions, the task at hand is broader with a focus on the values that shape public understanding and policy discourse. Values frame individuals' thinking but are typically shared such that they often define group membership. Infused with affect, they are relatively stable, transcend specific actions and situations, and influence perceptions, understanding, evaluation, and behaviour (Bergman, 1998; Schwartz and Bilsky, 1987). Alongside frames of thinking, political scientists have identified frames of communication that organize and shape public discourse about issues by proposing definitions, causal connections, and interpretations (Chong and Druckman, 2007; Lee et al., 2008). Increasingly, frames of communication are deliberately designed and used by policy actors, appealing to specific sets of values so as to encourage people to adopt certain opinions or attitudes with respect to particular issues or policy approaches. Politics, viewed through this lens, becomes a battle of competing frames with victory assured if the frame of communication being promoted becomes the majority's natural frame of thinking (D'Angelo, 2012; Knoepfel et al., 2007).

Figure 10.1 provides a schematic map of the processes explored in this chapter, differentiating between the framing of thinking and that of communication. It shows social behaviour (namely behaviour directed towards or referring to other people) shaming people in poverty. This behaviour reflects

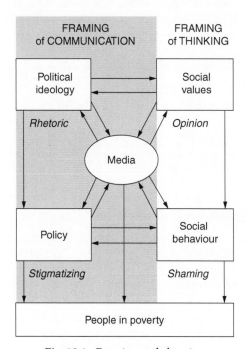

Fig. 10.1. Framing and shaming

social values (namely personal values that are shared by other people) expressed as opinion with respect to a particular idea, explicitly the nature and causes of poverty. The diagram similarly shows stigmatizing policies underpinned by political ideology that is conveyed as political rhetoric. It also allows for mass media, reflecting political ideology and social values, to affect policy and social behaviour, recursively to influence political ideology and social values, and also to respond to policy and social behaviour. The potential for the media directly to affect people in poverty is also evident in the diagram, but people in poverty are given no voice; this is, of course, an oversimplification but one that reflects a statistical reality. Information to populate the diagram is taken from the policy analyses described in Chapter 8 and media analyses conducted in five of the seven case-study countries. The latter generally entailed undertaking a content analysis of a sample of newspapers each day for twelve weeks spread systematically over a five- or ten-year period ending at the turn of the year 2011 to 2012.

RESONATING OR NOT WITH THE PUBLIC

While the story so far has emphasized marked similarity in the experience of people in poverty and considerable coincidence in the attitudes of those who are not, the interplay between policy, the media, and public opinion takes very different forms across the case-study countries. In China, Norway, and India media discourse, at least as glimpsed through the newsprint reviewed, seems for varying reasons to be rather detached from the values and concerns of the people participating in focus groups. Not so in Britain and Uganda, where the language of print echoes that heard in discussion.

Before addressing this conundrum directly, it is necessary to add to its complexity. Opinion polling reported in Chapter 9 indicated marked vari- ations in the proportion of people believing laziness to be a more important cause of poverty than unfairness. These differences were not always reflected in the focus group discussions where individualistic reasons for poverty were commonplace in most of the discussions except those in China. More recent attitudinal data reinforce the commonality of views as illustrated in 'cave plots' presented in Figures 10.2, 10.3, and 10.4. In the 'cave plots' 'stalagmites' indicate the proportion of people agreeing with a proposition, 'stalactites' the proportion disagreeing. Figure 10.2 captures the prevalence of the work ethic and work as a social responsibility. In 2005–2008, 80 per cent of respondents in Norway, China, and India believed that 'work was a duty towards society' as did 70 per cent of Britons and over 60 per cent of South Koreans. Furthermore, similarly high proportions thought that 'people who don't work turn lazy' (Figure 10.3), while large numbers considered it

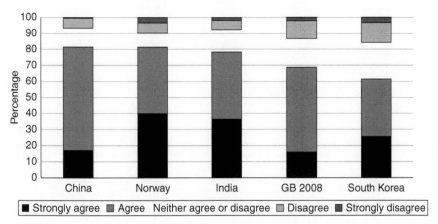

Fig. 10.2. 'Work is a duty towards society' (2005–2007)

World Values Survey 1981–2008; European Values Survey 2008

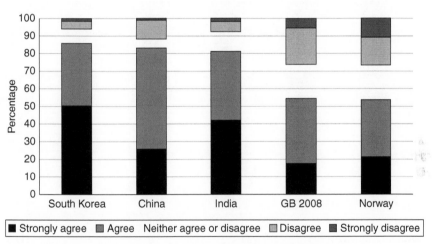

Fig. 10.3. 'People who don't work turn lazy' (2005–2007)

World Values Survey 1981–2008; European Values Survey 2008

'humiliating to receive money without having to work for it' (Figure 10.4) (which is particularly relevant to welfare policy). There were some differences between countries. For example, 'unconditional benefit' was somewhat less despised in Norway and Britain, and in these two countries only smallish majorities felt that lack of work induced laziness. Nevertheless, an attachment to individual self-reliance is strongly evident.

Finally, to focus the discussion back on poverty, Table 10.1 demonstrates that people's views are not independent of their own social standing. It shows, generally speaking, that the richer a person is the more likely they are to

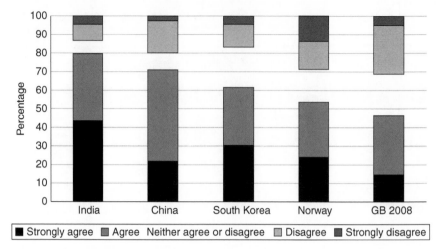

Fig. 10.4. 'Humiliating to receive money without having to work for it' (2005–2007)
World Values Survey 1981–2008; European Values Survey 2008

Table 10.1 Perceptions of the causes of poverty by level of relative household income

Percentages saying main cause of poverty is laziness and lack of willpower

		Income				
	Latest year	Low	Medium	High		Total
China	2001	51	55	68		58
India	2001	32	44	50		42
Norway	1996	33	35	41		35
Pakistan	2001	17	19	27		20
		Below	Average	Above		
Kenya	2013	20	25	54		26
		Low	Low medium	High medium	High	
Great Britain	2010	28	18	15	17	24

World Values Survey; British Social Attitudes Survey; Park et al. (2013b)

consider poverty to be the result of laziness and lack of willpower. The differences are particularly marked in India and Kenya, inserted in lieu of Uganda for which there are no data. But it is also noticeable that not inconsequential numbers of persons in the lowest third of the income distribution, half in China and a third in India and Norway, also attribute poverty to laziness, and in the unique case of Britain the fraction doing so exceeds that for people with higher incomes. Some of these survey respondents will be experiencing poverty while the others by definition will not be rich. Presuming not many attribute their own poverty to laziness, these statistics suggest that the process of othering discussed in Chapter 8 may be endemic. There appears to be an acceptance of negative stereotypes of poverty even among some on low incomes, and a willingness (or felt need) to blame others for being in poverty as part of a self-justifying discourse. This frame of thinking would seem to juxtapose the virtuousness of work against the evil of laziness, with the differential willingness to work being used to justify why one person is rich while another is poor. Poverty is seen as a due desert for not fulfilling one's duty to work, or even a natural punishment for idleness.

This frame of thinking, evident in varying degrees in all the case-study countries, is reinforced in Britain and Uganda by the frame of communication but not in China, India, or Norway. To understand the reasons it is necessary to be aware of the varying contribution made by print media in policy debates within these differing contexts.

In Britain, newspapers have to survive economically alongside almost universal coverage from television and radio that provide most people with their main source of news, and have increasingly to resist the advance of social media (Chase and Walker, 2014c). They achieve this by sectioning the market and differentially packaging news, entertainment, comment, and campaigning. Daily national newspapers divide into broadsheets with a primarily middle class readership (National Readership Survey social grades 1 and 2) and tabloids that are targeted at mainly working class readers (C2, D), including people not working (E), and have a combined readership of around nineteen million (Preston, 2011). Two media conglomerates, one international, one British, own most of the newspapers by market share and daily newspapers typically have a stable-mate Sunday newspaper, while many also have associated regional newspapers that are increasingly distributed free (paid for by advertising). Most UK national newspapers are positioned politically, four of the five national tabloids are located on the centre right of politics; they often interweave political comment and opinion with news, and many take pride in trying to swing elections. In so doing, they explicitly seek to frame social and policy issues from competing ideological perspectives that merge commercial and political advantage. As explained below, poverty and welfare benefits are often presented as problems in need of solutions.

Norwegian newspapers are also under pressure from new media but are still read daily by 64 per cent of the population (down from 84 per cent in 1991; Medianorway, 2013). Three companies control 65 per cent of the circulation but government provides subsidies, based on circulation, to maintain heterogeneity, and some 147 newspapers are currently in print (including Sunday, morning, and evening editions). Newspapers present themselves as politically independent although the second largest selling tabloid, *Dagbladet*, was until 1977 affiliated to the Liberal Party (Venstre), while *Aftenposten*, the leading newspaper in terms of sales, and which generally reflects mainstream Norwegian social democratic thought, was once aligned to conservative forces. More so than in Britain, newspapers serve as forums for debate driven by contributions from politicians, party members, and people writing for special interest groups. Broadly supportive of Norway's generous welfare state, this debate is nevertheless often critical of government and government policy. While poverty was a dominant issue in the late 1990s and early 2000s, it is now much less salient, typically being used to illustrate policy failure and as a vehicle through which to criticize government (Gubrium and Lødemel, 2014c).

The Ugandan newspaper readership is concentrated in urban areas and has not developed as quickly as the audience for broadcasting, especially FM radio and increasingly television (Bantebya-Kyomuhendo and Mwiine, 2014c). The industry is dominated by the New Vision Group, which was established by the government in 1986 and is still subject to control through a 53 per cent government holding in the group. It publishes: *New Vision* in English, the largest selling paper with a daily circulation of 32,000 but targeted at the urban elite; *Bukedde* in Luganda; *Orumuri* in Runyankole/Rukiga; *Etop* in Ateso; and *Rupiny* in Luo. Other newspapers include: the politically independent *Daily Monitor*, circulation 24,000; the *Weekly Observer*, launched in 2004 by a journalists' co-operative; and the *East African* based in Kenya. Political comment is constrained. While the enabling statute guarantees the *New Vision* editorial independence such that it does critique public policy, it nevertheless operates a strict gate-keeping role on opinion and veers towards moderation in its own self-regulation (Wasswa, 2005). Privately owned newspapers are bolder but freedom of the press is far from guaranteed. For example, the *Monitor* was temporarily closed in May 2013 and another independent newspaper, *Red Pepper*, effectively closed down after publishing letters critical of the government. In this climate, while the media repeatedly comment on the national embarrassment of continued high levels of poverty and the generic failure of schemes to address the problem, frequently attributed to corruption, people in poverty are themselves often presented as an impediment to economic development.

The news media in China are similarly constrained but on an entirely different scale. With over 1,900 newspapers reaching a daily readership of ninety-six million, China has the world's largest newspaper industry and is now being organized on commercial lines, spawning the emergence of some forty publishing groups (BBC, 2013). There are about a dozen national newspapers including the *People's Daily*, the official organ of the party-state, and *Cankao Xiaoxi*, which has the largest circulation (three million), but most newspapers are regional in their coverage. Journalistic styles vary markedly but all newspapers have to be approved by the government, which tightly controls their content through a system at provincial level that is based on directive and self-censorship. While this is generally recognized by the public, people tend to be more sceptical about the content of broadcast news. Newspapers announce government initiatives, launch approved debates, and sometimes actively carry forward policies such as drives against corruption.

Unsurprisingly, therefore, issues are viewed through an authorized official frame which, as it happens, is one that encourages compassion towards people in poverty and concern about the structural causes of poverty, but that is largely content with the limited welfare provision available (Yan, 2014c).

After China, India has the world's second largest news readership with seventy-nine million daily readers built up from 88,763 registered newspapers, out of which 5,383 are daily newspapers published in nineteen languages. Unlike China, the Indian press is largely free of state control, and indeed Amartya Sen (2001) has argued that the existence of India's free press helps to explain why less than a thousand people died of hunger in the 1950s and 1960s compared to perhaps three million in China. Some 400 newspapers are published in English, the top five having a combined readership of about 15.5 million. With a national rather than regional focus, and published in the language of governance, the English dailies tend to play a disproportionate role in policy debates. Their stance, a legacy of the fight for national independence and the commitment to development, is very often anti-government and almost invariably pro-poor (Pellissery and Mathew, 2014c). Almost diametrically opposed to media discourse in Uganda, the dominant frame applied by Indian English-language newspapers is that poverty is not the making of people in poverty but rather the product of an ineffectual state.

At the risk of oversimplification, the dominant communication framing of poverty is different in each of the five countries considered. In two, Norway and India, poverty is employed as a device to censure government: in Norway, the criticism is sometimes that there is too much welfare; in India, the argument is invariably that there is insufficient. In China, the concept of poverty is almost ethereal and people in poverty are placed beyond criticism; the state is portrayed as their protector. In contrast, in Uganda and Britain people in poverty are both a problem and the problem, but whereas criticism of government policy in Uganda tends to be muted, in Britain welfare policy is part of the political battleground: the party in government is almost always accused of failing, the opposition is persistently in search of convincing solutions. And yet, despite these profound differences in public discourse, public opinion in each country is remarkably similar: it would hold that in the final analysis, with structural factors put to one side, people are the cause of their own poverty.

FRAMING THE PROBLEM OF POVERTY

It is helpful to characterize the different ways in which poverty is framed in media discourses with respect to its definition and its presumed causes and consequences, and also to compare and contrast the different countries, starting with Uganda and Britain where the dominant discourse is that of denigration.

Reinforcing Frames

Based on analyses of five[2] newspapers covering ten years, Bantebya-Kyomuhendo and Mwiine (2014c) identify a consistent portrayal of poverty as 'total deprivation', inadequate material possessions, insufficient income, poor physical health, and low social status. People in poverty are correspondingly described as pathetic individuals, unsightly in appearance, dirty, smelly, dressed in rags, and frequently infested with jiggers (a parasitic arthropod, *Tunga penetrans*, that causes the inflammatory skin disease tungiasis and is associated with mud floors and insanitary conditions). While poverty is defined in absolute terms, understandable in a country where 65 per cent of people live on less that USD 2/day, commentators equally apply ideas as to what people 'ought to have' and what is 'acceptable in the community'. Moreover, faced with desperate circumstances, it is assumed that people in poverty resort to what are described as 'desperate actions' including: casual employment, illicit distilling, theft, homosexuality, and prostitution. Newspapers, particularly those in the vernacular, tend to link poverty to gender relations, citing poverty as the cause of women leaving their husbands ('I'm tired of sleeping on a one inch mattress'), and men's failure to provide the material things necessary to consummate a marriage. Families are also accused of using daughters like 'cash cows', 'selling them off' young into marriage. As a result, coverage of poverty is often accompanied by moral indignation as well as disgust at material deprivation.

Ugandan newspapers offer different explanations of the causes of poverty. Sometimes they acknowledge structural factors such as differential access to education and health care and the failure of government to stabilize basic commodity prices. During the 2011 presidential campaign, much attention was also paid to the failure of government policies as a cause of poverty. For the most part, though, newspapers echoed views heard in the focus groups reported in Chapter 9: poverty was a consequence of laziness, lack of focus, reckless living, spending on alcohol, tobacco, and illicit sex, or inherent bad luck (*ekisirani*). How, it was asked, could poverty exist in a land blessed 'with fertile soils, a good climate and abundant national resources'? The answers attributed to various politicians, officials, and church leaders at different times included money wasted on *boda bodas* (motorbikes), poor hygiene, keeping children home from school, laziness, and an unwillingness to change, to take up new opportunities, to adopt new methods, and to embrace modern attitudes to the economy and to families. Poverty was not just an embarrassment to an aspiring nation, people in poverty were actually holding back progress.

---

[2] New Vision, Daily Monitor, Weekly Observer, Bukedde, and Orumuri.

Similar arguments were espoused in a very different context in Britain. Chase and Walker (2014c), analysing sample issues of all national newspapers between 2006 and 2012, found that negative portrayals of poverty prevailed in the right-of-centre tabloids that dominate circulation (the *Daily Mail*, the *Sun*, the *Daily Express*, and the *Daily Star*), but were also found in the right-leaning broadsheets (the *Daily Telegraph*, the *Sunday Telegraph*, and the *Sunday Times*). Competing ideological perspectives were often presented in the *Daily Mirror*, the *Guardian*, the *Observer*, and the *Morning Star*, and to a lesser extent by the *Independent*, but these newspapers, the *Daily Mirror* excepted, had circulations less than a tenth of those of the tabloids (see also Baumberg et al., 2012).

What all the British newspapers appear to share is a view of poverty that more or less equates with receipt of welfare benefits. Hence, discussion about the causes and consequences of poverty is largely framed as a debate about the merits or otherwise of welfare provision that is, in turn, an ideological discourse between political left and right and between government and opposition. Children and sometimes the deserving elderly apart, people on benefits are almost universally taken to constitute a problem: there are too many, the cost for the taxpayer is too high, and everyone would be better off if they were working. This analysis is largely shared between newspapers on the left and right, but they differ in terms of attributing cause and effect. Those on the left, in their editorials and copy, acknowledge the structural causes of unemployment, the rise in poorly paid, insecure employment, increasing inequality, and limited access to good education and training. Newspapers on the right do likewise, and did so especially in the immediate aftermath of the 2008 Great Recession when fear of mass layoffs was at its greatest, but emphasize the benefit system itself as the cause of poverty, with Labour governments being responsible for its introduction and growth.

> The Labour government 'creates thousands more dependants willing to go to the polls and vote for them' and an 'everything for free culture'.
>
> *Sunday Express*, 24 April 2009

> The priority is to get Britain back to gainful employment, the 'millions of habitual welfare claimants' who must be taken off the 'intravenous drip of tax payer support and made to earn their keep'.
>
> *Daily Express*, 9 September 2009

Whereas historically people who are sick or living with disabilities have attracted less opprobrium than those who are healthy (Golding and Middleton, 1982; Briant et al., 2011), this is no longer the case and government activation policies now oblige recipients of incapacity benefits to engage in employment-orientated activities.

'Fit as a fiddler:...I am sickened at the amount of malingerers abusing our incapacity benefits system;...at last the sick note scroungers are to get a kick up the butt.

Sun, 22 November 2007

'Spot the malingerer'—the welfare system provides 'millions of pounds to those too fat, tired or spotty to work'.

Daily Mail, 20 November 2007

Echoing the ideas and language heard in focus groups (see Chapter 9), the dominant frame evident in the British media is that the negative consequences of welfare provision are not limited to instilling laziness and dependency. They are coupled, for example, with another *bête noir* of the political right, increased immigration:

It is certainly lamentable that while millions of Britons vegetate on out-of-work benefits, jobs that they should be fit for are taken in their hundreds of thousands by migrants.

Sunday Times, 29 August 2010

Likewise, benefits and benefits fraud are used to explain low employment rates, high taxation, and lack of economic growth:

'Disgrace of the shirkers': 'the welfare state has been hijacked by people too idle to do a proper day's work'. [It is] time [to] 'crackdown on' [those who] 'sponge off tax payers'.

Daily Express, 2 November 2011

We don't pay our taxes only to get ripped off by disability claimants.

Daily Star, 25 August 2010

Dole scroungers are regarded as the new middle class while the rest of us who struggle working to support them become new poverty-stricken social underclass.

Daily Express, 9 September 2007

Politically even more important, welfare benefits are co-opted to explain the unspecific, pessimistic fears of a middle class that feels its living standards to be under threat: beliefs that society is disintegrating with increased divorce, teenage pregnancy, child neglect, crime, antisocial behaviour, binge drinking, and drug abuse. The *Sun*, encapsulated these concerns in the phrase 'broken Britain', a motif that the Conservative Party subsequently took up and used in the 2010 general election campaign, engendering the full endorsement of the *Sun* for its policies (Wiki, 2013).

So in both Britain and Uganda, the dominant media frames reinforce the negative images of poverty evident from focus group discussions. Moreover, poverty is not only attributable to individual lack of effort, the very presence of poverty is seen to hold back economic growth and thereby the prosperity of those buying newspapers. Coverage of poverty simultaneously panders to the readership's fears about an increasingly dysfunctional and threatening society.

Supportive Frames

While in China, as in Britain and Uganda, there was considerable congruence between the dominant media framing and that of respondents in discussion groups, the dynamics were very different. The British media competed for political influence and readership by reflecting popular opinion, while in Uganda the focus of criticism was diverted from the specifics of government to poverty as a brake on economic prosperity. In notable contrast to both, the media in China carry the official Chinese Communist Party line. Based on an analysis of three national papers and four local Beijing ones, this official frame over the dozen years to 2012 seems to have been largely concerned with managing expectations (Yan, 2014c). It is unclear, in the Chinese political context, how far the coincidence of communication and personal frames reflects social pressure on respondents in discussion groups to echo public discourse, although the constraints on free expression are much less than they once were.

As already noted in Chapter 5, poverty varies markedly between urban and rural China. The official poverty line is an absolute level fixed according to the cost of living in rural areas and, set in 2011 at 6.3 yuan a day, is equivalent to between USD 1 and USD 1.88 per day depending on how it is adjusted for local costs (purchasing power parities) (Economist, 2013). Prior to 2011, the government had been using a standard set in the 1990s which registered just 2.8 per cent of the rural population as poor. The old standard was replaced, according to the *China Daily*, because 'it understated the poverty rate' 'which was lower than in many developed countries such as the US, which has a poverty rate of about 15 per cent' (*Daily Telegraph*, 2011). The new measure, despite being much more conservative than the US measure cited, nevertheless increased the poverty rate in rural areas to 12.4 per cent in 2011, but according to the official press agency *Xinhua* this had already fallen to 10.2 per cent a year later. In an intriguing parallel with the focus group discussions that debated whether poverty existed at all in urban China, there is no official measure of urban poverty. Instead newspapers refer to the numbers of people receiving social assistance (Dibao), the rate of which is typically higher in more prosperous cities 'either because they can afford them or because the [poverty] lines reflect relative rather than absolute poverty' (Park and Wang, 2010).

In the era before Deng Xiaoping's announcement of China's open-door policy in 1979, poverty existed in public discourse only to the extent that it was the product of capitalism that the revolution sought to eradicate. Policy was implemented at the level of the *Danwei* unit, or workplace, which provided employment and social protection to state employees. Officially unemployment did not exist, and the media referred only to 'households in difficulty' rather than to poverty (Guan, 1999). Dibao was not introduced until the 1990s, beginning in Shanghai in 1993, and was not much in evidence in rural areas until 2005 (Li et al., 2011). Moreover, poverty rates declined little in the five years before China joined the World Trade Organization in 2001. Thereafter, poverty fell quickly and Dibao featured regularly in the newspapers reviewed as a positive aspect of policy. With it, the party-state has come to represent itself, and to be represented in the news media, as the protector of the people, with Dibao being a 'protective umbrella' in the face of inevitable economic change (*People's Daily*, 9 October 2007). Urban poverty is presented as being inescapable in a modern society, especially one in the early stages of economic development. It is a product of necessary industrial restructuring resulting in unemployment in the context of limited social security that is exacerbated by global competition. While the state no longer offers guarantees such as full employment, the solution is seen to lie in further economic development, higher levels of production, and improved public policies.

Consistent with the media's structural analysis of the causes of poverty, people in poverty are represented as victims of necessary change. They are people in need of help and support who should be treated 'with a caring heart' and with 'sympathy and attention', and readers are encouraged to contribute to charities at special times of the year such as the Chinese New Year. Equally, recipients of Dibao are almost invariably described as being full of gratitude for the help that they receive. Furthermore, the sentiment is that people in poverty also need to be offered hope of change, and therefore it is important that they are encouraged to 'work hard toward the improvement of their own lives' (*People's Daily*, 18 November 2010).

While the structural analysis of poverty offered by state controlled newspapers echoes opinions expressed in focus groups, the conundrum remains that the majority of the Chinese public believe that poverty is attributable to individual laziness rather than to social unfairness. Possibly in a tightly controlled state there will always be a gulf between public discourse and private opinion, between words and deeds. Maybe the reality of poverty that shames resides in the hints of bullying in the classroom, in the *People's Daily's* edict that hope is engendered through self-help, in the lists of Dibao recipients posted in public, and in the charitable nature of the help available.

Discordant Frames

In India and Norway the conundrum is less the mismatch between words and deeds as that between newspaper coverage and the opinions expressed in focus groups. In India the benign and even pro-poor stance of the media reviewed by Pellissery and Mathew (2014c) contrasts with the derogatory tenor that characterized the discussions reported in Chapter 9. Partly this is attributable to the fact that the analysis of newsprint was restricted to English-language newspapers that help to shape political discourse but would not have been read by people attending the groups. Partly, though, it reflects a moral blindness born out of massive inequality in incomes and influence (Drèze and Sen, 2013).

As in Uganda, poverty is described in despairing terms in Indian newspapers, with people portrayed as living in abject poverty; hungry and ravaged by ill-health they are forced to sell their daughters or body parts in order to eat. But they are also presented as victims of exploitation, corruption, and government failure who are unable to access health care and good education. Thus people in poverty are rarely accused of laziness or blamed for their circumstances; rather, the spotlight is turned on government and governmental neglect and incompetence.

But, despite its pro-poor stance, the Indian press has also been accused of neglecting people in poverty, ignoring diagnosis of the injustice that perpetuates poverty (Drèze and Sen, 2013). One example cited is the debate over the poverty line following publication of the Tendulkar Committee Report in 2009 (GIPC, 2009), and whether new methodology had caused the line to be lowered or raised. This debate, focussed on technicalities, failed to ask why 350 million people, 30 per cent of the population, was still forced to live on a subsistence income (Rs 32 and Rs 26 per person per day in urban and rural areas, noticeably less than USD 1 in July 2011). Similarly, the media has been accused of acquiescence in the long debate about the National Food Security Bill giving people a right to 5 kg of food grain every month (eventually signed into law by President Pranab Mukherjee in July 2013). The media generally accepted the proposition that the proposal was too expensive, when the total cost was less than the revenue forgone by exempting gold and diamond imports from customs duties. The reason given by Drèze and Sen (2013) is that the media, dependent on advertising revenue, reflects the interests of the privileged and that its campaigning on behalf of 'the common people' largely benefits the less well-off among the already privileged rather than India's truly underprivileged.

The mismatch between public discourse and personal attitudes, therefore, might well reflect personal indifference or simple hypocrisy. Harsh Mander, cited in *The Hindu* (10 April 2012), has argued that the Indian elite are alienated from the country's underprivileged and indifferent to their suffering: 'an exile of the poor from our conscience and consciousness' (see also Mander, 2012a, 2012b). While public discourse treats 'the poor' (an exclusionary term used 223 times in the extracts reviewed by Pellissery and Mathews, 2014c) with respect, self-interest in the perpetuation of poverty acts as a brake on reform and leaves intact exploitation manifest in day-to-day dealings with people on low incomes:

When TN [the state of Tamil Nadu] introduced Rs 2 rice, most of the poor stopped working and were enjoying the government rice. Labour became a problem . . . [the National Food Security Bill] will destroy India fully and nobody will be ready to work.

The Times of India, 6 July 2013

While respondents in the focus groups may not have read the English-language press, the presumption is that the elites that do so privately share their contempt for people in poverty. This phenomenon was directly witnessed in focus groups in Pakistan when politicians and civil servants moved on from discussing policy to their own dealings with domestic staff, low-income relatives, and people begging.

In Norway the discrepancy is reversed, with a more critical media juxtaposed against a less judgemental public. This is probably explicable in terms of the open-door policy of newspapers that provides a platform for individuals and interest groups to engage in political debate (Gubrium and Lødemel, 2014c). Shared values, concerning the importance of egalitarianism, social cohesion, and welfare go largely unstated with debate focussed on the need for reform. Similarly to Britain, poverty is treated as being synonymous with receipt of benefit, although social assistance receipt is more often singled out from the insurance and other citizenship benefits that give most Norwegians a direct personal stake in their welfare state. Poverty is predominantly discussed in terms of policy failure and broken political promises. Voices on the left demand more generous benefits and those on the right claim that benefits may have induced 'passivity' on the part of people receiving benefits, and precipitated 'welfare tourism' resulting in increased immigration and dependency among immigrant groups.

The expression of shared values and social solidarity was much more to the fore in focus groups comprised of people who did not generally engage in public debate about reform. Negative criticism was largely reserved for the Roma community. Indeed, the groups were possibly generally even more compassionate towards the needs of migrant communities than to native Norwegians, who might have been expected to benefit from all the opportunities provided by an affluent egalitarian society. As Figure 10.5 reveals, Norwegian public opinion overwhelmingly blames poverty on structural factors. Moreover, even those who have not recently received welfare benefits and who are less likely to blame poverty on social injustice than those who have, choose bad luck rather than bad behaviour as the principal cause of poverty. (This is in marked contrast to their British counterparts.)

These comparisons indicate national differences in the congruence between communication frames (as revealed through analysis of newsprint) and frames of public thinking (as indicated by opinion surveys and focus groups). It seems that newspapers vary in the extent to which they reflect (as in the case of

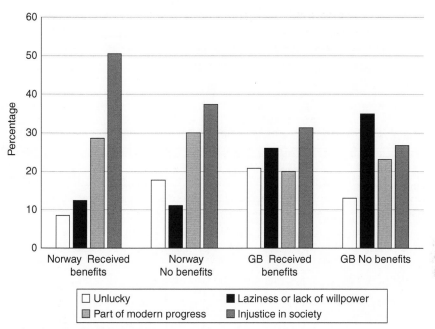

Fig. 10.5. Perceived causes of poverty by recent benefit receipt 2008
European Values Survey 2008

Britain and Uganda) or challenge (as exampled by China and India) public opinion. The reasons are inevitably complicated, but may well be partly due to differences in the way that policy is framed (the topic of the next section) and the media's role in this process.

FRAMING POLICIES

In considering the framing of antipoverty policy it is essential to understand policymakers' take on the manifestations and consequences of poverty that together provide the stimulus to act, and their analysis of the causes that, however poorly specified, affords a policy model for action. It is also necessary to consider the other goals of national and local policymaking, the policy-making institutions, and where accountability for poverty is deemed to lie. For example, successive governments in South Korea have prioritized strong economic growth above all else—'welfare' is equated with aggregate national prosperity, and until the 1997 Asian economic crisis poverty was politically invisible, something to be addressed within the realm of the family according to Confucian principles (Huh, 2009; Jo and Walker, 2013). Similarly in Pakistan, although for different reasons linked to political instability, war, and corruption, Choudhry (2013) concludes that people in poverty have 'continuously experienced neglect and were forsaken by the state' during the sixty-six years of the country's history.

China

While China in the last fifty years has achieved several step-change reductions in absolute poverty linked to economic growth, the market reforms from 1979 onwards (see Chapter 2), the associated large-scale closure of state owned enterprise, increased inequality and urban poverty, and large-scale rural migration raised fears of social unrest (Xue and Zhong, 2006). The introduction of Dibao, along with other reforms relating to wages, taxation, and old-age and unemployment insurance, was a direct response to these fears. It explicitly established a social safety net to ease labour risks, an adjustment mechanism for lessening income disparity, and a 'shock absorber' to ensure social stability (Anon, 2013). While Dibao is a measure against poverty, its premier function is, as explained by former Premier Li Peng, as 'an effective program that costs little but is beneficial to social stability' (quoted in Duoji, 2001, p. 178). It serves to regulate the labour market, maintain order, and target marginal workers while minimizing expenditure (Solinger and Hu, 2012).

As such, Dibao shares many of the features of British Poor Law relief, including requiring demonstrable moral behaviour from recipients and providing supplementary allowances up to a bare subsistence level that is less than the minimum wage in each city ('the principle of less eligibility'). Moreover, these have variously been shown to impart shame even in the Chinese context (Chen et al., 2013; Piven and Cloward, 1993). Implementation and funding at local level fosters territorial injustice and stigmatizing policies. It has been shown, for example, that poorer cities let recipients supplement their Dibao allowance with casual employment thereby reducing overall expenditure (Solinger and Hu, 2012). In contrast, policymakers in more prosperous cities use Dibao to encourage unskilled and less productive registered unemployed to leave the labour market and also to 'clean the streets' of casual labour and street traders by enforcing work restrictions.

The media's role is predominately that of conveyor of official messages. They report the contentment of recipients (contentment not always found by researchers; Chen et al., 2013) that demonstrates social stability and 'harmony'. Pitching benefit rates so low logically undermines newspapers' portrayal of compassionate treatment. But it clearly conveys the regulatory message 'work or else poverty' that is, in fact, consistent with the strong work ethic and willingness to blame the individual that are evident in surveys of Chinese public opinion, if less so in public discussion.

Uganda

As one of the poorest countries in the world, antipoverty policy in Uganda has been inextricably linked to development policy. While absolute poverty has halved since the early 1990s according to official measures that are low by global standards, over half of the population still remains poor or officially 'insecure'. Until recently poverty reduction and development strategy was based on the 1997 Poverty Eradication Action Plan (PEAP), which was financially underpinned by the World Bank and other donors with aspirations framed by the Millennium Development Goals. It delivered universal primary education (UPE) and the Plan for Modernization of Agriculture. Buoyed by the discovery of oil, PEAP was replaced in 2010 by the National Development Plan (NDP) under which poverty reduction takes second place to economic transformation. Indeed, the PEAP goal of reducing poverty to 10 per cent by 2017 has been substituted with Uganda attaining middle-income status by the same year (Hickey, 2011).

Although ostensibly a democratic presidential parliamentary system with universal suffrage, political parties were more or less banned for nineteen years until 2005. This fostered top-down, popularist policymaking that often left implementation falling short of the political promise. UPE, for example, was delivered without adequate funding, leading to a fall in quality that caused the middle classes to move their children to private education thereby stigmatizing state provision (see Chapter 7). Similarly, the rhetoric of agricultural reform was that it would address the plight of poor subsistence farmers but, in reality, the most vulnerable have had least access to programme resources because allocation committees have favoured farmers that were better resourced. Farmers interviewed levelled accusations of nepotism against those policing access to the scheme (Kyomuhendo and Mwiine, 2013). No social assistance programmes existed until 2010 when payment of Senior Citizens Grants (SCGs) and Vulnerable Family Grants (VFGs) began being piloted in sixteen districts largely funded by overseas donors. The payment represents only about 20 per cent of the monthly household consumption of the poorest of Uganda's population (MGLSD, 2013).

While Uganda is not a rich country, spending on social protection is less than half that of comparable countries such as Rwanda and Tanzania (ILO, 2010). In this, government policy reflects the dismissive, accusatory attitudes concerning people in poverty evident both in the media and in the focus groups conducted in Uganda. Poverty is everywhere in Uganda but positive action is largely missing from public policy.

India

If Uganda is characterized by a deficit of antipoverty policy, India might well have a surfeit, the result of political parties vying for votes. Yet 314 million people out of a total population of 1.13 billion are officially to be considered poor and more than half still live without sanitation. Poverty in India is shaped by geography, caste, and gender that variously mediate and contribute to poverty-related shame. Responsibility for antipoverty policy is vested in states within a federal democratic structure that complicates rational policy design (Pellissery and Mathew, 2013). Poverty was first prioritized with Indira Gandhi's 1971 election-winning slogan *Garibi Hatao* ('abolish poverty'). This initiated an ongoing tradition of short-lived patronage-based schemes that operate in parallel to a combination of federal and state social security and assistance programmes implemented, somewhat akin to Dibao in China, to cope with the negative social implications of a policy of economic liberalization pursued from 1991 onwards.

Policymaking in India is compromised by normative disconnections between key players: central policymakers committed to positivistic policymaking; politicians, especially at state and local level, who 'frequently invoke social institutions rather than policy instruments'; and technocrats brought in to reconcile conflicting views in multiparty governance who often fail to take account of the importance of social institutions (Pellissery and Mathew, 2013). An illustration is the BPL, which is used nationally as a poverty standard and locally as the eligibility criterion for social assistance provision. Technically constructed but politically debated and manipulated, it has been varied in order to massage poverty numbers, inadvertently altering entitlement to benefits and shifting people between 'deserving' and 'undeserving' categories. It has also been exploited by local gatekeepers to dispense patronage thereby bringing social assistance and its recipients into disrepute.

Among 100 or more schemes, the PDS and NREGA are numerically the most important and, like many of the others, rich in their shaming potential. The PDS distributes food grains and essential items to needy people through 500,000 'fair price' shops. Used politically to demonstrate the largess of the state, it stigmatizes people as poor and arguably brings greatest benefit to food producers through guaranteed public purchasing. NREGA provides one-hundred days of guaranteed employment and thereby offers an alternative to forced labour. However, abiding by the principle of 'less eligibility', NREGA pays less than the minimum wage and supplies basic work rather than fulfilling employment as a form of state charity, 'giving alms to the beggar without any intention to help him acquire a better status' (Rao, 2009).

Antipoverty programmes reflect the complex moralities and immoralities that characterize Indian society. They are framed, largely top-down, by political interests, and often shaped in implementation according to vested interests that typically exclude the voices of recipients. In their potential to shame, the policies more accurately reflect the derogatory language heard in focus groups than the pro-poor stance of newspapers.

Norway

Poverty, even when defined in relative terms, is rare in Norway, which is a very prosperous and egalitarian society. Ideals of equality, social justice, social security, solidarity, and social integration have largely been realized based on the prerequisite of a strong work ethic and commitment to full employment (Gubrium and Lødemel, 2013a; Halvorsen and Stjernø 2008). However, while most provision is universal it is often premised on an employment history with relatively residual social assistance support for those without. This creates a major fault line between deserving and undeserving in an otherwise closely integrated society. It is a division that resonated even in focus groups that were generally inclusive in their language but which witnessed native Norwegians in receipt of social assistance being pilloried, contrasted with immigrants who were thought to be more deserving in that they had not had the same opportunities in life.

Historically, employment and insurance schemes were run nationally and were separate from locally administered social assistance that always included a heavy social-work input in which cash payments were used to regulate behaviour. Recently there has been a partial merger to create municipal offices of work and welfare (NAV) that served politically to reconcile differences between left and right, previously aired in the press and present in the coalition government, by increasing the work conditionality of benefits. A newly implemented system (the Qualification Programme, QP) creates a series of steps from benefit into full-time employment, and associated categories into which benefit recipients are placed and between which they are expected to progress. As explained in Chapters 7 and 9, benefit recipients or 'clients' perceive finely graded distinctions of shame and stigma resulting from this system, made worse by the fact that outcomes for clients are dependent on discretionary judgements made by officials.

Whether the regulation and stigmatization inherent in the QP and the psychic pain experienced as a consequence would find approval among the Norwegian public is unclear. While stigma associated with the old Poor Law and paupers has lingered on in Norwegian social assistance, very few Norwegians experience it or know of its reality (Lødemel, 1997). On the other hand, the public commitment to the work ethic and support for the principle of work as a duty is very strong indeed (Figure 10.2).

Britain

It is in Britain that the legacy of the Poor Law is most evident both in welfare provision and in the public psyche. As explained in Chapter 1, the National Health Service (NHS) and basic state pension is virtually all that remains of the immediate post-World War II experiment with universal provision. The distinctions between deserving and undeserving have been reintroduced in various guises at different times ('genuine' poverty in the 1980s, 'dependency' and (ir)'responsibility' in the 1990s, worklessness in the 2000s) largely defined with respect to a person's willingness to work. Furthermore, work conditionality has been extended in the last fifteen years to cover virtually all benefits available for people of working age (Griggs et al., 2013; Walker and Chase, 2013).

Poverty has long been defined in relative terms but an official definition of poverty was not formally introduced until 2010. It was then accompanied by a quasi-absolute measure (a relative measure not adjusted for rising median incomes) and one combining income poverty and material deprivation (which both tend to yield lower estimates). In 1999, the Labour Prime Minister Tony Blair unexpectedly committed the government to eradicating child poverty within a generation, choosing to target child poverty because of evidence of its negative lifetime consequences but also in a none too successful attempt to build popular support by avoiding the blame attached to adult poverty (Blair, 1999). Legislation ensures that the eradication target is still in place, but there is no evidence of a sustained government commitment to meet it. Both poverty and child poverty, measured as a percentage of median household incomes, are high relative to other European countries, although Britain's relative position has improved following the 2008 global financial crisis (OECD, 2013). In 2012, the government announced another review of poverty measurement, and suggested introducing a multidimensional measure that gives less weight to lack of income (Cm. 2012).

Accompanying the secular trend towards increased income targeting, greater conditionality, and more residual provision, the tone of the public debate has fluctuated, with peaks of negativity in the 1980s, the late 1990s, and late 2000s that Baumberg et al. (2012) have linked to periods of policy reform. Fraud was a key motif in the 1990s but was to some extent superseded in the 2000s by a set of more fundamental concerns captured in the concept of 'broken Britain': worklessness, lack of effort, people receiving 'something for nothing', large families, bad parenting, and antisocial behaviour. Baumberg et al. (2012) have also convincingly demonstrated that people's opinions are affected by reading negative stories in newspapers, and moreover that once changed their new opinions become self-sustaining. Given this dynamic triad comprising politics, the media, and public opinion, the pauperization of poverty has intensified as frames of thinking and communication intersect and interact. Politicians seeking votes sound out public opinion through their own polls and focus groups, learn what will appeal to the electorate, and either offer what the electorate wants or else package policies in ways that are likely to prove most palatable. Shriller language and stricter policies become the foundation for the next phase of reform such that the language of the street— for example, that worklessness 'breeds' intergenerational poverty and creates a 'semi-permanent underclass'—has become the language of government reports (DWP, 2011).

REPRODUCING SHAME AND STIGMA

This chapter has shifted attention from the private realm of individual attitudes and behaviour to the public realm of media discourse, politics, and policy. Alerted to the reality of more affluent people actively shaming those in poverty, and the often stigmatizing delivery of antipoverty programmes and social assistance described in Chapters 7 and 9, it has sought to discover whether the same negativity is apparent in newspaper coverage and in the framing of public policy. It has also begun to explore the interactions between public policy, policy discourse, and individual attitudes and behaviour.

There is much that is complex but the simple facts are that there is strong, albeit varying, public attachment to the work ethic in each of the countries considered, and a strong tendency for people (in private if not in public) to say that poverty is often attributable to lack of effort. These values are universally reflected in the framing of antipoverty policy, either explicitly (as in Britain and Korea), or in the underlying assumptions and policy structures that prioritize work incentives (as in China, Norway, and India) or in terms of policy neglect (as in Pakistan and Uganda). However, the tenor of public debate and the language used in public discourse varies markedly, as does the part played by print journalism in the dynamic between politics and public opinion.

Figure 10.6 simplifies these dynamics. It shows that in Britain they are mutually reinforcing, ratcheting up negativity towards people in poverty, translating it into public policy, and legitimating it in private behaviour. Political parties converge on policies that appeal to the electorate and create a common discourse that it is amplified by a press that leans, measured in terms of number of readers, to the political right. The dynamics are similarly reinforcing in Uganda but seem principally to reinforce public attitudes and behaviour; the media has a limited impact on policy since government ownership of newspapers constrains policy debate. Nevertheless, the absence of effective policy might reasonably be interpreted as an appropriate policy response to the dismissive tone of public discussion. Government control of

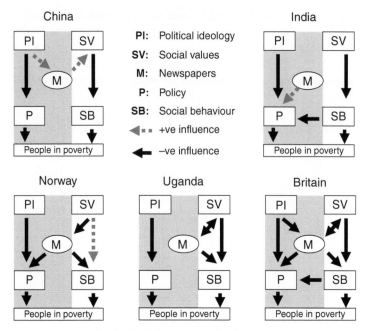

Fig. 10.6. Policy and media dynamics

the media in China introduces a different dynamic in that newspapers speak the words of government, encouraging respect for people in poverty, arguably as an alternative to delivering adequate policy. Respectful public discourse may well hide quite negative private attitudes that are reflected in policies that would appear stigmatizing to Western eyes, and are clearly experienced as such by some Dibao recipients. Similar double messaging, if hypocrisy is too strong a label, is evident in Indian politics. The more affluent public has little time for people in poverty and is prone to exploit them as cheap domestic labour. Politicians similarly use people in poverty to their own advantage and bureaucratic corruption steals subsidized food, figuratively and sometimes literally, from the tables for which it is intended. The media sides with 'the poor' in its assumed institutional role which is to criticize government, but not to the point where it is likely to disturb the status quo. Finally, in Norway, where social solidarity and universal policies have pushed poverty to the margins of society and the public consciousness, poverty is nevertheless used rhetorically in the media to criticize government. Being comparatively rare, policies targeted at people in poverty are inherently exclusionary and also stigmatizing in their implementation.

The shaming and stigmatizing of people in poverty that has been demonstrated in previous chapters persists despite these different institutional dynamics. Maybe this is because, as suggested in Chapter 1, poverty invariably poses a threat to the status quo because its continued existence alongside considerable wealth is generally acknowledged to be morally unacceptable. A convenient defence, offered by the relatively wealthy against accusations of selfishness and exploitation, is that the distribution of resources is based on merit and effort. Hence, it is argued that people in poverty deserve to be poor and could have been rich had they (or their forebears) worked sufficiently hard.

11

Poverty, Shame, and Society

> The worst thing about living in extreme poverty is the contempt—that they treat you like you are worthless, that they look at you with disgust and fear and that they even treat you like an enemy. We and our children experience this every day, and it hurts us, humiliates us and makes us live in fear and shame.
>
> ATD Fourth World, 2013a

This powerful reflection on what it means to live in poverty succinctly captures the arguments of Chapters 1–10. The words could have been spoken by respondents in any of the seven countries investigated: Britain, China, India, Norway, Pakistan, South Korea, or Uganda. In fact, they are the words of a mother living in extreme poverty on another continent (Latin America) that were to resonate around Conference Room 1 in the United Nations building, New York, on 27 June 2013 (ATD Fourth World, 2013b). The conference was organized by the international NGO ATD Fourth World to inform thinking about what might replace the Millennium Development Goals when they come to an end in 2015. In addition to this mother from Peru, voice was briefly given to people from seven countries, all of whom had experience of what it is currently like to live in poverty.

As evidenced in Chapter 2, academics and policymakers have been rather slow to listen carefully to the accounts of people with direct experience of poverty about what their lives are like and what they would find to be of greatest assistance. Indeed, novelists, and film-makers arguably exhibit a better understanding than academics and policymakers about what it means to be poor (Chapters 5 and 6). Instead, researchers have been keen to measure the extent of poverty and policymakers often to demonstrate policy success. Income is comparatively straightforward to measure, and even multidimensional definitions and indices of poverty have only recently begun to embrace the psychosocial aspects of poverty. For a host of reasons, objective measures have been equated with truth while the views and understanding of the people affected by poverty have been labelled as subjective, and by implication considered suspect if not simply wrong. In point of fact, people experiencing poverty must be the experts on their own condition even if, without further information, they may not be able fully to contextualize what they know or to isolate individual and structural causes and correlates. Studying poverty and making policy in the absence of such insights, while commonplace, is logically indefensible and likely to result in distortion and to policies that are ineffectual and even counterproductive.

For the Peruvian mother cited above, the external component of shaming, 'contempt', is the worst thing about poverty because it makes her and her children live in fear and shame. While respondents in the very different national and cultural settings covered in this volume were not asked to rank the negative aspects of poverty, shame was, with subtle variations, certainly a very important component of their life experience. They, too, often felt ashamed because of the limitations imposed by their poverty and were regularly made to feel ashamed, often on a daily basis. Amartya Sen (1983), it will be recalled, places shame at the 'irreducible absolutist core in the idea of poverty' and, although the evidence presented above cannot be taken as definitive proof of the universality of Sen's dictum, it suggests that failure to take adequate account of shame has resulted in a distorted understanding of the experience of poverty. The communality of experience reported across diverse settings in seven countries is striking. Almost irrespective of objective living standards, people defined as being poor according to local norms felt similarly about themselves, experienced their circumstances in comparable ways, and responded to them in an analogous fashion. This constitutes powerful evidence in support of the appropriateness of relative conceptions of poverty. It also points to the legitimacy of coupling debates about poverty in the global North and South; while the material poverty is not equivalent, the emotional pain and psychosocial consequences for the people affected are much more directly comparable than might previously have been thought.

The distortions introduced by not paying adequate attention to shame are myriad. They have, for example, focussed attention on material aspects of poverty, downplaying the psychic anguish experienced by adults and children that lowers self-esteem and saps morale. They have allowed beliefs concerning the shamelessness of people in poverty to go unchallenged. The fact that people are deeply ashamed of being poor is incompatible with notions that such people willingly choose poverty in preference to working hard, living moral lives, and paying their social dues. The persistence of such negative stereotypes, combined with notions that poverty is simply a lack of resources, has permitted policymakers to adopt policies that exclusively address material deprivation without regard to the negative consequences of stigma (see Chapters 3, 9, and 10). Indeed, policies have been introduced that deliberately stigmatize, seemingly oblivious of the fact that people in poverty are already heavily stigmatized and feeling profoundly ashamed.

Moving beyond Sen's recognition of an immutable conjunction between poverty and shame, the life experiences of people in poverty recounted in this volume and evident in the primary research upon which it is based (Chase and Bantebya-Kyomuhendo, 2014) are largely consistent with the model presented as Figure 4.1, which suggests that shame not only makes poverty harder to bear but could make it more persistent. Respondents were generally coping well, managing whenever possible to add to their resources and to eke out those that they already had through very careful organization. Equally, many were exhibiting several of the classic negative consequences of shame: self-deception, anxiety, despair, depression, social isolation, and loss of self-confidence (see Chapters 7 and 8). Given that these conditions are known to reduce personal efficacy, people in poverty would have been able better to manage their affairs had they not simultaneously been battling against the psychological manifestations of shame.

While the shame of poverty is often sorely felt it is also imposed, the contempt that the Peruvian mother hated so much (see Chapters 9 and 10). This is the structural dimension of poverty-related shame that hurts in its own right, feeds the debilitating consequences of internal shame, and, if the lives of people in poverty are to be improved, needs to be challenged in the same way as other stereotypical forms of discrimination have been challenged such as those based on ethnicity, gender, and sexual orientation. Challenging beliefs that people experiencing poverty are lazy, disgusting, and disreputable and rightly suffering for their own sins or those of their forebears will not prove easy. Not only have they been in existence for millennia (see Chapter 1), they also reflect and inform key regulatory principles in hierarchical societies that are organized on the basis of income and wealth (Higgins, 1978). The existing hierarchy is justified with respect to merit and effort, but allowances for the possibility of individual advancement and social change occur through application of the work ethic, regulated by the threat of shame to stimulate effort and its application to reinforce the costs of failure. The relatively affluent therefore take comfort from social and political discourses that justify their favourable position in an unequal society and may even feel virtuous in shaming others to work harder.

This volume has explored a neglected aspect of poverty, namely shame, which people in poverty consider to be vitally important. The evidence assembled leads inexorably to three provocative conclusions and calls for action. Firstly, there is a need at the very least to reflect again on the nature of poverty, and on its causes and consequences. Secondly, nothing will change unless shame is recognized as a key mechanism in perpetuating the structures of self-interest that support the unequal distribution of resources in society and resist meaningful attempts to eradicate poverty. Finally, there is a need to challenge the governments and interest groups that support them which pay lip service to tackling poverty while clinging to the status quo (Killeen, 2008).

THE SOCIAL REALITY OF THE POVERTY–SHAME NEXUS

Cutting through the complex debates on definition and measurement rehearsed in Chapter 2, poverty is taken to comprise the deprivations resulting from inadequate resources. These deprivations include material ones, such as insufficient food and inadequate housing, and more complex social ones that individually or together prevent individuals from fully participating in society or, to adapt Sen's (1999) terminology, from having the freedom to achieve capabilities to which they aspire and that are consistent with enjoyment of their human rights.

The evidence presented indicates that the capabilities to which people aspire are remarkably similar across different cultures, albeit framed by prevailing living standards determined nationally and locally. Individuals desire resources sufficient to enable them to be good husbands, wives, partners, and parents, and reliable relatives, neighbours, citizens, and workers. The repercussions of failing to achieve these aspirations are also comparable. While they differ in terms of their immediate consequences for individuals' nutrition, physical health, and absolute life expectancy, they are similarly experienced as shame arising from the failure either to live up to one's image of self or to fulfil the rightful expectations of others. While many people fail to fulfil their life ambitions and are disappointed and even ashamed as a result, the shame experienced by people in poverty who are unable to achieve the basics in life is different in degree and arguably in kind. There is profound shame in being unable to provide for self and family, to reciprocate where needed, and to socialize and participate in community events. Such shame is similarly felt by British mothers and fathers who cannot afford school uniforms for their children and by parents in Uganda who send their children to school barefoot. Moreover, as demonstrated in Chapters 7, 9, and 10, this shame is internally felt but also often externally imposed.

The findings presented on the experience of poverty shift the emphasis from the traditional focus on material hardship to its psychosocial consequences. In so doing, it reflects the priority of respondents with direct experience of poverty, and reminds academics and policymakers alike that poverty is experienced not just as cold and hunger but as loss of manhood, maternal pride, and basic humanity. Shame hurts and 'often persists like a psychic scar that stubbornly refuses to heal' (Ho et al., 2004, p. 76). It is repeatedly drawn to people's attention when they are cold-shouldered in the family, ignored in the street, short-changed by the moneylender, exploited by the employer, and whenever their bluff is called and they are publicly humiliated because they lack the resources that they need. People in poverty have to manage this pain alongside a limited budget. Most succeed in doing so, although often at the cost of engaging in pretence and withdrawing socially. But for some the self-loathing, scapegoating, and loss of self-esteem turn into despair, depression, and thoughts of suicide. In some documented cases death is the preferred alternative to the shame of being unable to provide for kith and kin (see Chapter 8 and Mathews, 2010).

When the core research began no data were available on the extent of shame associated with poverty, and their importance could only be judged by the salience in people's accounts of the experience of poverty. Quantitative estimates of shame are now beginning to emerge, although they have to be treated with care. Asking about shame can itself be shaming and, as noted in Chapter 3, the term is conspicuous by its comparative absence from everyday speech. Embarrassment and, reflecting a stronger response, being 'made to feel small' were euphemisms often used by British respondents. Figure 11.1 reports information from a British survey on poverty and social exclusion (Bailey et al., 2013) indicating that 78 per cent of people assessing their income to be 'well below average' report ever having been embarrassed because of low income, with 62 per cent saying that they had been made to feel small for a similar reason. The same study indicated that the proportion reporting shame-like feelings increased in line with the degree of deprivation, reaching in excess

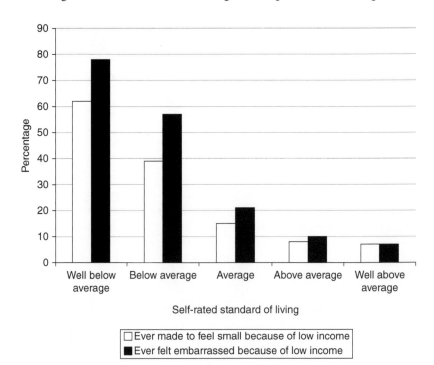

Fig. 11.1. Poverty and shame in Britain, 2012
Bailey et al. (2013)

of 90 per cent for those who were most deprived. These data suggest that in Britain poverty-related shame is prevalent as well as salient. The Oxford Poverty and Human Development Initiative (OPHI), in order to operationalize Sen's capabilities approach, is also including measures of shame in its multidimensional index. Respondents are asked directly about shame attributable to poverty, and preliminary results for Chile appear to indicate that 45 per cent of the population experience poverty-related shame and that adding measures of shame increases the overall multidimensional poverty rate by eleven percentage points (Los Rios and Los Rios, 2010).

Turning to external shame, Figure 11.2 synthesizes the complex attitudes of people in Kenya who are affluent enough to own a television set (namely the richest 58 per cent or so). Most Kenyans in this study believe that wealth is important in according status and identity and that poverty erodes dignity, but fewer recognize that people might be embarrassed by poverty or be stigmatized in their dealings with officialdom. Most saw nothing to be ashamed of in being poor and very few believed that they would feel ashamed if they were ever to become poor. The failure to appreciate that people in poverty might be shamed by their loss of dignity was investigated in focus groups that accompanied the survey work. As among the affluent groups in the case-study countries (see Chapter 9), Kenyans appreciated the structural reasons for poverty but often dwelt on factors such as laziness, ignorance, poor parenting, prostitution, and alcohol abuse. However, if they were ever to be poor themselves, they believed that it would be for structural reasons rather than as a result of personal failings since they considered themselves to be both competent and hardworking.

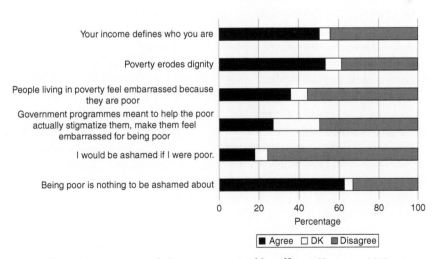

Fig. 11.2. Poverty and shame as perceived by affluent Kenyans, 2013

Park et al. (2013a)

The day-to-day shaming imposed on people in poverty in their encounters with others, sometimes manifest even in the words and behaviour of close relatives, is reinforced in some countries by negative stereotypes reproduced in the mass media and is almost invariably accompanied by stigmatization imposed by bureaucracies (see Chapter 10). Such stigmatization and discrimination has recently been acknowledged by the UN. A UN report observes that 'those living in poverty are also subject to discriminatory attitudes and stigmatization from public authorities and private actors precisely because of their poverty' and 'that discrimination is both a cause and a consequence of poverty' (Sepúlveda Carmona, 2012a, p. 6). The primary cause of poverty—lack of income variously attributable to complex combinations of restricted employment opportunities, limitations of health, age, education and development, and cultural and security constraints—is added to by the mix of stigmatization and external and internal shame that can exacerbate, deepen, and perpetuate the problem.

This is not to say that people in poverty are without agency; mere survival is often demonstrable evidence of considerable skill and fortitude in the face of major impediments. Nor is it necessary fully to accept Waxman's (1977) thesis, referred to in Chapter 4, that stigma and discrimination condemn people in poverty to 'getting by' rather than 'getting on'. Equally, as illustrated in Chapters 7, 8, and 9, people in poverty are regularly confronted by prejudices and stereotypes underpinned by self-justifying beliefs that most, if not all, people in poverty are lazy, irresponsible, or dishonest. These beliefs are institutionalized in provisions that adopt the undeserving as the base case, provide the minimum of assistance possible so as not to create 'dependency', and effectively require all individuals to demonstrate that they are not abusing or defrauding the system. Treated with minimal respect and accustomed to often low service standards, people in poverty are prone to respond to authorities with disdain, hostility, and even fear that may lead them into confrontation. But perhaps more often, shame causes them either to refrain from approaching officialdom or not to fully engage with it (Sepúlveda Carmona, 2011). By distancing themselves from authorities they avoid further stigma and discrimination, albeit at the cost of losing out on services that could potentially be of considerable benefit. If this is the extreme case, the experiences of people in poverty summarized above and considered in detail in the companion volume (Chase and Bantebya-Kyomuhendo, 2014) indicate that it is not unusual. Moreover, while the tenor of discourse varies across cultures and political systems, blatant stigmatization was evident in all seven countries and the relatively affluent were prone to be abusive about people in poverty whenever etiquette permitted.

Shame, then, may be a consequence of poverty, a cause, or both. It is certainly a painful, psychic wound that often blights the lives of people living in poverty. It is a wound that society inflicts, often deliberately, sometimes inadvertently. It is a wound deepened by the words and actions of many of the people who happen not to be living in poverty.

AFFLUENCE, POVERTY, AND SOCIETY'S FRAGILE BONDS

The prevalence of poverty-related shame is perhaps less surprising than the limited attention that it has previously attracted. Shame, sociologists and social psychologists opine, is a fundamental social element that regulates individual behaviour and defends social institutions. While shame is understated to the point of invisibility, individuals nevertheless generally choose to conform rather than to risk shame that would make them social outcasts. Shame is a tool of the powerful for exerting control over the less powerful. Only rarely, as in the case of complex rituals of reciprocity that determine relationships between castes, are the powerful at risk of shaming by the powerless (see Chapters 5 and 7). In societies in which financial resources are synonymous with power and status, especially those that are committed to maximizing economic growth, poverty is synonymous with failure, powerlessness, and dependency on others. The threat of shame is used to encourage effort commensurate with the work ethic and shame is applied to those who fail economically, as judged by their poverty status, and especially to those who claim welfare benefits. As evidenced in Chapter 10, authoritarian governments can impose this dynamic, making economic success a nationalistic goal and personal economic achievement a badge of citizenship, while in democracies government is but one actor, albeit a very powerful one, competing to frame social and political thinking. Nevertheless, the work ethic was a predominant value in all seven exemplar countries regardless of the prevailing political system.

The above model accurately describes, albeit in much simplified form, the social dynamics of each of the case-study countries that have been promoted since at least the origins of Confucianism in Asia and the emergence of the Poor Law system in sixteenth-century Europe (see Chapter 1). Moreover, this model has been enthusiastically advocated in modern times by those on the radical right (Murray, 1984), the centre right (Smith, 2010; Heidenreich, et al. 2013), and the centre left (Blair, 1997). Yet, as explained in Chapters 3 and 4, modern sociology and social psychology demonstrate that the model is based on false premises that condemn it to failure—failure that is demonstrated empirically through the life experiences of the people in poverty cited in this volume. It presumes that the benefits to society outweigh the costs to individuals threatened with shame since the latter will come to work harder, contribute more to economic growth, and cost society less by making fewer claims on welfare. The scientific evidence reported in Chapters 3 and 4 demonstrates that behaviour is seldom if ever changed by the threat of shame and that, once shame is imposed, a person is excluded socially and potentially becomes a free agent, unfettered and uncontrollable by the imposition of social norms and expectations. Ironically, it is just this fear of people in poverty living outside societies' normative frameworks that sparked rhetoric about the ghetto and underclass in the US (Mead, 1986; Murray, 1984), concern about a 'broken Britain' (CSJ, 2006; Wiki., 2013), the moral panic over poverty in Norway in the early to mid-2000s (Hagen and Lødemel, 2010), and the current fear of crime and HIV/Aids in the 'slums' of Kampala, (AllAfrica, 2012; Guyson, 2011; MLHUD, 2013), alongside demands for greater conditionality, regulation, and public shaming.

As demonstrated in Chapters 7 and 8, the individual costs of shame are very considerable and it is not clear that these are ever fully accounted for given the primary focus of policy on poverty relief or changed behaviour. Moreover, as predicted by social psychologists, the evidence indicates that individuals' attempts to manage the shame associated with poverty are often counterproductive in terms of personal efficacy. Shame results from a negative appraisal of character and, while Confucius would not have agreed, according to Western science the pain associated with shame partly arises from the immutable nature of character that is not readily amenable to change. This is exacerbated in the case of poverty-related shame by the inability of the vast majority of people in poverty to do more than they are already doing to escape from poverty because of structural constraints over which they have no control. Moreover, the important distinction between the threat and implementation of shame is often blurred in the case of poverty-related shame, which means that the exclusionary consequences of shame are more evident than integrative ones. Children, for instance, do not escape shame despite having little control over their own material circumstances, while the recurrent and long-term nature of some poverty means that adults are often simultaneously confronted by both the threat and imposition of shame. Poverty-related shame is also often directed at entire groups—'the poor', 'them', benefit 'bums', and 'scroungers'—such that action by individuals is unlikely to remove them from the glare of shame and shame converges with stigma, being divisive and discriminatory rather than recuperative.

The belief in blaming and shaming—even a commitment to naming and shaming as evident in some social assistance provision (see Chapter 9)—is strong. Given the unwavering attachment to work, the work ethic, and the desirability of families being self-sufficient, this may stem from faith in the effectiveness of shaming in changing behaviour, albeit faith that is ill informed. Equally, though, the work ethic is directly enforced by conditionality in social security and social assistance legislation and typically always has been. Indeed, Anderson (2013) has traced distinctions in Britain based on work back to at least 1349 when, in the context of a labour shortage precipitated by the Black Death, the Ordinance of Labourers required able-bodied men and women to work on penalty of imprisonment and made giving alms to beggars a criminal offence. Therefore, behavioural change may not be the only objective in shaming people in poverty. Societies define themselves with respect to shared ideals and ideal patterns of behaviour and differentiate between 'good' and 'failed' citizens, between 'us' and 'them' (Anderson, 2013). Shaming may, in this instance, be a restatement of difference, establishing more or less permanent boundaries that reflect the status quo between 'respectable' citizens who are not in poverty and others who are, namely 'them'. Being discriminatory, this shaming is akin to stigma, even constituting a form of punishment for economic failure without any intent to secure behavioural change or rehabilitation. Moreover, in the context of high and often increasing income inequality, the work ethic provides a protective and self-congratulatory discourse policed by shame. Through this the respectable and privileged can claim to justify outcomes that have much to do with the lottery of birth. It likewise provides an argument for not raising levels of welfare—people in poverty do not deserve it—and for not further increasing taxes because the money that would be taxed is hard earned.

Despite the hurt and additional hardship imposed by shame on people experiencing poverty, the analysis in Chapter 10 underlines why this belief structure is likely to prove resistant to change. Antipoverty programmes in all the study countries include stigmatizing components and are mostly supported by the public's negative view of all or some people in poverty. Killeen (2008) has labelled this phenomenon 'poverty-ism'. In Britain, the dynamic is mutually reinforcing and cumulative with politicians competing for votes by echoing the public's poverty-shaming discourse. Even in India, the ostensibly pro-poor media are careful to avoid alienating the growing middle class, while in China pro-poor public discourse is widely accepted as rhetoric orchestrated by the Chinese Communist Party that belies under-lying attitudes and discriminatory policy structures. To defend themselves against shaming discourses, people in poverty find others to scapegoat as morally inferior, thereby creating hierarchies based on perceptions of shamelessness (see Chapter 8; Chase and Walker, 2013). Scheff (1997) argued that shame is a glue holding society together. Poverty-related shame might be better described as cement reinforcing structures of in-equality and perpetuating poverty. Shame-laden discourse sees governments pandering to the self-serving views of the affluent while people in poverty are divided among themselves.

PROMOTING DIGNITY IN THE POLICY WORLD

That change is resisted by self-interested groups does not mean that it is impossible. Campaigns against slavery, racism, and gender prejudice, for example, have proved successful, although they have taken time and progress has required defence against reactionary forces. And lest these comparisons seem far-fetched, it should be recalled that prejudice against people in poverty has been traced back to at least the second millennium BCE (see Chapter 1) and that the goal of eradicating poverty is inherently political and a challenge to the status quo since, defined in relative terms, it requires a redistribution of resources away from the affluent and politically influential. Viewed from a global perspective, successfully to attain the Millennium Development Goals and any successors ultimately requires resources to be transferred from economically richer countries to poorer ones.

There are two strong arguments to support an assault on the prejudice that underpins poverty-related shame. Firstly, shaming people in poverty is likely to be counterproductive, reducing their self-efficacy and arguably reducing the effectiveness of antipoverty programmes. Secondly, the structural manifestations of shame that take the form of stigmatizing policy and discrimination are an infringement of human rights and arguably illegal (Killeen, 2008).

There is already evidence that, when combined, these two arguments can be persuasive. In June 2012 the ILO agreed Recommendation 202 that requires all 185 member states to provide a nationally defined minimum level of income security for its older citizens, for those of active age who are unable to earn a sufficient income, and for children. The Recommendation also establishes a set of fundamental principles that governments are expected to apply in the design and implementation of relevant policies. The initial draft was devoid of any recognition of poverty-related shame, but an amendment was accepted before the final vote that governments should have 'respect for the rights and dignity of people covered by the social security guarantees' (ILO, 2012, p. 5). Informed by preliminary findings from the research synthesized in this volume relating to policy effectiveness, the amendment was tabled by trade union representatives supported by employers. The vote was also aided by a letter by Magdalena Sepúlveda Carmona (2012b), the UN Special Rapporteur on extreme poverty and human rights, arguing that the amendment was consistent with a human rights-based approach to social protection. Clearly inclusion of a sentence in an international treaty is not in itself going to bring about policy change, let alone a fundamental change in global public opinion. Indeed, the relevant British minister opined, it would seem without much reflection, that 'it is not envisaged that this recommendation will have any impact on the UK' (Hoban, 2013; Walker et al., 2012). Nevertheless, Recommendation 202 provides a set of evaluative criteria that can be used by policy activists to critique polices and proposed reforms.

Shaming is Counterproductive

The model of the poverty–shame nexus, presented in Figure 4.1 and developed from the research summarized in Chapters 3 and 4, indicates that the shame heaped on people in poverty not only hurts but is counterproductive. It reduces self-confidence, social capital, and agency, all characteristics that are likely to make escape from poverty more difficult. Similarly the stigmatization of poverty programmes is likely to make them less effective; lacking the political support necessary for adequate resourcing as a result of institutional stigma, personal stigma is likely to lower take-up and reduce compliance among beneficiaries (see Chapter 4). This model is clearly consistent with prior theory and is strongly supported by the core of evidence cited in this book and detailed in Chase and Bantebya-Kyomuhendo (2014), which derives directly from the experience of people living in poverty. However, it is too soon to be able to offer definitive proof of the causal linkages.

Nevertheless, interest in the connection between poverty and shame is growing. One pioneering study has already explored the effects of poverty-related shame on children's educational outcomes in India, Ethiopia, Peru, and Vietnam (Dornan and Portela, 2013). Shame was measured at the age of 12 in terms of embarrassment and shame felt at a lack of smart clothes and possessions and, except in Ethiopia, increased markedly with declining household income. Performance in mathematics, vocabulary, and the ability to read and write were all negatively associated with shame even after taking account of other factors including household expenditure (a measure of poverty). More tellingly still, scores in mathematics and vocabulary measured three years later when children were aged 15 remained lower, markedly so in India and Vietnam where the associations with shame were highly statistically significant.

This study is important in suggesting that poverty-related shame may contribute to intergenerational poverty by inhibiting the acquisition of human capital. Moreover, the authors were careful to distinguish between shame caused by poor educational performance and poor results attributable to shame. However, it is important to ascertain whether, as predicted, adult behaviour and efficacy are also sensitive to poverty-related shame. While research is beginning to suggest that the prevalence of shame among people experiencing poverty is high, it is not universal. Psychologists, whose academic interests tend to prioritize felt shame over external shaming, have linked shame-proneness to personality (Cohen et al., 2011; Schoenleber and Berenbaum. 2010) and upbringing (Wells and Jones, 2000), and suggested that proneness leads to different responses to shaming situations (Crystal et al., 2001; Thompson et al., 2004), although the evidence is mostly based on studies of university students and so not directly applicable to poverty.

Nevertheless, it is therefore vital to disentangle the extent to which the negative effects of poverty-related shame are mediated by personality and other individual characteristics. Plans are afoot to include questions on poverty-related shame in panel surveys that also carry personality and genetic information.

There is additional research in train focussed on policy. Gubrium and Lødemel (2013b) have reviewed the policy analyses referred to in Chapters 9 and 10 concerning evidence of shaming and stigma in the framing, structure, and delivery of antipoverty programmes, and begun to develop global principles that should minimize the extent of shaming and instead foster dignity. These include: recognition that poverty is relational rather than an identity, and that people applying for assistance would like to have high aspirations for themselves and for service provision; that users should be given voice in the design and implementation of policy; that policy should recognize the everyday needs and constraints of users; and that conditionally-based provision subject to 'bureaucratic discretion both in a positive sense (with a charitable function) and a negative one (with a punitive function to weed out the "undeserving") is inherently demeaning'. Proposals have also been made, working with Oxfam and ATD Fourth World, to engage people with direct experience of poverty to reinterpret and operationalize ILO Recommendation 202 as a set of evaluative criteria and as a charter establishing the responsibilities of service providers corresponding to the requirements typically imposed on users. Additional research is underway in China, Norway, the UK, the US, India, and Uganda to triangulate the perspectives of users with those of providers of services targeted towards people in poverty, involving observations of service delivery as well as interviews with staff, users, and policymakers (Lødemel, 2013). The next step is then to transform the principles into shame-free policy models to be tested against standard implementations so as to establish directly whether, as predicted, policies that enhance dignity are more effective in reducing poverty than those that are stigmatizing.

Shaming is Wrong, and Probably Illegal

Treating people in poverty in a way that ensures their dignity may well make for increased policy effectiveness, but it is equally a matter of justice. This, combined with the understanding that 'eradicating extreme poverty is not only a moral duty but also a legal obligation under existing international human rights law' (Sepúlveda Carmona, 2012a, p. 4), as endorsed by the General Assembly of the United Nations in 2013 (UN, 2013b), rules out the status quo as a viable option even without the possibility of enhanced policy effectiveness.

There may be debate about whether 'dignity' is an appropriate antonym for shame, but it is a suitable antidote. Lawyers have turned to the concept of dignity partly to address limitations attaching to equality as a guiding principle. It provides a defence against levelling down: 'equality based on dignity must enhance rather than diminish the status of individuals' (Fredman, 2011, p. 21); it offers a basis for a flexible and inclusive response to the coverage of discrimination legislation and overcomes the need always to have a comparator when someone is treated unfairly. Equally, it is important that loss of dignity is not added as an additional requirement in proving discrimination.

The 2013 resolution of the UN General Assembly on extreme poverty (UN, 2013b, p. 3), basing its affirmation on numerous pieces of international human rights legislation including the Universal Declaration of Human Rights, the International Covenant on Civil and Political Rights, and the International Covenant on Economic, Social and Cultural Rights, stipulates that:

> extreme poverty and exclusion from society constitute a violation of human dignity and that urgent national and international action is therefore required to eliminate them.

It also reminds governments that in September 2012 the UN Human Rights Council adopted a set of guiding principles on extreme poverty and human rights and 'encourages' governments and all other policy actors to:

> consider the guiding principles in the formulation and implementation of their policies and measures concerning persons affected by extreme poverty
>
> UN, 2013b, p. 5

The guiding principles are powerful and comprehensive and include five that go to the heart of the issues addressed in this book:

> Respect for the inherent dignity of those living in poverty must inform all public policies. State agents and private individuals must respect the dignity of all, avoid stigmatization and prejudices, and recognize and support the efforts that those living in poverty are making to improve their lives . . .
>
> Public policies to overcome poverty must be based on respecting, protecting and fulfilling all the human rights of persons living in poverty in equal manner. No policy, in any area, should exacerbate poverty or have a disproportionate negative impact on persons living in poverty . . .
>
> Persons living in poverty have a right to be protected from the negative stigma attached to conditions of poverty. States must prohibit public authorities, whether national or local, from stigmatizing or discriminating against persons living in poverty and must take all appropriate measures to modify sociocultural patterns with a view to eliminating prejudices and stereotypes. States must put in place educational programs, in particular for public officials and the media, to promote non-discrimination against persons living in poverty . . .

Persons living in poverty must be recognized and treated as free and autonomous agents. All policies relevant to poverty must be aimed at empowering persons living in poverty. They must be based on the recognition of those persons' right to make their own decisions and respect their capacity to fulfil their own potential, their sense of dignity and their right to participate in decisions affecting their life . . .

Effective and meaningful participation is an affirmation of the right of every individual and group to take part in the conduct of public affairs. It is also a means of promoting social inclusion and an essential component of efforts to combat poverty, not least by ensuring that public policies are sustainable and designed to meet the expressed needs of the poorest segments of society.

UN, 2012, pp. 6–8

What will be apparent is that these principles are not being adhered to in any of seven case-study jurisdictions reviewed in this volume. The resolution only requires institutions to consider the principles but not necessarily to follow them. This volume therefore additionally constitutes a portfolio of evidence documenting the personal and social costs of not adopting these globally approved principles.

The astute reader will also note that the UN Resolution refers to 'extreme' poverty. This is partly the lasting legacy of Father Wresinski who, as it was explained in Chapter 2, was so influential in promoting a human rights approach to poverty within the UN. It also poses a potential constraint on using human rights legislation to promote the dignified treatment of all people in poverty. Active before much of the analysis of poverty dynamics had been undertaken, Wresinski identified long duration as being the crucial determinant of multidimensional and incapacitating poverty and this is echoed in the definition of extreme poverty still used within the UN:

the combination of income poverty, human development poverty and social exclusion . . . where a prolonged lack of basic security affects several aspects of people's lives simultaneously, severely compromising their chances of exercising or regaining their rights in the foreseeable future.

Sepúlveda Carmona, 2012a, p. 4

What poverty dynamics has subsequently demonstrated is that only a minority of poverty is persistent even in low-income countries (see Chapter 2), and that even short spells of poverty can have lasting negative and multidimensional consequences (Arranz, and Cantó, 2012; Tomlinson and Walker, 2009, 2010). Moreover, the evidence presented in this volume reveals that persons selected as being in poverty but not necessarily in extreme poverty are prone to suffer many of the same limitations and diminution of rights that were of concern to Father Wresinski. Furthermore, all five of the UN's guiding principles cited above are an appropriate response to the shaming, stigma, and discrimination experienced by people in poverty in each of the seven case-study countries and could not reasonably be denied to any person experiencing poverty anywhere.

The inclusion of the adjective 'extreme' should not be used to limit the applicability of the UN principles. Nor is it legitimate for governments in middle- and higher-income countries to declare that the 2013 resolution is irrelevant to them, as some have done with respect to ILO Recommendation 202. The UN Resolution (UN, 2013b, pp. 2 and 5) recognizes that 'extreme poverty persists in ALL countries of the world' (emphasis added) and the evidence assembled in this book speaks to the universality of the poverty experience. It demonstrates that, despite massive differences in material conditions, the psychosocial experience of poverty is very similar and is much shaped by the shaming to which people in poverty are exposed and the stigmatizing and discriminatory practises to which they are frequently subjected. There can be no excuse, therefore, for any government or nation to ignore the UN's guiding principles on extreme poverty and human rights. In this context, the shame of poverty that has been documented in this volume is a shame on everyone.

References

Abel-Smith, B. and Townsend P. (1965) *The Poor and the Poorest*, London: Bell.

Abercrombie, N., Hill, S., and Turner, B. (eds) (1990) *Dominant Ideologies*, London: Unwin Hyman.

Alicke, M. and Sedikides, C. (2009) 'Self-Enhancement and Self-Protection: What They Are and What They Do'. *European Review of Social Psychology* 20(1): 1–48.

Alkire, S. (2007) 'The Missing Dimensions of Poverty Data: Introduction to the Special Issue'. *Oxford Development Studies* 35(4): 347–59; <http://www.ophi.org.uk/wp-content/uploads/MPI_2011_Methodology_Note_4-11-2011_1500.pdf?cda6c1> accessed January 2014.

Alkire, S., Roche, J., Santos, M., and Seth S. (2011) *Multidimensional Poverty Index 2011: Brief Methodological Note*, Oxford: Oxford Poverty and Human Development Initiative (OPHI).

Alkire, S., Roche, J., and Sumner, S. (2013) *Where Do the World's Multidimensionally Poor People Live?*, Oxford: OPHI Working Paper 61.

All Africa (2012) *Uganda: Kampala is One Big Slum*, 31 October; <http://allafrica.com/stories/201210310503.html?viewall=1> accessed January 2014.

Anderson, B. (2013) *Us and Them? The Dangerous Politics of Immigration Control*, Oxford: Oxford University Press.

Anok (2008) *Is Poverty a Personal Choice?*, 20 November; <http://identitycheck-anok.blogspot.co.uk/2008/11/is-poverty-personal-choice.html> accessed January 2014.

Anon (2013) 'A Social Safety Net for Urban and Rural Residents Has Taken Shape in China'. *Qiushi* 1: 72–7 (written by the 'Leading Party Members' Group of the Ministry of Human Resources and Social Security').

Arranz, J. and Cantó, O. (2012) 'Measuring the Effect of Spell Recurrence on Poverty Dynamics—Evidence from Spain'. *The Journal of Economic Inequality* 10(2): 191–217.

ASPE (2012) *The 2012 Poverty Guidelines*; <http://aspe.hhs.gov/poverty/12poverty.shtml#guidelines> accessed January 2014.

ATD (2013) *Ending the Violence of Extreme Poverty: A Must for Sustainable Societies*; Pierrelaye: International Movement ATD Fourth World; <http://www.atd-fourthworld.org/IMG/pdf/rio_updated_proposals.pdf> accessed January 2014.

ATD Fourth World (2013a) *Towards Sustainable Development that Leave No One Behind: The Challenge of the Post-2015 Agenda*, New York: International ATD Fourth World Movement.

ATD Fourth World (2013b) *Knowledge from Experience: Building the Post-2015 Sustainable Development Agenda with People Living in Extreme Poverty*.

Atkinson, A. (1989) 'How Should We Measure Poverty? Some Conceptual Issues', in Atkinson, A. (ed.) *Poverty and Social Security*, Hemel Hempstead: Harvester-Wheatsheaf.

Atkinson, A., Cantillon, B., Marlier, E., and Nolan, B. (2002) *Social Indicators: The EU and Social Exclusion*, Oxford: Oxford University Press.

Bagozzi, R., Verbeke, W., and Gavino, Jr. J. (2003) 'Culture Moderates the Self-Regulation of Shame and its Effects on Performance: The Case of Sales Persons in the Netherlands and the Philippines'. *Journal of Applied Psychology* 88(2): 219–33.

Bailey, N., Besemer, K., Bramley, G., and Livingston, M. (2013) *How Neighbourhood Context Shapes Poverty: Some Results from the Poverty and Social Exclusion UK Survey 2012*, paper presented to the 'Poverty Neighbourhoods' workshop, European Network for Housing Research conference, Tarragona, 19–22 June 2013.

Bandyopadhyaya, J. (2007) *Class and Religion in Ancient India*, London: Anthem Press.

Banks, J. and Johnson, P. (1994) 'Equivalence Scales and Public Policy'. *Fiscal Studies* 15(1): 1–23.

Bantebya-Kyomuhendo, G. and Mwiine, A. (2013) '"Food that Cannot Be Eaten": The Shame of Uganda's Anti-Poverty Policies', in Gubrium, E., Pellissery, S., and Lødemel, I. (eds) *The Shame of It: Global Perspectives on Anti-Poverty Policies*, Bristol: Policy Press.

Bantebya-Kyomuhendo, G. and Mwiine, A. (2014a) 'Literary and Oral Tradition Portrayals of Poverty: The Evolution of Poverty-Shame in Uganda', in Chase, E. and Bantebya-Kyomuhendo, G. (eds) *Poverty and Shame: Global Experiences*, Oxford: Oxford University Press.

Bantebya-Kyomuhendo, G. and Mwiine, A. (2014b) '"Poverty is Not an Identity": Expressionism of People in Poverty', in Chase, E. and Bantebya-Kyomuhendo, G. (eds) *Poverty and Shame: Global Experiences*, Oxford: Oxford University Press.

Bantebya-Kyomuhendo, G. and Mwiine, A. (2014c) 'Poor and Indispensable: Co Existing With Those in Poverty in Rural Uganda', in Chase, E. and Bantebya-Kyomuhendo, G. (eds) *Poverty and Shame: Global Experiences*, Oxford: Oxford University Press.

Barbalet, J. (1998) *Emotion, Social Theory and Social Structure: A Macrosociological Approach*, Cambridge: Cambridge University Press.

Barrientos, A. and Neff, D. (2010) *Attitudes to Chronic Poverty in the 'Global Village'*, Hamburg: GIGA German Institute of Global and Area Studies, Working paper 134.

Baumberg, B., Bell, K., and Gaffney, D. (2012) *Benefits stigma in Britain*, London: Turn2Us.

BBC (2013) *Q&A: China's Newspaper Industry*; <http://www.bbc.co.uk/news/business-20970543> accessed January 2014.

Bedford, O. (2004) 'The Individual Experience of Guilt and Shame in Chinese Culture'. *Culture and Psychology* 10: 29–52.

Bell, D. (2000) *The End of Ideology: On the Exhaustion of Political Ideas in the Fifties: With 'The Resumption of History in the New Century'*, Cambridge, MA: Harvard University Press.

Benedict, R. (1946) *The Chrysanthemum and the Sword*, New York: Houghton Mifflin.

Bennett, F. with Roberts, M. (2004) *From Input to Influence: Participatory Approaches to Research and Inquiry Into Poverty*, York: Joseph Rowntree Foundation.

Ben-Yehuda, N. and Goode, E. (1994) *Moral Panics: The Social Construction of Deviance*, Oxford: Blackwell.

Beresford, P., Green, D., Lister, R., and Woodward, K. (1999) *Poverty First Hand: Poor People Speak for Themselves*, London: CPAG.

Bergman, M. (1998) 'A Theoretical Note on the Differences Between Attitudes, Opinions, and Values'. *Swiss Political Science Review* 4(2): 81–93.

Berthoud, R., Bryan, M., and Bardasi, E. (2004) *The Relationship Between Income and Material Deprivation Over Time*, Leeds: Department for Work and Pensions, Research Report 219, Corporate Document Services.

Beth, S. (2007) 'Hindi Dalit Autobiography: An Exploration of Identity'. *Modern Asian Studies* 41: 545–74.

Biewen, M. and Steffes, S. (2010) 'Unemployment Persistence: Is There Evidence for Stigma Effects?'. *Economics Letters* 106(3): 188–90.

Blair, T. (1997) 'The 21st Century Welfare State'. Speech to the Social Policy and Economic Performance Conference, Amsterdam, 24 January.

Blair, T. (1999) 'Beveridge Revisited: A Welfare State for the 21st Century', in Walker R. (ed.) *Ending Child Poverty: Popular Welfare for the 21st Century*, Bristol: The Policy Press.

Blume, L. (2002) *Stigma and Social Control*, Vienna: Institute for Advanced Studies, Economics Series 119.

Booth, C. (1892) *Life and Labour of the People in London* (1889–1903), London: Macmillan.

Bos, A. van den and Stapel, D. (2009). 'Why People Stereotype Affects How They Stereotype: The Differential Influence of Comprehension Goals and Self-Enhancement Goals on Stereotyping'. *Personality and Social Psychology Bulletin* 35(1): 101–13.

Boulding, K. (1987) 'The Economics of Pride and Shame'. *Atlantic Economic Journal* 15(1): 10–19.

Bradshaw, J., Middleton, S., Davis, A., Oldfield, N., Smith, N., Cusworth, L., and Williams, J. (2008) *A Minimum Income Standard for Britain: What People Think*, York: Joseph Rowntree Foundation.

Breugelmans, S. and Poortinga, Y. (2006) 'Emotion Without a Word: Shame and Guilt Among Rarámuri Indians and Rural Javanese'. *Personality Process and Individual Differences* 91(6): 1111–22.

Brewer, M. (1988) 'A Dual Process Model of Impression Formation', in Srull, T. and Wyer, Jr, R. (eds), *Advances in Social Cognition*, Hillsdale, NJ: Erlbaum.

Brewer, M., Duncan, A., Shephard, A., and Suárez, M. J. (2006) 'Did Working Families' Tax Credit Work? The Impact of In-Work Support on Labour Supply in Great Britain'. *Labour Economics* 13: 699–720.

Briant, E., Watson, N., and Philo, G. (2011) *Bad News for Disabled People: How the Newspapers are Reporting Disability*, Glasgow: Strathclyde Centre for Disability Research and Glasgow Media Unit in association with Inclusion London; <http://eprints.gla.ac.uk/57499/1/57499.pdf> accessed January 2014.

British Social Attitudes Survey (Various) <http://www.britsocat.com> accessed January 2014.

Bulwer-Lytton, E. (1830) *Paul Clifford*, Rockville, MD: Wildside Press (republished 2007).

Burke, E. and Stanlis, P. (2000) *The Best of Burke: Selected Writings and Speeches of Edmund Burke*, Washington, DC: Regnery.

Burke, J. and Mihany, K. (2012) *Financial Literacy, Social Perception and Strategic Default*, Arlington, VA: Rand Working Paper WR937.

Busch, M. (1898) *Bismarck: Some Secret Pages from his History*, New York: Macmillan.

Calandrino, M. (2003) *Low-Income and Deprivation in British Families*, London: Department for Work and Pensions, Working Paper 10.

Cameron, D. (2010) 'A New Welfare Contract'. Speech at Burton on Trent, 20 April; <http://www.conservatives.com/News/Speeches/2010/04/David_Cameron_A_New_Welfare_Contract.aspx> accessed January 2014.

Castell, S. and Thompson, J. (2007) *Understanding Attitudes to Poverty in the UK: Getting the Public'S attention*, York: Joseph Rowntree Foundation.

Cattell, V. (2001) 'Poor People, Poor Places, and Poor Health: The Mediating Role of Social Networks and Social Capital'. *Social Science and Medicine* 52: 1501–16.

Chambers, R (1994) 'The Origins and Practice of Participatory Rural Appraisal'. *World Development* 22 (7): 953–69.

Chase, E. and Bantebya-Kyomuhendo, G. (eds) (2014) *Poverty and Shame: Global Experiences*, Oxford: Oxford University Press.

Chase, E. and Walker, R. (2013) 'The Co-Construction of Shame in the Context of Poverty: Beyond a Threat to the Social Bond'. *Sociology* 47(4): 739–54.

Chase, E. and Walker, R. (2014a) 'Portrayals of Poverty and Shame in Literature and Film in the UK', in Chase, E. and Bantebya-Kyomuhendo, G. (eds) *Poverty and Shame: Global Experiences*, Oxford: Oxford University Press.

Chase, E. and Walker, R. (2014b) 'The Co-Construction of Shame in the Context of Poverty in the UK', in Chase, E. and Bantebya-Kyomuhendo, G. (eds) *Poverty and Shame: Global Experiences*, Oxford: Oxford University Press.

Chase, E. and Walker, R. (2014c) '"Happy on Benefits"? Public Perceptions of People Living in Poverty in the UK', in Chase, E. and Bantebya-Kyomuhendo, G. (eds) *Poverty and Shame: Global Experiences*, Oxford: Oxford University Press.

Chen, Y., Ngai, N.-P., and Tang, K.-L. (2013) *Does Social Policy Respond to Multi-Stress of the Urban Aged Poor in China? Qualitative Evidence from Beijing*. Paper presented at the EASP 10th Annual Conference, Beijing, July.

Chong, D. and Druckman, J. (2007) 'Framing Theory'. *Annual Review of Political Science* 10: 103–26.

Choudhry, S. (2013) 'Pakistan: A Journey of Poverty-Induced Shame', in Gubrium, E., Pellissery, S., and Lødemel, I. (eds) *The Shame of It: Global Perspectives on Anti-Poverty Policies*, Bristol: Policy Press.

Choudhry, S. (2014a) 'The Wealth of Poverty-Induced Shame in Urdu Literature', in Chase, E. and Bantebya-Kyomuhendo, G. (eds) *Poverty and Shame: Global Experiences*, Oxford: Oxford University Press.

Choudhry, S. (2014b) 'Tales of Inadequacy from Pakistan', in Chase, E. and Bantebya-Kyomuhendo, G. (eds) *Poverty and Shame: Global Experiences*, Oxford: Oxford University Press.

Choudhry, S. (2014c) 'How Best to Shame Those in Poverty in Pakistan', in Chase, E. and Bantebya-Kyomuhendo, G. (eds) *Poverty and Shame: Global Experiences*, Oxford: Oxford University Press.

Clark, D. (2006) 'Capability Approach', in Clark, D. (ed.) *The Elgar Companion to Development Studies*, Cheltenham: Edward Elgar.

Clasen, J., Gould, A., and Vincent, J. (1998) *Voices Within and Without: Responses to Long-Term Unemployment in Germany, Sweden and Britain*, Bristol: The Policy Press.

Clery, E., Lee, L., and Kunz, S. (2013) *Public Attitudes to Poverty and Welfare, 1983–2011*, London: NatCen Social Research for the Joseph Rowntree Foundation.

Cm. (2012) *Measuring Child Poverty: A Consultation on Better Measures of Child Poverty*, London: Presented to Parliament by the Secretary of State for Work and Pensions by Command of Her Majesty, Cm 8483.

Cohen T., Wolf, S., Panter, A., and Insko, C. (2011) 'Introducing the GASP Scale: A New Measure of Guilt and Shame Proneness'. *Journal of Personality and Social Psychology* 100(5): 947–66.

Collier, P. (2007) *The Bottom Billion: Why the Poorest Countries Are Failing and What Can Be Done About It*, New York: Oxford University Press.

Collins, M., Mac Mahon, B., Weld, G., and Thornton, R. (2012) *A Minimum Income Standard for Ireland: A Consensual Budget Standards Study Examining Household Types Across the Lifecycle*, Dublin: Trinity College Dublin, Studies in Public Policy 27.

Congregational Union (1883) *The Bitter Cry of Outcast London: An Inquiry Into the Condition of the Abject Poor*, London: Congregational Union.

Corbo, C. (2006) *Paupertas: La legislazione tardoantica (IV-V sec. d.c.)*, Naples: Satura Editrice.

Corden, A. (1995) *Changing Perspectives on Benefit Take-Up*, London: HMSO.

Coser, L. (1963) *Sociology Through Literature*, Englewood Cliffs: Prentice-Hall International.

Coudouel, A., Jesko, S., Hentschel, J., and Wodon, Q. (2003) 'Poverty Measurement and Analysis', in Klugman, J. (ed.) *A Sourcebook for Poverty Reduction Strategies* (2 Vol. Set), Washington, DC: World Bank.

CPRC (2004) *The Chronic Poverty Report 2004–05*, Manchester: Chronic Poverty Research Centre, University of Manchester; <http://www.chronicpoverty.org/up loads/publication_files/CPR1_ReportFull.pdf> accessed January 2014.

Crystal, D., Parrott, W., Okazaki, Y., and Watanabe, H. (2001) 'Examining Relations Between Shame and Personality Among University Students in the United States and Japan: A Developmental Perspective'. *International Journal of Behavioral Development* 25(2): 113–23.

CSJ (2006) *Breakdown Britain: Interim Report on the State of the Nation*, London: Centre for Social Justice.

D'Angelo, P. (2012) 'Studying Framing in Political Communication with an Integrative Approach'. *American Behavioral Scientist* 56: 353–64.

Daily Telegraph (2011) 'China Raises Poverty Line Increasing Official Poor'. *Daily Telegraph*, 30 November; <http://www.telegraph.co.uk/news/worldnews/asia/china/8925011/China-raises-poverty-line-increasing-official-poor.html> accessed January 2014.

Davis, A., Hirsch, D., Smith, N., Beckhelling, J., and Padley, M. (2012) *A Minimum Income Standard for the UK in 2012: Keeping Up in Hard Times*, York: Joseph Rowntree Foundation.

Dawnay, E. and Shah, H. (2005) *Behavioural Economics: Seven Principles for Policy-Makers*, London: New Economics Foundation.

Dearing, R., Stuewig, J., and Tangney, J. (2005) 'On the Importance of Distinguishing Shame from Guilt: Relations to Problematic Alcohol and Drug Use'. *Addictive Behaviors* 30(7): 1392–404.

DellaVigna, S. and Kaplan, E. (2008) 'The Political Impact of Media Bias', in Islam, R. (ed.) *Information and Public Choice: From Media Markets to Policymaking*, Washington, DC: World Bank.

Devins, S. (2013) *Meeting Julia on the Road to Peace*, New York: Fourth World Movement; <http://www.4thworldmovement.org/povertyisviolence.php> accessed January 2014.

Dharwadker, V. (1994) 'Dalit Poetry in Marathi'. *World Literature Today*. 68(2): 319–24.

Diamond, P. and Lodge, G. (2013) *European Welfare States After the Crisis: Changing Public Attitudes*, London: Policy Network.

Dickerson, S., Gruenewald, T., and Kemeny, M. (2004) 'When the Social Self is Threatened: Shame, Physiology, and Health'. *Journal of Personality* 72(6): 1191–216.

Donald, A. and Mottershaw, E. (2009) *Poverty, Inequality and Human Rights: Do Human Rights Make a Difference?* York: Joseph Rowntree Foundation.

Dorling, D., Rigby, J., Wheeler, B., Ballas, D., Thomas, B., Fahmy, E., Gordon, D., and Lupton, R. (2007) *Poverty, Wealth and Place in Britain, 1968 to 2005*, Bristol: Policy Press.

Dornan, P. and Portela, M. (2013) *Childhood Experience of Shame and Human Capital*, Oxford: Young Lives Study, Mimeo.

Douglas-Fairhurst, R. (2010) 'London Labour and the London Poor by Henry Mayhew'. *The Guardian*, 16 October; <http://www.guardian.co.uk/books/2010/oct/16/rereading-henry-mayhew-london-poor> accessed January 2014.

Dovidio, J., Major, B., and Crocker, J. (2000) 'Stigma: Introduction and Overview', in Heatherton, T., Kleck, R., Hebl, M. et al. (eds) *The Social Psychology of Stigma*, New York: Guilford Press.

Drèze, J. and Sen, A. (2013) *An Uncertain Glory: India and its Contradictions*, London: Allen Lane.

Du Bois, W. (1899) *The Philadelphia Negro, a Social Study*, Philadelphia: The University of Pennsylvania Press (Republished 1996).

Duoji, C. (2001) *Research and Practice of the Minimum Standard of Living Scheme in China*, Beijing: People's Press.

DWP (2007) *Opportunity for All: Indicators Update 2007*, London: Department for Work and Pensions.

DWP (2011) *Universal Credit: Welfare that Works*, London: Department for Work and Pensions, Cm. 795.7.

Ebrey, P. (1999) *The Cambridge Illustrated History of China*, Cambridge: Cambridge University Press.

Economist (2013) 'China's Poor: World-Class Poverty', *Economist*, 27 February; <http://www.economist.com/blogs/analects/2013/02/chinas-poor> accessed January 2014.

Edin, K., Lein, L., Nelson, T., and Clampet-Lundquest, S. (2000) *Talking to Low-Income Fathers*, Chicago: University of Chicago, Joint Center for Poverty Research Newsletter 4, 2.

Eisenberger, R., Huntington, R., Hutchison, S., and Sowa, D. (1986) 'Perceived Organizational Support'. *Journal of Applied Psychology* 71(3): 500–7.

Elias, N. (1969) *The Civilizing Process: Volume 1, The History of Manners*, Oxford: Blackwell.

Elias, N. (1982) *The Civilizing Process: Volume 2, State Formation and Civilization*, Oxford: Blackwell.

Elison, J. and Harter, S. (2007) 'Humiliation: Causes, Correlates and Consequences', in Tracy, J., Robins, R., and Tangney, J. (eds) *The Self-Conscious Emotions*, New York: Guilford Press.

Eurostat (2013) *People at Risk of Poverty or Social Exclusion*; <http://epp.eurostat.ec. europa.eu/statistics_explained/index.php/People_at_risk_of_poverty_or_social_ex clusion> accessed January 2014.

Fernández-Villaverde, J., Greenwood, J., and Guner, N. (2010) *From Shame to Game in One Hundred Years: An Economic Model of the Rise in Premarital Sex and its De-Stigmatization*, Boston: NBER Working Paper 15677; <http://www.nber.org/pa pers/w15677> accessed January 2014.

Ferragina, E., Tomlinson, M., and Walker, R. (2013) *Poverty, Participation and Choice: The Legacy of Peter Townsend*, York: Joseph Rowntree Foundation.

Fessler, D. (2007) 'From Appeasement to Conformity: Evolutionary and Cultural Perspectives on Shame, Competition and Cooperation', in J. Tracy, Robins, R., and Tangney, J. (eds) *The Self-Conscious Emotions*, New York: Guilford Press.

Field, F. (1997) *Reforming Welfare*, London: Social Market Foundation.

Finley, M. (1973) *The Ancient Economy*, Berkeley: University of California Press.

Finn, D., Mason, D., Rahim, N., and Casebourne, J. (2008) *Problems in the Delivery of Benefits, Tax Credits and Employment Services*, York: Joseph Rowntree Foundation; <http://www.jrf.org.uk/publications/problems-delivery-benefits-tax-credits-and-employment-services> accessed January 2014.

Finn, R. (2006) 'Portraying the Poor', in Atkins, M. and Osborne, R. (eds) *Poverty in the Roman World*, Cambridge: Cambridge University Press.

Fiske, S. (1998) 'Stereotyping, Prejudice and Discrimination' in D. Gilbert and S. Fiske (eds) *The Handbook of Social Psychology*, second edition, Boston, MA: McGraw Hill.

Fontaine, J. R., Luyten, P., De Boeck, P., Corveleyn, J., et al. (2006) 'Untying the Gordian Knot of Guilt and Shame: The Structure of Guilt and Shame Reactions Based on Situation and Person Variation in Belgium, Hungary, and Peru'. *Journal of Cross-Cultural Psychology*, 37(3): 273–92.

Foster, J. and Santos, M. (2012) *Measuring Chronic Poverty*, Oxford: Oxford Poverty and Human Development Initiative (OPHI) Working Paper, 52.

Fredman, S. (2011) *Discrimination Law*, Oxford: Oxford University Press.

Frenkel-Brunswick, E. (1950) 'The Interview as an Approach to the Prejudiced Personality', in Adorno, T., Frenkel-Brunswick, E., Levinson, D., and Sanford, N. (eds) *Authoritarian Personality*, New York: Harper and Row.

Fukuyama, F. (1992) *The End of History and The Last Man*, New York: Free Press.

Fung, H., Lieber, E., and Leung, P. (2003) 'Parental Beliefs about Shame and Moral Socialization in Taiwan, Hong Kong and the United States', in Yang K. and Hwang, K. (eds) *Progress in Asian Social Psychology: Conceptual and Empirical Contributions*, Westport, CT: Praeger/Greenwood Press.

Furukawa, E., Tangney, J., and Higashibara, F. (2012) 'Cross-Cultural Continuities and Discontinuities in Shame, Guilt and Pride: A Study of Children Residing in Japan, Korea and the USA'. *Self and Identity* 11(1): 90–113.

Gallagher, C. and Greenblatt, S. (2000) *Practicing New Historicism*, Chicago: Chicago University Press.

Gallie, D., Paugam, S., and Jacobs, S. (2003) 'Unemployment, Poverty and Social Isolation: Is there a Vicious Circle of Social Exclusion?'. *European Societies* 5(1): 1–32.

Garnsey, P. (1989) *Famine and Food Supply in the Graeco-Roman World: Responses to Risk and Crisis*, Cambridge: Cambridge University Press.

Garroway, C. and Laiglesia, de J. (2012) *On the Relevance of Relative Poverty for Developing Countries*, Paris: OECD Development Centre, Working Paper 314.

Gaulejac, de V. (1989) 'Honte et pauvreté'. *Santé mentale au Québec* 14(2): 128–37.

Gibbs, L. (2008) 'Zeus and Shame', No. 528 in A*esop's Fables: A New Translation*, Oxford: Oxford University Press.

Gilbert, P. (1997) 'The Evolution of Social Attractiveness and its Role in Shame, Humiliation, Guilt and Therapy'. *British Journal of Medical Psychology* 70(2): 113–47.

Gilens, M. (1999) *Why Americans Hate Welfare: Race, Media, and the Politics of Antipoverty Policy*, Chicago: University of Chicago Press.

GIPC (2009) *Report of the Expert Group to Review the Methodology for Estimation of Poverty*, New Delhi: Government of India Planning Commission, November 2009.

Glennerster, H. (2004) 'The Context for Rowntree's Contribution', in Glennerster, H., Hills, J., Piachaud, D., and Webb, J. (eds) *One Hundred Years of Poverty and Policy*, York: Joseph Rowntree Foundation.

Godinot, X. with Viard, T. (2010) *Extreme Poverty and World Governance*, Forum for a new World Governance; <http://www.world-governance.org/IMG/pdf_Extreme_Poverty_and_World_Governance_-2.pdf> accessed January 2014.

Goetz, J. and Keltner, D. (2007) 'Shifting Meanings of Self-conscious Emotions Across Culture', in Tracy, J., Robins, R., and Tangney, J. (eds) *The Self-Conscious Emotions*, New York: Guilford Press.

Goffman, E. (1955) 'On Face-Work: An Analysis of Ritual Elements in Social Interaction'. *Psychiatry: Journal of Interpersonal Relations* 18(3): 213–31.

Goffman, E. (1963) *Stigma: Notes on the Management of Spoiled Identify*, Englewood Cliffs, NJ: Prentice Hall.

Golding, P. and Middleton, S. (1982) *Images of Welfare: Press and Public Attitudes to Poverty*, Oxford: Martin Robertson.

Goldthorpe, J. (2013) 'Understanding—and Misunderstanding—Social Mobility in Britain: The Entry of the Economists, the Confusion of Politicians and the Limits of Educational Policy'. *Journal of Social Policy* 42(3): 431–50.

Gordon, D. (2006) 'The Concept and Measurement of Poverty', in Pantazis, C., Gordon, D., and Levitas, R. (eds), *Poverty and Social Exclusion in Britain: The Millennium Survey*, Bristol: Policy Press.

Gordon, D., Adelman, L., Ashworth, K., Bradshaw, J., et al. (2000) *Poverty and Social Exclusion in Britain*, York: Joseph Rowntree Foundation.

Gordon, D., Mack, J., Lansley, S., Main, G., Nandy, S., Patsios, D., and Pomati, M. (2013) 'The Impoverishment of the UK PSE UK First Results: Living Standards'. Bristol: Bristol University; <http://www.poverty.ac.uk/system/files/attachments/The_Impoverishment_of_the_UK_PSE_UK_first_results_summary_report_March_28.pdf> accessed January 2014.

Gordon, D. and Pantazis, C. (1997) *Breadline Britain in the 1990s*, Aldershot: Ashgate.

GPP (2013) *The Global Poverty Project*, London; <http://globalpovertyproject.com/pages/presentation> accessed January 2014.

Green, D. (2010) 'Are Women Really 70% of the World's Poor? How Do We Know?'. *Oxfamblogs*; <http://www.oxfamblogs.org/fp2p/?p=1797> accessed January 2014.

Grig, L. (2006) 'Throwing Parties for the Poor', in Atkins, M. and Osborne, R. (eds) *Poverty in the Roman World*, Cambridge: Cambridge University Press.

Griggs, J., Hammond, A., and Walker, R. (2013) 'Activation for All: Welfare Reform in the UK', in Lødemel, I., and Moreira, A. (eds) *Workfare revisited: The Political Economy of activation reforms*, New York: Oxford University Press.

Guan, X. (1999) *Study on Urban Poverty Problem in China*, Changsha: Hunan People's Publishing House.

Gubrium, E. and Lødemel, I. (2013a) '"Not Good Enough": Social Assistance and Shaming in a Strong Welfare State', in Gubrium, E., Pellissery, S., and Lødemel, I. (eds) *The Shame of It: Global Perspectives on Anti-Poverty Policies*, Bristol: Policy Press.

Gubrium, E. and Lødemel, I. (2013b) 'Towards Global Principles for Dignity-Based Anti-Poverty Policies', in Gubrium, E., Pellissery, S., and Lødemel, I. (eds) *The Shame of It: Global Perspectives on Anti-Poverty Policies*, Bristol: Policy Press.

Gubrium, E. and Lødemel, I. (2014a) '"Then" and "Now": Literary Representations of Shame, Poverty and Social Exclusion in Norway', in Chase, E. and Bantebya-Kyomuhendo, G. (eds) *Poverty and Shame: Global Experiences*, Oxford: Oxford University Press.

Gubrium, E. and Lødemel, I. (2014b) '"Relative" Poverty in a Rich Welfare State: Experiences from Norway', in Chase, E. and Bantebya-Kyomuhendo, G. (eds) *Poverty and Shame: Global Experiences*, Oxford: Oxford University Press.

Gubrium, E. and Lødemel, I. (2014c) '"No One Should Be Poor": Social Shaming in Norway', in Chase, E. and Bantebya-Kyomuhendo, G. (eds) *Poverty and Shame: Global Experiences*, Oxford: Oxford University Press.

Gubrium, E., Pellissery, S., and Lødemel, I. (eds) (2013) *The Shame of It: Global Perspectives on Anti-Poverty Policies*, Bristol: Policy Press.

Guyson, N. (2011) 'Slums Surround Uganda's Capital City'. *AfricaNews*, 27 June.

Hagen, K. and Lødemel, I. (2010) 'Fattigdomstiåret 2000–2010: Parentes eller ny kurs for velferdsstaten?', in Frønes, I. and Kjølsrød, L. (eds), *Det Norske Samfunn*, Oslo: Gylendal Akademisk.

Halvorsen, K. and Stjernø, S. (2008) *Work, Oil and Welfare*, Oslo: Universitetsforlaget.

Harel, A. and Klement, A. (2007) 'The Economics of Stigma: Why More Detection of Crime May Result in Less Stigmatization'. *The Journal of Legal Studies* 36(2): 355–77.

Harrington, M. (1962) *The Other America: Poverty in the United States*, New York: Macmillan.

Hart, D. and Matsuba, M. (2007) 'The Development of Pride and Moral Life', in Tracy, J., Robins, R., and Tangney, J. (eds) *The Self-Conscious Emotions*, New York: Guilford Press.

Heidenreich, M., Petzold, N., Natili, M., and Panican, A. (2013) *Active Inclusion in Times of Crisis: Minimum Income, Active Labour Market and Social Investment Policies in Three European Countries*, contribution to the research stream 'Poverty and Social Assistance Dynamics from a Comparative Perspective', 11th Annual ESPAnet Conference in Poznań.

Heller, Á. (1985) *The Power of Shame: A Rational Perspective*, London: Routledge.

Hernanz, V., Malherbet, F., and Pellizzari M. (2004) *Take-Up of Welfare Benefits in OECD Countries: A Review of the Evidence*, Paris: OECD, Social, Employment and Migration Working Papers 17.

Hickey, S. (2011) *Beyond the Poverty Agenda? Insights from the New Politics of Development in Uganda*, Manchester: Institute for Development Policy and Management.

Hiebert, P. (1985) *Anthropological Insights for Missionaries*, Grand Rapids, MI: Baker Book House.

Higgins, J. (1978) 'Regulating the Poor Revisited'. *Journal of Social Policy* 7(2): 189–98.

Himmelfarb, G. (1984) 'The Idea of Poverty: England in the Early Industrial Age'. *History Today*, 34(2): 23–30.

Ho, D., Fu, W., and Ng, S. (2004) 'Guilt, Shame and Embarrassment: Revelations of Face and Self'. *Culture and Psychology* 10(1): 64–84.

Hoban, M. (2013) *Work and Pensions: International Labour Conference*, Hansard, 7 February: Column 32WS.

Hoggett, P., Wilkinson, H., and Beedell, P. (2013) 'Fairness and the Politics of Resentment'. *Journal of Social Policy/FirstView Article*: 1–19; DOI <http://dx.doi.org/10.1017/S0047279413000056> accessed January 2014.

Holley, L., Stromwall, L., and Bashor, K. (2012) 'Reconceptualizing Stigma: Toward a Critical Anti-Oppression Paradigm'. *Stigma Research and Action* 2(2): 51–61.

Hooper, C.-A., Gorin, S., Cabral, C., and Dyson, C. (2007) *Living with Hardship 24/7: The Diverse Experiences of Families in Poverty in England*, London: The Frank Buttle Trust.

Huh, S. (2009) 'The 10th Anniversary of Enactment of National Basic Livelihood Security Act: The Limits and Tasks'. *Citizen and World* 16(12): 274–89.

Hulme, D., Moore, K., and Shepherd, A. (2001) *Chronic Poverty: Meanings and Analytical Frameworks*, Manchester: Chronic Poverty Research Centre, CPRC, Working Paper 2.

Hunter, R. (1904) *Poverty*, New York: Macmillan.

ILO (2010) *World Social Security Report 2010/11: Providing Coverage in Times of Crisis and Beyond*, Geneva: ILO.

ILO (2012) *Recommendation Concerning National Floors of Social Protection*, adopted by the Conference at its one hundred and first session, 14 June 2012. Geneva: ILO, Recommendation 202.

ILO (2013) *China*. Geneva: ILO Social Security Department; <http://www.ilo.org/dyn/ ilossi/ssimain.home?p_lang=en&p_geoaid=156> accessed January 2014.

Jenkins, S. (2011) *Changing Fortunes: Income Mobility and Poverty Dynamics in Britain*, Oxford: Oxford University Press.

Jo, Y.-N. (2013) 'Psycho-Social Dimensions of Poverty: When Poverty Becomes Shameful'. *Critical Social Policy*, 33: 514–31.

Jo, Y.-N. (2014a) 'Portrayals of Poverty in Popular Films of South Korea', in Chase, E. and Bantebya-Kyomuhendo, G. (eds) *Poverty and Shame: Global Experiences*, Oxford: Oxford University Press.

Jo, Y.-N. (2014b) 'Hearing from their Own Voice: Living in Poverty in South Korea', in Chase, E. and Bantebya-Kyomuhendo, G. (eds) *Poverty and Shame: Global Experiences*, Oxford: Oxford University Press.

Jo, Y.-N. and Walker, R. (2013) Self-Sufficiency, Social Assistance and the Shaming of Poverty in South Korea', in Gubrium, E., Pellissery, S., and Lødemel, I. (eds) *The Shame of It: Global Perspectives on Anti-Poverty Policies*, Bristol: Policy Press.

Jung, I.-Y. (2007) *Social Assistance in Nine OECD Countries*, paper presented at the 4th East Asian Social Policy research network (EASP) Conference: Restructuring Care Responsibility—Dynamics of Welfare Mix in East Asia University of Tokyo, Japan, 20–21 October.

Jury, A. (2009) *Shame on Who: Experiential and Theoretical Accounts of the Constitution of Women's Shame Within Abusive Relationships*, Palmerston North: Massey University, PhD Thesis in Sociology.

Kakwani, N. and Silber, J. (eds) (2008) *Quantitative Approaches to Multidimensional Poverty Measurement*, Basingstoke: Palgave Macmillan.

Killeen, D. (2008) *Is Poverty in the UK a Denial of People's Human Rights?*, York: Joseph Rowntree Foundation; <http://www.jrf.org.uk/sites/files/jrf/2183.pdf> accessed January 2014.

Kingdom, J. (2011) *Agendas, Alternatives and Pubic Policies*, Boston: Longman.

Knoepfel, P., Larrue, C., Varone, F., and Hill, M. (2007) *Public Policy Analysis*, Bristol: Policy Press.

Kothari, R. (2001) 'Short Story in Gujarati Dalit Literature', *Economic and Political Weekly*, 36(45): 4308–11.

Kyomuhendo, G. and Mwiine, A. (2013) 'Food that Cannot be Eaten: The Shame of Uganda's Anti-Poverty Policies', in Gubrium, E., Pellissery, S., and Lødemel, I. (eds) *The Shame of It: Global Perspectives on Anti-Poverty Policies*. Bristol: Policy Press.

Lal, D. (2013) *Poverty and Progress: Realities and Myths about Global Poverty*, Washington, DC: Cato Institute.

Larsen, C. (2008) 'The Institutional Logic of Welfare Attitudes: How Welfare Regimes Influence Public Support'. *Comparative Political Studies* 41(2): 145–68.

Larsen, C. and Dejgaard, T. (2012) *The Institutional Logic of Images of the Poor and Welfare Recipients: A Comparative Study of British, Swedish and Danish Newspapers*, Aalborg: Centre for Comparative Welfare Studies (CCWS), working paper 2012–78.

Lawrence, B. (2013) 'Shameless writer Paul Abbott: "Everything I've won Baftas for was written on drugs"'. *Telegraph*, 26 February; <http://www.telegraph.co.uk/

culture/tvandradio/9889123/Shameless-writer-Paul-Abbott-Everything-Ive-won-Baftas-for-was-written-on-drugs.html> accessed January 2014.

Lay, S. (2002) *British Social Realism: From Documentary to Brit-Grit*, London: Wallflower Press.

Lee, N., McLeod, D., and Shah, D. (2008) 'Framing Policy Debates: Issue Dualism, Journalistic Frames, and Opinions on Controversial Policy Issues'. *Communication Research* 35(5): 695–718.

Lee, W. (2010) 'Depression and Welfare Transitions of the National Basic Livelihood Protection Program'. *Korean Journal of Social Welfare* 62(4): 249–74.

Lee-Gong, E. (2011) *The Role of NGOs in Welfare Delivery: The Case of South Korea*, paper presented at the Social Policy Association Annual Conference, 4–6 July.

Lewis, D., Rodgers, D., and Woolcock, M. (2008) 'The Fiction of Development: Literary Representation as a Source of Authoritative Knowledge'. *Journal of Development Studies* 44(2): 198–216.

Lewis, O. (1968) *A Study of Slum Culture*, New York: Random House.

Lewis, O. (1969) 'Culture of Poverty', in Moynihan, D. (ed.) *On Understanding Poverty: Perspectives from the Social Sciences*, New York: Basic Books.

Li, J., Wang, L., and Fischer, K. (2004) 'The Organization of Chinese Shame Concepts'. *Cognition and Emotion* 18: 767–97.

Li, S., Luo, C., and Sicular, T. (2011) *Overview: Income Inequality and Poverty in China, 2002–2007*, London: University of Western Ontario, CIBC Centre for Human Capital and Productivity, Working Paper 201110.

Li, S. and Yang, S. (2009) 'Impact of the Urban MSLS in China on Income Distribution and Poverty'. *Chinese Population Science* 5: 19–27.

Lind, J. (2007) 'Fractionalization and the Size of Government'. *Journal of Public Economics* 91(1): 51–76.

Link, B. and Phelan, J. (2001) 'Conceptualizing Stigma'. *Annual Review of Sociology* 27: 363–85.

Lipsky, M. (1980) *Street-Level Bureaucracy: Dilemmas of the Individual in Public Services*, New York: Russell Sage Foundation.

Lister, R. (2004) *Poverty*, Cambridge: Polity Press.

Lister, R. (2008) *A Human Rights Conceptualisation of Poverty*, Paris: International Conference on Exclusion, a Challenge to Democracy. How relevant is Joseph Wresinski's Thinking? Paris: Paris Institute of Political Studies, 19 December.

Lødemel, I. (1997) *The Welfare Paradox*, Oslo: Scandinavian University Press.

Lødemel, I. (2013) *Poverty and Shame: Perspectives and Practices Concerning Anti-Poverty Measures*. Oslo: Velferd, arbeidsliv og migrasjon (VAM); <http://www.forskningsradet.no/servlet/Satellite?c=Prosjekt&cid=1253986402290&pagename=vam/Hovedsidemal&p=1232443453186> accessed January 2014.

Los Rios, de C. and Los Rios, de J. (2010) *A Sensitivity Assessment of Multidimensional Poverty to Various sets of Missing Dimensions' Indicators: The Chilean Case*, Oxford: OPHI Research in Progress.

Loseke, D. and Kusenbach, M. (2007) 'The Social Construction of Emotions', in Holstein, J. and Gubrium, J. (eds) *Handbook of Constructionist Research*, New York: Guilford Press.

Lynd, H. (1958) *On Shame and the Search for Identity*, London: Routledge and Kegan Paul.

Ma, J. and Zhao, S. (2006) 'Exploratory Study on the Disincentive Effects of MSLS'. *Journal of Chongqing University of Science and Technology* (Social Science Edition) 4(1): 43–6.

Manchester, C. and Mumford, K. (2012) *How Costly is Welfare Stigma? Separating Psychological Costs from Time Costs in Food Assistance Programs;* <http://www.krannert.purdue.edu/faculty/kjmumfor/papers/stigma.pdf> accessed January 2014.

Mander, H. (2012a) *Ash in the Belly: India's Unfinished Battle Against Hunger*, New Delhi: Penguin.

Mander, H. (2012b) *A Fractured Freedom: Chronicles of India's Margins, 2004–2011*, New Delhi: Three Essays.

Manza, J. and Brooks, C. (2012) 'How Sociology Lost Public Opinion: A Genealogy of a Missing Concept in the Study of the Political'. *Sociological Theory* 30(2): 89–113.

Massaro, T. (1991) Shame, Culture, and American Criminal Law'. *Michigan Law Review* 89(7): 1880–944.

Mathews, L. (2010) 'Coping with Shame of Poverty, Analysis of Farmers in Distress'. *Psychology and Developing Societies* 22(2): 385–407.

Mattinson, D. (2010) *Talking to a Brick Wall: How New Labour Stopped Listening to the Voter and Why We Need a New Politics*, London: Biteback.

Maxwell, S. (1999) *The Meaning and Measurement of Poverty*, London: Overseas Development Institute, ODI Poverty Briefings.

Mayhew, H. (1851) *London Labour and the London Poor*, London: G. Woodfall and Son.

McGinn, T. (1998) *Prostitution, Sexuality, and the Law in Ancient Rome*, Oxford: Oxford University Press.

Mead, L. (1986) *Beyond Entitlement: The Social Obligations of Citizenship*, New York: The Free Press.

Medianorway (2013) *Facts and Figures on Norwegian Media;* <http://medienorge.uib.no/english/> accessed January 2014.

MGLSD (2013) *Direct Income Support*. Kampala: Ministry of Gender, Labour and Social Development: Expanding Social Protection Programme (ESP) Uganda; <http://www.socialprotection.go.ug/What%20is%20SAGE%20all%20about.php> accessed January 2014.

Michielse, H. (1990) 'Policing the Poor: J. L. Vives and the Sixteenth-Century Origins of Modern Social Administration'. *Social Service Review* 64(1): 1–21.

Middleton, S., Ashworth, K., and Walker, R. (eds) (1994) *Family Fortunes: Pressures on Parents and Children in the 1990s*, London: CPAG.

Mills, R. (2005) 'Taking Stock of the Developmental Literature on Shame'. *Developmental Review* 25(1): 26–63.

MLHUD (2013) *Uganda National Urban Policy*, Kampala: CME Consult Group Ltd for Ministry of Lands, Housing and Urban Development.

Moffitt, R. (1983) 'An Economic Model of Welfare Stigma'. *The American Economic Review* 73(5): 1023–35.

Morley, N. (2006) 'The Poor in the City of Rome', in Atkins, M. and Osborne, R. (eds) *Poverty in the Roman World*, Cambridge: Cambridge University Press.

Muggah, R. (2012) *Researching the Urban Dilemma: Urbanization, Poverty and Violence*, Ottawa: International Development Research Centre.

Murray, C. (1984) *Losing Ground: American Social Policy 1950–1980*, New York: Basic Books.

Murray, C. (2009) 'Stigma Makes Generosity Feasible'. *AEI ideas*, 30 November; <http://www.aei-ideas.org/2009/11/stigma-makes-generosity-feasible/> accessed January 2014.

Narayan, D., Chambers, R., Shah, M., and Petesch, P. (2000a) *Voices of the Poor: Crying Out for Change*, New York: Published for the World Bank, Oxford University Press.

Narayan, D. with Patel, R., Schafft, K., Rademacehr, A., and Koch-Schulte, S. (2000b) *Voices of the Poor: Can Anyone Hear Us?*, New York: Published for the World Bank, Oxford University Press.

Neubeck, K. and Casenave, N. (2001) *Welfare Racism: Playing the Race Card Against America's poor*, New York: Routledge.

Neubourg, de C., Castonguay, J., and Roelen K. (2007) *Social Safety Nets and Targeted Social Assistance: Lessons from the European Experience*, Washington, DC: World Bank, Social Protection Discussion Paper 0718.

Nolan, B. and Whelan, C. (1996) *Resources, Deprivation and Poverty*, Oxford: Clarendon Press.

Nolan, B. and Whelan, C. (2010) 'Using Non-Monetary Deprivation Indicators to Analyze Poverty and Social Exclusion: Lessons from Europe?'. *Journal of Policy Analysis and Management* 29(2): 305–25.

Nolan, B. and Whelan, C. (2011) *Poverty and Deprivation in Europe*, Oxford: Oxford University Press.

Notes (2003) 'Shame, Stigma, and Crime: Evaluating the Efficacy of Shaming Sanctions in Criminal Law'. *Harvard Law Review* 116(7): 2186–207.

Nussbaum, M. (2000) *Women and Human Development: The Capabilities Approach*, Cambridge: Cambridge University Press.

Oberholzer-Gee, F. (2008) 'Nonemployment Stigma as Rational Herding: A Field Experiment'. *Journal of Economic Behavior and Organization* (65)1: 30–40.

OECD (1994) *The Jobs Study*, Paris: OECD.

OECD (2013) *Crisis Squeezes Income and Puts Pressure on Inequality and Poverty*, Paris: OECD.

OED (2013) *Oxford English Dictionary: The Definitive Record of the English Language*, Oxford: Oxford University Press, Oxford Dictionaries Online.

Ogilive, D. (1987) 'The Undesired Self: A Neglected Variable in Personality Research'. *Journal of Personality and Social Psychology* 52: 379–88.

OHCHR (2004) *Human Rights and Poverty Reduction: a Conceptual framework*, New York and Geneva: Office of the United Nations High Commissioner for Human Rights.

Oorschot, van W. (1991) 'Non Take-Up of Social Security Benefits in Europe'. *Journal of European Social Policy* 1(1): 15–30.

Oorschot, van W. (1998) 'Failing Selectivity: On the Extent and Causes of Non-Take-Up of Social Security Benefits', in Andress, H. (ed.) *Empirical Poverty Research in a Comparative Perspective*, Aldershot: Ashgate.

Oorschot, van W. (2000) 'Who Should Get What, and Why? On Deservingness Criteria and the Conditionality of Solidarity Among the Public'. *Policy and Politics* 28(1): 33–48.

Oorschot, van W. (2006) 'Making the Difference in Social Europe: Deservingness Perceptions Among Citizens of European Welfare States'. *Journal of European Social Policy* 16(1): 23–42.

Oorschot, van W., Opielka, M., and Pfau-Effinger, B. (eds)(2008) *Culture and Welfare State: Values of Social Policy from a Comparative Perspective*, London: Edward Elgar.

OPHI (2013) *Oxford Poverty and Human Development Initiative*, Oxford; <http://www.ophi.org.uk/> accessed January 2014.

Orshansky, M. (1988) 'Counting the Poor: Another Look at the Poverty Profile'. *Social Security Bulletin* 51(10): 25–51.

Osborne, R. (2006) 'Roman Poverty in Context', in Atkins, M. and Osborne, R. (eds) *Poverty in the Roman World*, Cambridge: Cambridge University Press.

Page, R. (1984) *Stigma: Concepts in Social Policy 2*, London: Routledge.

Panic, M. (2005) *Reconstruction, Development and Sustainable Peace: A Unified Programme for Post-Conflict Countries*. New York: United Nations, Committee for Development Policy, Background Paper No. 8, ST/ESA/2005/CDP/8.

Pantazis, C., Gordon, D., and Levitas, R. (eds) (2006) *Poverty and Social Exclusion in Britain: The Millennium Survey*, Bristol: The Policy Press.

Park, J., Chase, E., and Walker, R. (2013a) *Soaps, Poverty and Attitudes in Kenya*, Oxford: Oxford Institute of Social Policy, Mimeo.

Park, J., Walker, R., and Chase, E. (2013b) *Exploring the Impact Makutano Junction on Poverty-Related Shame*, Oxford: Oxford Institute of Social Policy, Mimeo

Park, A. and Wang, D. (2010) 'Migration and Urban Poverty and Inequality in China'. *China Economic Journal* 3(1): 49–67.

Parkin, A. (2006) '"You do Him no Service": An Exploration of Pagan Almsgiving', in Atkins, M. and Osborne, R. (eds) *Poverty in the Roman World*, Cambridge: Cambridge University Press.

Parvez-Video (2013) *Zakat: First Universal Welfare System*, available online, 9 September; <http://www.parvez-video.com/islam/economy/page1/> accessed January 2014.

Pawson, R. (2002) 'Evidence and Policy and Naming and Shaming'. *Policy Studies* 23(3): 211–30.

Payne, S. (2006) 'Mental Health, Poverty and Social Exclusion', in Pantazis, C., Gordon D., and Levitas R. (eds) *Poverty and Social Exclusion in Britain: The Millennium Survey*, Bristol: The Policy Press.

Pellissery, S. (2007) 'Local Processes of National Corruption: Elite Linkages and Their Effects on Poor People in India'. *Global Crime* 8(2): 131–51.

Pellissery, S. (2009) *The Politics of Social Protection in Rural India*, Saarbrücken: VDM Verlag.

Pellissery, S., Lødemel, I., and Gubrium, E. (2013) 'Shame and Shaming in Policy Processes', in Gubrium, E., Pellissery, S., and Lødemel, I. (eds) *The Shame of It: Global Perspectives on Anti-Poverty Policies*, Bristol: Policy Press.

Pellissery, S. and Mathew L. (2013) 'Thick Poverty, Thicker Society and Thin State: Policy Spaces for Human Dignity in India', in Gubrium, E., Pellissery, S., and Lødemel, I. (eds) *The Shame of It: Global Perspectives on Anti-Poverty Policies*, Bristol: Policy Press.

Pellissery, S. and Mathew, L. (2014a) 'Film and Literature as Social Commentary in India', in Chase, E. and Bantebya-Kyomuhendo, G. (eds) *Poverty and Shame: Global Experiences*, Oxford: Oxford University Press.

Pellissery, S. and Mathew, L. (2014b) 'Experiences of Shame in Contexts of Dense and Deep Poverty in India', in Chase, E. and Bantebya-Kyomuhendo, G. (eds) *Poverty and Shame: Global Experiences*, Oxford: Oxford University Press.

Pellissery, S. and Mathew, L. (2014c) 'Shame or Humiliation: Divergent Roads in India's Hierarchical Society', in Chase, E. and Bantebya-Kyomuhendo, G. (eds) *Poverty and Shame: Global Experiences*, Oxford: Oxford University Press.

Piachaud, D. (1981) 'Peter Townsend and the Holy Grail', *New Society* 10 September: 419–21.

Pinker, R. (1971) *Social Theory and Social Policy*, London: Heinemann Educational.

Piven, F. and Cloward, R. (1993) *Regulating the Poor*, New York: Vintage Books.

Praag, van. B. and Ferrer-i-Carbonell, A. (2008) 'A Multi-Dimensional Approach to Subjective Poverty', in Kakwani, N. and Silber, J. (eds) *Quantitative Approaches to Multidimensional Poverty Measurement*, Basingstoke: Palgave-Macmillan.

Pradban, M. and Ravallion, M. (2011) *Measuring Poverty Using Subjective Poverty Lines*, Washington, DC: World Bank, Policy Research Working Paper.

Preston, P. (2011) 'Leveson and Public Interest? 20m Tabloid Readers Can't Be Wrong'. *Observer*, 4 December.

PSE (2013) *Methods Development*, Bristol: PSE Poverty and Social Exclusion; <http://www.poverty.ac.uk/pse-research/pse-uk/methods-development> accessed January 2014.

Rao, V. (2009) *Policy Making in India for Rural Development*, paper presented during the Fourth Annual International Conference on Public Policy and Management at the Indian Institute of Management, Bangalore.

Ravallion, M. (2012) *Poor, or Just Feeling Poor? On Using Subjective Data in Measuring Poverty*. Washington, DC: World Bank, Policy Research Working Paper 5968.

Ravallion, M., Chen, S., and Sangraula, P. (2009) 'Dollar a Day Revisited'. *World Bank Economic Review* 23(2): 163–84.

Rea, J. (ed.) (1972) *The Oxyrhynchus Papyri XL*, London: The British Academy.

Richardson, A. and Naidoo, J. (1978) *The Take-up of Supplementary Benefits*, London: unpublished paper prepared for the Department of Health and Social Security.

Ridge, T. (2002) *Childhood Poverty and Social Exclusion: From a Child's Perspective*, Bristol: The Policy Press.

Ringen, S. (1988) 'Direct and Indirect Measures of Poverty'. *Journal of Social Policy* 17(3): 351–65.

Ringen, S. (2009) *Poverty: The Rowntree Project Revisited*, Cambridge, MA: Kennedy School of Government, Malcolm Wiener Inequality and Social Policy Seminar Series, 10 April.

Ringgren, H. (2003) *Theological Dictionary of the Old Testament: 'zz-panîm, Volume 11*, Grand Rapids, MI: Eerdman.

Robeyns, I. (2005) 'The Capability Approach: A Theoretical Survey'. *Journal of Human Development* 6(1): 93–114.

Robinson, N. (1999) *Islam: A Concise Introduction*, Richmond: Curzon Press.

Robles, G. (2013) *Targeting Efficiency and Take-Up of Oportunidades, a Conditional Cash Transfer, in Urban Mexico in 2008*, Oxford: DPhil Thesis, University of Oxford.

Room, G. (ed.) (1995) *Beyond the Threshold: The Measurement and Analysis of social exclusion*, Bristol: The Policy Press.

Ross, L. (1977) 'The Intuitive Psychologist and His Shortcomings: Distortions in the Attribution Process', in Berkowitz, L. (ed.) *Advances in Experimental Social Psychology*, Volume 10, New York: Academic Press.

Roth, N. (2003) *Medieval Jewish Civilization: An Encyclopedia*, New York: Routledge.

Rowntree, B. (1901) *Poverty: A Study of Town Life*, London: Macmillan.

Rowntree, B. (1941) *Poverty and Progress: A Second Social Survey of York*, London: Longmans.

Rowntree, B. and Lavers, G. (1951) *Poverty and the Welfare State: A Third Social Survey of York Dealing Only with Economic Questions*, London: Longmans.

Scheff, T. (1995) 'Conflict in Family Systems: The Role of Shame', in Tangney, J. and Fischer, K. (eds) *Self-Conscious Emotions: The Psychology of Shame, Guilt, Embarrassment and Pride*, New York: Guilford Press.

Scheff, T. (1997) *Emotions, the Social Bond and Human Reality*, New York: Cambridge University Press.

Scheff, T. (2000) 'Shame and the Social Bond'. *Sociological Theory* 18: 84–98.

Scheff, T. (2001) 'Social Components in Depression'. *Psychiatry* 64(3): 212–24.

Scheff, T. (2002) 'Working Class Emotions and Relationships: Secondary Analysis of Sennett, Cobb, and Willis', in Phillips, B., McKinnon, H., and Scheff, T. (eds) *Toward a Sociological Imagination: Bridging Specialized Fields*, Lanham, MD: University Press of America.

Scheff, T. (2003) 'Shame in Self and Society'. *Symbolic Interaction* 26(2): 239–62.

Scheff, T. and Retzinger, S. (1991) *Emotions and Violence: Shame and Rage in Destructive Conflicts*, Lexington, MA: Lexington Books.

Scheff, T. and Retzinger, S. (2000) 'Shame as the Master Emotion of Everyday Life'. *Journal of Mundane Behavior*, 1(3).

Schoenleber, M. and Berenbaum, H. (2010) 'Shame Aversion and Shame-Proneness in Cluster C Personality Disorders'. *Journal of Abnormal Psychology* 119(1): 197–205.

Schwartz, S. and Bilsky, W. (1987) 'Toward a Universal Structure of Human Values'. *Journal of Personality and Social Psychology* 53: 550–62.

Schwarz, J. (1997) *Illusions of Opportunity: The American Dream in Question*, New York: W. W. Norton and Company.

Seiler, M., Seiler, V., Lane, M., and Harrison, D. (2012) 'Fear, Shame, and Guilt: Economic and Behavioral Motivations for Strategic Default'. *Real Estate Economics* 40(s1): S199–S233.

Sen, A. (1983) 'Poor, Relatively Speaking'. *Oxford Economic Papers* 35: 153–69.

Sen, A. (1999) *Commodities and Capabilities*, Delhi: Oxford University Press.

Sen, A. (2001) *Development as Freedom*, Oxford: Oxford University Press.

Sen, A. (2005) 'Human Rights and Capabilities'. *Journal of Human Development* 6(2): 151–66.

Sennett, R. and Cobb, J. (1972) *The Hidden Injuries of Class*, Cambridge: Cambridge University Press.

Sepúlveda Carmona, M. (2011) *Report of the Special Rapporteur on Extreme Poverty and Human Rights*, New York: United Nations General Assembly, Sixty-Sixth Session, Item 69 (b) of the Provisional Agenda, Promotion and Protection of Human Rights: Human Rights Questions, Including Alternative Approaches for Improving the Effective Enjoyment of Human Rights and Fundamental Freedoms.

Sepúlveda Carmona, M. (2012a) *Final Draft of the Guiding Principles on Extreme Poverty and Human Rights*, submitted by the Special Rapporteur on extreme poverty and human rights, New York: United Nations General Assembly, Human Rights Council, Twenty-First Session, Agenda Item 3.

Sepúlveda Carmona, M. (2012b) *Promotion Of and Respect For Rights and Dignity: A Briefing Note*, Geneva: letter and enclosure sent to the permanent missions to the United Nations Office in Geneva, 12 April.

Shaver, P., Wu, S., and Schwartz, J. (1992) 'Cross-Cultural Similarities and Differences in Emotion and its Representation: A Prototype Approach', in Clark, M. (ed.) *Review of Personality and Social Psychology*, Newbury Park, CA: Sage.

Shepherd, A. (2011) *Tackling Chronic Poverty: The Policy Implications of Research on Chronic Poverty and Poverty Dynamics*, Manchester: Chronic Poverty Research Centre.

Shropshire, J. and Middleton, S. (1999) *Small Expectations: Learning to Be Poor?*, York: York Publishing Services for the Joseph Rowntree Foundation.

Siegrist, J. (2003) *Subjective Wellbeing: New Conceptual and Methodological Developments in Health-Related Social Sciences*, paper presented to ESF SCSS exploratory workshop, Income, Interactions and Subjective Wellbeing, Paris, 25–26 September.

Simmel, G. (1908) 'The Poor' (trans. Jacobson, C.). *Social Problems* 13: 118–39.

Simmel, G. (1950) *The Sociology of Georg Simmel* (trans. and ed. Wolff, K. H.), New York: Free Press.

Simonsen, E. and Ericsson, K. (2005) *Children of World War II: The Hidden Enemy Legacy*, Oxford: Berg Publishers.

Smith, A. (2009) *An Enquiry into the Nature and Causes of the Wealth of Nations* [1776], Lawrence, KS: Digireads.com.

Smith, I. Duncan (2010) *Universal Credit: Welfare That Works*, speech at launch of the White Paper, 11 November.

Smith, I. Duncan (2012) *Leonard Steinberg Memorial Lecture*, Policy Exchange, Westminster, London, 9 May.

Smith, R., Webster, J., Parrott, W., and Eyre, H. (2002) 'The Role of Public Exposure in Moral and Nonmoral Shame and Guilt'. *Journal of Personality and Social Psychology* 83(1): 138–59.

Solinger, D. (2010) 'The Urban *Dibao*: Guarantee for Minimum Livelihood or for Minimal Turmoil?', in Wu, F. and Webster, C. (eds) *Marginalization in Urban China: Comparative Perspectives*, Basingstoke: Palgrave Macmillan.

Solinger, D. and Hu, Y. (2012) 'Welfare, Wealth and Poverty in Urban China: The Dibao and its Differential Disbursement'. *The China Quarterly* 211: 741–64.

Spicker, P. (1984) *Stigma and Social Welfare*, London: Croom Helm.

Stedman Jones, G. (2004) *An End to Poverty?* London: Profile Books.

Stiles, P. (2008) *The Negative Side of Motivation: The Role of Shame*, Cambridge: Judge Business School, Working Paper Series 07/2008.

Stuber, J. and Schlesinger, M. (2006) 'Sources of Stigma for Means-Tested Government Programs'. *Social Science and Medicine* 63: 933–45.

Stuenkel, D. and Wong, V. (2012) 'Stigma', in Lubkin, I. and Larsen, P. (eds) *Chronic Illness*, Burlington, MA: Jones and Bartlett Publishers.

Stuewig, J. and McCloskey, L. (2005) 'The Impact of Maltreatment on Adolescent Shame and Guilt: Psychological Routes to Depression and Delinquency'. *Child Maltreatment* 10(4): 324–36.

Stuewig, J. and Tangney, J. (2007) 'Shame and Guilt in Antisocial and Risky Behaviors', in Tracy, J., Robins, R., and Tangney, J. (eds) *The Self-Conscious Emotions: Theory and research*, New York and London: The Guilford Press.

Surender, R. (2013) 'The Role of Historical Contexts in Shaping Social Policy in the Global South', in Surender, R. and Walker, R. (eds) *Social Policy in a Developing World*, Cheltenham: Edward Elgar.

Sutherland, J. and Felty, K. (2010) *Cinematic Sociology: Social Life in Film*, California: Sage Publications.

Svallfors, S. (ed.) (2012) *Contested Welfare States: Welfare Attitudes in Europe and Beyond*, Stanford: Stanford University Press.

Tangney, J. and Dearing, R. (2003) *Shame and Guilt*, New York: Guilford Press.

Tangney, J., Marschall, D., Rosenberg, K., Barlow, D., and Wagner, P. (1994) *Children's and Adults' Autobiographical Accounts of Shame, Guilt and Pride Experiences: An Analysis of Situational Determinants and Interpersonal Concerns*, Fairfax: George Mason University, unpublished manuscript.

Tangney, J., Stuewig, J., and Mashek, D. (2007a) 'What's Moral About the Self-Conscious Emotions?', in Tracy, J., Robins, R., and Tangney, J. (eds) *The Self-Conscious Emotions*, New York: Guilford Press.

Tangney, J., Stuewig, J., and Mashek, D. (2007b) 'Moral Emotions and Moral Behavior'. *Annual Review of Pscyhology* 58: 345–72.

Taylor, D. (2011) 'Wellbeing and Welfare: A Psychosocial Analysis of Being Well and Doing Well Enough'. *Journal of Social Policy* 40(4): 777–94.

Taylor-Gooby, P. (2013) 'Why Do People Stigmatise the Poor at a Time of Rapidly Increasing Inequality, and What Can Be Done About It?'. *Political Quarterly* 84(1): 31–42.

Teichman, D. (2005) 'Sex, Shame, and the Law: An Economic Perspective on Megan's Laws'. *Harvard Journal on Legislation* 42: 355–415.

Thompson, T., Altmann, R., and Davidson, J. (2004) 'Shame-Proneness and Achievement Behaviour'. *Personality and Individual Differences* 36(3): 613–27.

Titmuss, R. (1971) 'Welfare "Rights", Law and Discretion'. *Political Quarterly* 42(1): 113–32.

Todman, L., Taylor J., Cochrane K., Arbaugh-Korotko, J., et al. (2009) 'Social Exclusion Indicators for the United States'. *Journal of Individual Psychology* 65(4): 330–59.

Tomlinson, M. and Walker, R. (2009) *Coping with Complexity: Child and Adult Poverty*, London: CPAG.

Tomlinson, M. and Walker, R. (2010) *Recurrent Poverty: The Impact of Family and Labour Market Changes*, York: Joseph Rowntree Foundation.

Townsend, P. (1979) *Poverty in the United Kingdom*, Harmondsworth: Penguin.

Tracy, J. and Robins, R. (2004) 'Putting the Self Into Self-Conscious Emotions: A Theoretical Model'. *Psychological Inquiry* 15(1) 103–25.

Tracy, J. and Robins, R. (2007) 'The Self-Conscious Emotions: A Cognitive Appraisal Approach', in Tracy, J., Robins, R., and Tangney, J. (eds) *The Self-Conscious Emotions*, New York: Guilford Press.

Tsai, J. (2006) *Cultural Differences in the Valuation of Shame and Other Complex Emotions*, cited in Wong, Y. and Tsai, J. 'Cultural Models of Shame and Guilt', in Tracy, J., Robins, R., and Tangney, J. (eds) *The Self-Conscious Emotions*, New York: Guilford Press.

Turner, J. and Maryanski, A. (2013) 'The Evolution of the Neurological Basis for Sociality', in Franks, D. (ed.) *Handbook of Neurosociology*, New York: Springer.

Turner, J. and Stets, J. (2005) *The Sociology of Emotion*, Cambridge: Cambridge University Press.

UN (2011) *Report of the Special Rapporteur on Extreme Poverty and Human Rights*, New York: United Nations General Assembly, Sixty-Sixth Session, Item 69 (b) of the Provisional Agenda; A/66/265; <http://www.ohchr.org/Documents/Issues/Poverty/A.66.265.pdf> accessed January 2014.

UN (2012) *Report of the Special Rapporteur on Extreme Poverty and Human Rights*, New York: United Nations General Assembly Sixty-Seventh Session, Item 70 (b) of the Provisional Agenda; A/67/278; <http://daccess-ods.un.org/TMP/467728.637158871.html> accessed January 2014.

UN (2013a) *The Millennium Development Goals Report 2013*, New York: United Nations.

UN (2013b) *Resolution Adopted by the General Assembly, 67/164. Human Rights and Extreme Poverty*, New York: United Nations General Assembly (on the report of the Third Committee (A/67/457/Add.2 and Corr.1)), general distribution 13 March.

UNDP (1997) *Human Development to Eradicate Poverty*, New York: Oxford University Press for the United Nations Development Programme.

UNDP (2013) *Human Development Report 2013: The Rise of the South: Human Progress in a Diverse World*, New York: United Nations Development Programme.

UNHR (2013) *Participation of Persons Living in Poverty*, Geneva: Office of the High Commission for Human Rights; <http://www.ohchr.org/EN/Issues/Poverty/Pages/ParticipationOfPersonsLivingInPoverty.aspx> accessed January 2014.

Veit-Wilson, J. (1986) 'Paradigms of Poverty: A Rehabilitation of J.S. Rowntree'. *Journal of Social Policy* 15(1): 69–99.

Voipio, T. (2010) 'Building Social Floors for Decent Societies'. *Global Social Policy* 10(2): 158–61.

Walker, R. (1978) *Canvassing Rent Allowances in Bristol and Westminster*, London: Housing Development Directorate, Department of the Environment.

Walker, R. (2005) *Social Security and Welfare: Concepts and Comparisons*, Milton Keynes: Open University Press/McGraw-Hill.

Walker, R. (2008) 'European and American Welfare Values: Case-Studies in Cash Benefits Reform', in Oorschot, W. van, Opielka, M., and Pfau-Effinger, B. (eds) *Culture and Welfare State Values of Social Policy from a Comparative Perspective*, London: Edward Elgar.

Walker, R. with Ashworth, K. (1994) *Poverty Dynamics: Issues and Examples*, Aldershot: Avebury.

Walker, R., Bantebya-Kyomuhendo, G., Chase, E., Choudhry, S., et al. (2013) 'Poverty in Global Perspective: Is Shame a Common Denominator?'. *Journal of Social Policy* 42(2): 215–33.

Walker, R. and Chase, E. (2013) 'Separating the Sheep from the Goats: Tackling Poverty in Britain for Over Four Centuries', in Gubrium, E., Pellissery, S., and Lødemel, I. (eds) *The Shame of It: Global Perspectives on Anti-Poverty Policies*, Bristol: Policy Press.

Walker, R., Chase, E., and Lødemel, I. (2012) 'The Indignity of the Welfare Reform Act'. *Poverty* 143: 9–12.

Walker, R. and Kellard, K. (2001) *Staying in Work: Policy Overview*, Sheffield: Department for Education and Employment.

Walker, R., Lawson, R., and Townsend, P. (eds) (1984) *Responses to Poverty: Lessons from Europe*, London: Heinemann.

Wallbott, H. and Scherer, K. (1995) 'Cultural Determinants in Experiencing Shame and Guilt', in Tangney, J. and Fischer, K. (eds) *Self-Conscious Emotions: The Psychology of Shame, Guilt, Embarrassment, and Pride*, New York: Guilford Press.

Wasswa, J. (2005) *The Exploration of the Impact of State Ownership on Uganda's New Vision Newspaper's Social Role*, Grahamstown: Rhodes University.

Waxman, C. (1977) *The Stigma of Poverty: A Critique of Poverty Theories and Policies*, New York: Pergamon Press.

WCED (1987) *Our Common Future*, Oxford: Oxford University Press, World Commission on Environment and Development.

Wells, M. and Jones, R. (2000) 'Childhood Parentification and Shame-Proneness: A Preliminary Study'. *The American Journal of Family Therapy* 28(1): 19–27.

Whelan, C. and Maître, B. (2012) *Understanding Material Deprivation in Europe: A Multilevel Analysis*, Amsterdam: AIAS, GINI Discussion Paper 37.

Wiesfeld, G. (1999) 'Darwinian Analysis of the Emotion of Pride/Shame', in Dennen, J. van der, Smillie, D., and Wilson, D. (eds) *The Darwinian Heritage and Socio-Biology*, Westport: Praeger/Greenwood Press.

Wiki (2013) 'Broken Britain'. *Wikipedia*; <http://en.wikipedia.org/wiki/Broken_Brit ain> accessed January 2014.

Wilkinson, R. and Pickett, K. (2010) *The Spirit Level: Why Equality Is Better for Everyone*, Harmondsworth: Penguin Books.

Williams, B. (1993) *Shame and Necessity*, Berkeley, CA: California University Press.

Willis, P. (1977) *Learning to Labour*, Farnborough: Saxon House.

Wiseman, M. (2003) 'Welfare in the United States', in Walker, R. and Wiseman, M. (eds) *The Welfare We Want? The British Challenge for American Reform*, Bristol: Policy Press.

Woden, Q. (ed.) (2000) *Extreme Poverty and Human Rights: Essays on Joseph Wresinski*, Washington, DC. World Bank; <http://www-wds.worldbank.org/external/

default/WDSContentServer/WDSP/IB/2004/02/25/000265513_20040225165617/
Rendered/PDF/wdr27915.pdf> accessed January 2014.

Wong, Y. and Tsai, J. (2007) 'Cultural Models of Shame and Guilt', in Tracy, J., Robins, R., and Tangney, J. (eds) *The Self-Conscious Emotions*, New York: Guilford Press.

World Bank (2010) *Extreme Poverty Rates Continue to Fall*, Washington DC: World Bank; <http://data.worldbank.org/news/extreme-poverty-rates-continue-to-fall, Accessed 11th September 2013> accessed January 2014.

World Bank (2013) *PovcalNet: An Online Poverty Analysis Tool*, Washington, DC: World Bank; <http://iresearch.worldbank.org/PovcalNet/index.htm?0> accessed January 2014.

World Values Survey (Various) <http://www.worldvaluessurvey.org/> accessed January 2014.

Wresinski, J. (1989) 'Les plus pauvres, révélateurs de l'indivisibilité des droits de l'homme', in *Commission nationale consultative des droits de l'homme, 1989: Les droits de l'homme en questions*, Paris: La Documentation Française, trans. Fingleton, K. and Courtney, C.; <http://www.joseph-wresinski.org/IMG/pdf/THE_VERY_POOR.pdf> accessed January 2014.

Wright, S. (2003) 'The Street Level Implementation of Unemployment Policy', in Millar, J. (ed.) *Understanding Social Security: Issues for Policy and Practice*, Bristol: Policy Press.

Wright, T. (1868) *The Great Unwashed*, New York: Augustus M. Kelly (republished 1970).

Xu, X., Zhu, F., O'Campo, P., Koenig, M., Mock, V., and Campbell, J. (2005) 'Prevalence of and Risk Factors for Intimate Partner Violence in China'. *American Journal of Public Health* 95(1): 78–85.

Xue, J. and Zhong, W. (2006) 'Unemployment, Poverty and Income Disparity in Urban China', in Shi, L. and Sato, H. (eds) *Unemployment, Inequality and Poverty in Urban China*, London and New York: Routledge.

Yahoo (2013) *Do People Choose to be Poor?*; <http://answers.yahoo.com/question/index?qid=20080104190714AAWUTpp> accessed January 2014.

Yan, M. (2013) 'New Urban Poverty and New Welfare Provision: China's Dibao System', in Gubrium, E., Pellissery, S., and Lødemel, I. (eds) *The Shame of It: Global Perspectives on Anti-Poverty Policies*. Bristol: Policy Press.

Yan, M. (2014a) 'Literature as a Window to Conceptions of Poverty and Shame in China', in Chase, E. and Bantebya-Kyomuhendo, G. (eds) *Poverty and Shame: Global Experiences*, Oxford: Oxford University.

Yan, M. (2014b) 'Experiences of Poverty and Shame in a Rising China', in Chase, E. and Bantebya-Kyomuhendo, G. (eds) *Poverty and Shame: Global Experiences*, Oxford: Oxford University Press.

Yan, M. (2014c) 'Views of the Non-Poor on Those in Poverty in Urban China', in Chase, E. and Bantebya-Kyomuhendo, G. (eds) *Poverty and Shame: Global Experiences*. Oxford: Oxford University Press.

Yavetz, Z. (1969) *Plebs and Precepts*, New Brunswick: Transaction.

Yeo, E. (2004) 'Family Support Obligation Rules and Those Excluded From the National Basic Livelihood Security Law'. *Health and Social Welfare Review*. 24(1): 3–29.

Zetterholm, S. (1994) 'Introduction: Cultural Diversity and Common Policies', in Zetterholm S. (ed.) *National Cultures and European Integration: Exploratory Essays on Cultural Diversity and Common Policies*, Oxford: Berg.

Zhou, S. (2012) *Selectivity, Welfare Stigma, and the Take-Up of Social Welfare: How do Chinese People Manage Welfare Stigma?*, Cambridge: Harvard-Yenching Institute Working Paper Series.

Zhu, J. and Lin, M. (2010) 'Social Construction of Welfare Stigma: A Case Study of the Urban MSLS Families in Zhejiang Province'. *Zhejiang Journal* 3: 201–6.

Zysow, A. (2009) 'Zakāt', in Bearman, P., Bianquis, T., Bosworth C., van Donzel, E., and Heinrichs. W. (eds) *Encyclopædia of Islam*, Leiden: E. J. Brill. Available at Brill Online, 31 December 2012; <http://www.brillonline.nl/subscriber/entry?entry= islam_COM-1377> accessed January 2014.

Index

Entries in bold indicate references to tables or figures.

Abbott, P. 89–90
Abel-Smith, B. 17
Abercrombie, N. 69
adult respondents 112, 113–14
African Americans 57
agency 2, 31, 65, 66, 67, 89, 116, 127, 188, 193
Ali, M.:
  Brick Lane 80
Alicke, M. 58
alienation 20, 36t3.1, 46, 108
Alkire, S. 20, 22, 29
altruism 5–6, 130
American Dream 63
Ancient Rome 8, 13–14, 49
Anderson, B. 191
anger 35, 40, 42, 47–8, 52, 66, 70, 126, 127,
    128, 130, 131
  shame 63–4, 88–9, 106
Anglo Saxon countries 135
antipoverty programmes 4, 58, 60, 115, 117,
    145–6, 147, 155, 173, 179, 191
  Uganda 175
anxiety 11, 33, 40, 47, 70, 112, 120, 130, 184
Arranz, J.–196
arts 70, 74
Asian Financial crises 26
ATD Fourth World 23, 64, 128
ATD Quart Monde 24
Atkinson, A. 17, 18, 30
Augustus, first Roman Emperor 8–9
avoidance 87, 126

Bagozzi, R. 42
Bailey, N. 186
Band Aid 4
Banks, J. 17
Bantebya-Kyomuhendo, G. 55, 56, 60, 61, 68,
    70, 71, 87, 100, 121, 123, 132, 138, 150,
    164, 166, 184, 188, 193
Barbalet, J. 37
Barrientos, A. 134
Baumberg, B. 54, 56, 57–8, 59, 167, 178
Bedford, O. 38
beggars/ing 9, 93, 94, 104, 113, 123,
    129–30, 172
behaviour 45, 87, 138, 152, 157, 159–60,
    190, 191

antisocial 97
avoidance 126, 126
  criminal 66
  individual 189
  shame 62, 88, 89, 90–1, 134, 154, 190
Bell, D. 30
Ben-Yehuda, N.
Benedict, R. 42
benefits 12, 37, 39, 54, 58, 141, 168
  badge of poverty 55
  and charity 54–5
  with giving of gifts 54
  negativity to 57
  receipts 58, 59, 60, 63, **173**
Bennett, F. 31
Berenbaum, H. 193
Beresford, P. 118
Bergman, M. 159
Berthoud, R. 19
Beth, S. 91
Biewen, M. 45
Bilsky, W. 159
Bismarck, Chancellor 12
Blair, T. 178, 189
blame, and 'othering' 129
Blume, L. 46
Booth, C. 15, 16, 18
borrowing 82, 104, 123
Bos, A. van den 58
Boulding, K. 43
Bradshaw, J. 19
Breugelmans, S. 42
Brewer, M. 50, 150
Briant, E. 167
bribery 81
Britain 5, 15, 17, 57, 61, 63, 68, 74, 98,
    103, 104, 123, **136**, 136, 148, 150,
    167, 191
  and benefits 55, 101
  capitalism 87
  and children 109, 110, 128
  films 77, 81, 86, 88, 91–2
  housing 150
  institutional stigma 58
  and jobs 112, 113, 123–4
  and literature 73, 76, 80, 91–2
  and Poor Law 11, 12

Britain (*cont.*)
respondents 99, 101, 106, 108, 109–10, 114,
116–17, 122–3, 124, 125, 129, 137–8,
140–1
shame 186*f11.1*, 186–7
social realism 87
television comedy drama 89–90
welfare policies 12
Brooks, C. 158
Brundtland Commission on Sustainability
and the Environment (WCED) 19
Buddhism 34, 71–2, 92, 93
Bulwer-Lytton, E. 95
Burke, E. 158
Burke, J. 45
Busch, M. 12

Calandrino, M. 19, 20
Cantó, O. 196
capitalism 63
Casenave, N. 57
caste 80–1, 93, 106
see also India, caste
Castell, S. 118
Cathy Come Home (Britain) 78
Cattell, V. 20
causality 134
causation 73
Central Asia 26
Chambers, R. 19
charitable giving 9
charity 44, 54–5, 113
Chase, E. 12, 43, 55, 56, 58, 59, 60, 70, 86, 101,
121, 122, 129, 131, 137, 150, 167, 178,
184, 188, 191, 193
*Shame of Poverty: Global Experiences,
The* (Chase and Bantebya-
Kyomuhendo) 2, 31, 49, 52–3, 68
Chen, Y. 107, 125, 174
children 79, 83, 99, 103, 109, 190
malnourished 73
obligation to feed 77
and parents 109
and poverty 98
starving 89
violence 79
Chile 29, 187
China 5–6, 13, 26, 37, 38, 55, 56, 59–60, 63,
68, 72–3, 76, 79, 83, 100, 106–7,
118–19, 137, 169
Dibao 55, 57, 59, 61
economic growth 174
literature 71, 74, 77, 79, 85–6, 87, 94, 96
migrants 57
and respondents 112–13, 116, 128, 133,
138–9, 140, 142

urban 98
and wisdom 6
see also Confucius
Chinese Communist Party 91, 169, 191
Chong, D. 159
Choudhry, S. 61, 68, 70, 89, 122, 138, 151, 174
Christ 9
Christian texts 9
Christianity 13–14, 34, 104
chronic poverty 28, **28**, 29
church charity 11, 12
citizenship 60, 189
Clark, D. 102
Clasen, J. 118
class exploitation 91
Cloward, R. 174
Cobb, J. 41
Cohen, T. 193
collectivist cultures *see* cultures
Collier, P. 26
Collins, M. 17
communication 159, 163, 178–9
communism 71–2, 94
concealment 40, 72, 77, 82, 83, 87, 90, 124
conditional cash transfers 60, 152–3
Condorcet 5
Confucius 5–6, 43, 71–2, 74, 91, 135, 189, 190
family 107, 116
philosophy 13
principles 6–7, 173–4
traditions 13, 71
Congregational Union:
*Bitter Cry of Outcast London: An Inquiry
Into the Condition of the Abject Poor,
The* 16
Conservative Party 168
Corbo, C. 9
Corden, A. 55
Coser, L. 69
Coudouel, A. 31, 69
Crystal, D. 193
cultures 1, 35, 40, 42, 47, 48, 67, 69, 70, 72, 74,
83, 98, 118, 135, 188
collectivist 37, 38, 42, 47, 79, 83, 86, 109, 110
different 90, 96, 99, 185
individualist 38, 79
institutional 150–1
modern 83
national 82–3, 183
poverty across 72

D'Angelo, P.159
Dalit 80, 81, 91, 92
Daoism 71–2, 74, 91, 92
Davis, A. 19
Dawnay, E. 44

Dearing, R. 38, 40, 50, 120
debts 104, 109–10
decision making 43–4, 64
Dejgaard, T. 56, 57
DellaVigna, S. 158
denigration 23, 165–6
depression 41, 52, 63–4, 66, 87, 97, 131, 186
deprivation 4–5, 18–19, 20–1, 83, 111–12,
    186–7
Devins, S. 24
Dharwadker, V. 91
Diamond, P. 57
Dibao 17, 55, 57, 59–60, 61, 115, 150, 151,
    169, 170, 174, 180
Dickerson, S. 33, 40
dignity 194–5
discrimination 52, 64–5, 114, 151, 184, 188,
    191, 195
  language 142–3
dole queue 81, 88, 92
Donald, A. 23
Dorling, D. 21
Dornan, P. 193
Douglas-Fairhurst, R. 16
Dovidio, J. 50
Drèze, J. 171
Druckman, J. 159
drug abuse 40, 57, 108, 115, 122, 126, 129,
    137, 168
Du Bois, W. E. B. 15
Duoji, C. 152, 174

East Asia 28, 29–30
Ebrey, P. 6
economic growth 17, 18, 26, 30, 59, 72, 87, 94,
    107, 135, 138, 142, 146, 155, 168, 173,
    174, 189–90
Edin, K. 21, 118
education 60–1, 112, 153, 154, 193
  Uganda 111
educational attainment 22, 29
Eisenberger, R. 45
Elias, N. 42
Elison, J. 33, 34
embarrassment 34, 42, 47, 186, 193
emotions 35–6, 37, 43–4, 72, 82, 121
  self-conscious 38, 42, 47
  social 44
  within workplace 45
empathy 40
Emperor Han Wu-ti 6
employment 81, 114, 177
  low 168
  status 124
English 6, 37
Erfu, Z. 74, 91, 94

Ericsson, K. 49–50
Ethiopia 193
Europe 20, 26, 56, 57
  migrants 57
European Anti-Poverty Network 23, 128
European Union 1, 4
exclusion 20–1, 187
external shame 108, 154
extreme poverty 25, 196, 197

family 110, 122, 173–4
  and men 119
fear 35
Felty, K. 69
Fernández-Villaverde, J. 42, 44
Ferragina, E. 20, 43
Ferrer-i-Carbonell, A. 21
Fessler, D. 34–5
Field, F. 59
films 70, 74, 76, 83, 94–5, 97, 98, 121, 128
financial crisis 178
Finley, M. 10
Finn, R. 9
Fiske, S. 51
Fontaine, J. R. 42
food 102, 185
  requirements 17
  shortage 8
Foster, J. 28
framing 159
Fredman, S. 195
French Social Catholicism 20
Frenkel-Brunswick, E. 54–5
frumentatio 8–9
  and citizens 9
Fukuyama, F. 30
The Full Monty 77, 81, 92, 123
Fung, H. 38
Furukawa, E. 40, 42, 120

G8 summit (2005) 4
Gallagher, C. 70
Gallie, D. 20
Garnsey, P. 9
Garroway, C. 18, 26
Gaskell, E.:
    Mary Barton 88
Gaulejac, de V. 42
gender 110
Germany 12, 20, 59
  and Hitler 41
Gibbs, L. 32
Gilbert, P. 33
Gilens, M. 57
Glennerster, H. 16
Global North 4

global poverty 26
God 9, 11, 13–14, 73–4, 74, 93
Godinot, X. 24
Goetz, J. 3
Goffman, E. 36, 50, 64
Golding, P. 167
Goldthorpe, J. 43
Goode, E. 46
Gordon, D. 19
Gouride liangshi [Damned Grains]
    (Heng) 76, 82, 89
Greek city state 8
Greenblatt, S. 70
Greenwood, W. 76, 81
Grig, J. 10
Griggs, J. 178
Guan, X. 169–70
Gubrium, E. 55, 57, 61, 68, 77, 101, 122, 133,
    137, 147, 164, 172, 177
guilt 33–4, 35–6, **36**, 38, 39–40, 42, 47–8
Guyson, N. 190

Hagen, K. 190
Halvorsen, K. 177
happiness 32, 34, 93, 104–5, 112, 124
    Indian films 93
Hardy, T. 79
Harel, A. 46
Harrington, M. 17
Hart, D. 34
Harter, S. 33, 34
health 60–1
    status 21, 22
healthcare 154
    universal 60
Heidenreich, M. 189
Heller, Á. 46
Heng, L. 76, 82, 89, 91
Hernanz, V. 55, 62
Hickey, S. 175
Hiebert, P. 3
Higgins, J. 184
Himmelfarb, G. 12, 58
Hinduism 7, 93
Ho, D. 185
Hoban, M. 192
Hoggett, P. 58
Holley, L. 51–2
Hooper, C.-A. 21
household income 193
    relative **162**
'Houses of Correction' 58–9
housing:
    inadequate 185
    mortgage repayments 45
    poor 21

Hu, Y. 174
Huh, S. 152, 174
Hulme, D. 21
human capital 193
Human Development Index (HDI) 19, 99,
    99, 195
human rights 23, 25, 31, 153, 185, 192, 194,
    196, 197
humanitarian issues 13
humiliation 34
hunger 165
Hunger (Hansum) 77
Hunter, R. 15

identity 57
ideology 30, 63, 65, 167
    political 160
immigration 168
Imperial Examination System 6
income inequalities 28
income poverty 20
incomes 1, 10–11, 17, 112, 122
    and deprivation 20
    lack of 85
    low 18, 26, 102, 104, 163, 171–2
    middle 26
    minimum level of security 192
    relative to median 28
India 6–7, 13, 60, 64, 68, 77, 83, 94, 98, 99,
    106, 112, 137–8, 148
    accommodation 102–3
    benefit receipt 116
    caste structure 7, 57, 71, 91, 112, 143
    children 122
    corruption 116
    elites 171
    family life 79–80, 109
    films 69, 70, 71, 76, 79
        Mother India 80, 91
    literature 74, 79
    migrants 57
    nationalist writings 73–4
    respondents 100, 110, 127, 133
    social assistance 152–3
    women 78, 126
individualist cultures 38–9, 47
inequality 43, 51, 171, 174
institutional stigma 54, 55, 58
    public debate on 57–8
internal shame 106, 117, 132,
    184, 185
International Bill of Human Rights 23
International Labour Organization (ILO) 19,
    24, 61
Internet 61
Islam 10–1, 13–14, 104, 113

Japan 42
Jenkins, S. 22
Jews 49–50
Jo, Y.-N. 43, 61, 68, 72, 87, 101, 107, 125, 153, 174
jobs 81, 107–8
  failed applications 115–16
  multiple 91
  queue 112
'Jobs Study' 59
Johnson, P. 17
Jones, R. 193
Jones, S. 5
Judeo-Christian Tradition 10, 13–14
Jung, I.-Y. 154
Jury, A. 41

Kakwani, N. 22
Kale, Kishore Shantabai 76–7, 78
Kaplan, E. 158
karma 8, 13, 93
keeping up appearances 123–4, 147
Kellard, K. 64
Keltner, D. 3
Kenya 135–6, 164, 187
  poverty and shame **187**
Killeen, D. 184, 191, 192
Kingdom, J. 158
Klement, A. 46
Knoepfel, P. 30, 158, 159
Korea 98–9
Korea (Seoul) 98
Kothari, R. 91
Kusenbach, M. 56
Kwa-Zulu Natal 29
Kyomuhendo, G. 175

labour 9
  shortage of 191
Labour government 58, 59, 167, 178
labour market 112
Labour Party 59
Laeken indicators 18
Laiglesia, de J. 18, 26
Lal, D. 26
language 23, 37, 50, 58, 59, 61, 80, 157, 165, 168, 177, 179
  abusive 142–3
  body 70
  negative 155
  of shaming 142
  skills 113
  of stigma 65, 69, 137, 157
Larsen, C. 56, 57
Latin America 28
Lavers, G. 16

Lawrence, B. 90
Lay, S. 86
laziness 134, **134**, 134–5, 138, 139, 140–1, 142, 143, 160, 161, 162, 163, 166, 171, 187
Lee, N. 159
Lee, W. 152
Lee-Gong, E. 153, 155–6
lending 82
Lewis, D. 69
Lewis, O. 64, 95
Li, J. 37, 152, 170
Lin, M. 150, 153
Lind, J. 56
Link, B. 50–1, 52
Lipsky, M. 61
Lister, R. 20, 23, 24, 53–4, 129, 131
literature 74, 76, 83, 94–5, 97, 121, 128
livelihoods 19
Loach, K. 86–7
Lødemel, I. 57, 61, 68, 77, 101, 122, 137, 164, 172, 177, 190
Lodge, G. 57
Los Rios, de C. 187
Los Rios, de J. 187
Loseke, D. 56
Love on the Dole (Greenwood) 76, 81
low-status jobs 37
Luke 6:20 14
Lynd, H. 35–6

McCloskey, L. 40
McGinn, T. 49
Ma, J. 153
Maître, B. 20
Make Poverty History Campaign 4
management systems 45
Manchester, C. 54
Mandarin 70–1
Mander, H. 171
Manza, J. 158
Maoism 74
Maryanski, A. 35
Massaro, T. 46
material deprivation 20
Matsuba, M. 34
Mathew, L. 68, 69, 70, 91, 100, 122, 126, 138, 150, 165, 170–1
Matthew 26:11 56
Mattinson, D. 59
Maxwell, S. 19
Mayhew, H.:
  London Labour and the London Poor (Mayhew) 15–16
Mead, L. 95

Mecius 6
media 141, 156, 158, 159, 160, 165, 168–9,
    170–1, 172, 174, 178–9
  and stereotypes 188
Megan's Law 45–6
men 119
Mencius 71
meritocracy 6
Mexico:
  Oportunidades 61
Michielse, H. 11
Middleton, S. 21, 109,
Mihany, K. 45
military campaign 8
Millennium Development Goals 1, 4, 24,
    26, 175, 182
  $1 a day measure 17, 26
Mills, R. 33
minimum wages 153
modernity 11
Moffitt, R. 54
monasteries, in Britain 11
moral blindness 171
moral reciprocity 5–6
Morley, N. 9
Mottershaw, E. 23
Muggah, R. 128
multidimensional poverty 18, 21–3, 29, **29**, 30
Multidimentional Poverty Index (MPI) 22
Munford, K. 54
Murray, C. 62, 63, 189
Mwiine, A. 61, 68, 71, 87, 100, 123, 138, 150,
    164, 166, 175

Naidoo, J. 55
Narayan, D. 21, 60, 118
  Voices of the Poor 61, 118
National Health Service (NHS) 12, 178
Neff, D. 134
Neubourg, de C. 12
Neubeck, K. 57
'New Historicism' 70
newspapers 163–5, 166, 167, 168–9, 172–3
  China 164, 169–70, 180
  in English language 165, 171, 172
  India 165
  national 167
  Uganda 164, 166
Nolan, B. 19
non-poor 64, 155
Norway 56, 61, 68, 72, 74, 76, 77, 79, 81, 83,
    89, 98–9, 101, 137, 150, 180
  authors 88
  child respondents 103, 111–12, 115
  and jobs 112
  literature 91

newspapers 163–4
  respondents 108, 109, 112, 114, 122, 123,
    124, 125, 127, 128, 129, 138, 141, 148
  social assistance 177
  structural factors 172
  welfare state 91, 164
Nussbaum, M. 102

'Obamacare' 60
Oberholzer-Gee, F. 45
obesity 122
OECD 28, 59, 152, 178
officialdom 114, 132–3, 147, 149, 154,
    157, 187
Ogilive, D. 3
Oorschot, van W. 55, 56, 57, 62, 69
oral traditions 121
Orshansky, M. 17
Osborne, R. 8, 9, 10
othering 131, 141, 162
Oxford Poverty and Human Development
    Initiative (OPHI) 187

Pacific 26, 29–30
Page, R. 54, 55
Paine, T. 5
Pakistan 60, 61, 68, 73, 83, 98–9, 113–14, 125,
    138, 142, 172, 174
  abusive language 143
  accommodation 103
  caste 112
  children 99, 114, 122, 128
  literature 77
  and religion 151
  respondents 106, 109, 116, 133, 138
  schools 112
  women 110, 127
panel data 22
Panic, M. 128
Pantazis, C. 17, 19, 20–1
parents 110
Park, A. 169
Park, J. 136
Parkin, A. 9
Parvez-Video 11
'paupers' 12
Pawson, R. 39
Payne, S. 21
Pellissery, S. 57, 60, 68, 69, 70, 91, 100, 122,
    138, 150, 151, 165, 170–1
pensions 17, 128, 139, 178
people, and cause of proverty 165
personal failure 74, 94, 111, 114, 118, 149, 187
Personal Responsibility and Work
        Opportunities Reconciliation Act
        (PRWORA) 63

personal stigma 54
Peru 182, 183, 184
Phelan, J. 50–1, 52
Philippines 42
Piachaud, D. 18
Pickett, K. 43
Pinker, R. 54
Piven, F. 174
policy **180**, 194
  agendas 158
politics 2–3, 17–18, 159, 178–9
  and human rights 23
polygamy 110
Poor Law ('Pauper Law') 11, 12, 16, 174,
  177–8, 189
Poor Law Guardians 58
Poor People's Economic Human Rights
  Campaign
Poortinga, Y. 42
Portela, M. 193
poverty 1, 3–4, **28**
  absolute measures of 1, 17, **27**, 30
  definitions 18–19, 30, 178
  deprivation 4–5
  extreme 196
  as policy problem 13
  political 8, 49
  relative 30
  scientific construction of 30
  and shame 75, **75**
  studies 15
  subjective 21
Poverty Eradication Action Plan
  (PEAP) 175
poverty-related shame 154, 184, 187, 189,
  190, 192
poverty-shame nexus 65, **66**, 82, 85, 92, 95,
  96, 98, 193
Praag, van B. 21
Pradban, M. 30
prayers 8
Preston, P. 163
pride 34, 36, 44
primary poverty 16–17
print media 163
prostitution 78
proverbs 74, 93, 97
Proverbs 19:17 14
psychology 32–3
  pain 40
  and shame 184
  symptoms 33, 34
public assistance *see* social assistance
public opinion:
  China 175
punishment 46

Qing, L. 79, 89, 91, 92, 94
  Chuangyeshi [The Violent Storm] 92–3, 94
Qualification Programme (QP) 177

Ravallion, M. 17, 18, 21, 30, 31
Rea, J. 9
Recommendation 202 192
religions 13
respondents 98, **98**, 99, 108, 115, 121, 122,
  124–5
  basic necessities 102
  lives 105
  withdrawal 124–5
retreat 87
Retzinger, S. 41, 50, 88
Richardson, A. 55
Ridge, T. 109
Ringen, S. 4, 5, 10, 18, 20
Roberts, M. 31
Robeyns, I. 20
Robins, R. 32, 33
Robinson, N. 11
Robles, G. 55, 61, 150
Roma 57, 137, 141, 172
Roman legal code 9
Room, G. 20
Ross, L. 45
Roth, N. 49–50
Rowntree, S. 15, 16, 17
Ruganda, J. 80, 81
rural areas 138–9

sadness 35, 87
Saladin tithe 10
sales staff 42
sanctions 45, 46
  and family 110
Sandel, C. 76
  Collected Short Stories 89
Santos, M. 28
Scheff, T. 32, 35–6, 37, 40–1, **41**, 42, 43, 47,
  50, 85, 88, 120, 127, 131, 191
Scherer, K. 42
Schlesinger, M. 54
Schoenleber, M. 193
schools 79, 84, 97, 101, 111, 112, 150
Schwartz, J. 118, 159
secularism 13
Sedikides, C. 58
Seiler, V. 45
self-esteem 38, 81, 185–6
  low 40, 66, 120
Sen, A. 2, 19–20, 25, 65, 75, **76**, 96, 102, 105,
  120, 165, 171, 183, 185, 187
Seneca 65
Sennett, R. 41

Sepúlveda Carmona, M. 188, 192, 194, 196
sex 42
  offenders 45, 61, 84
  premarital 44–5
  prostitution 77
Shah, H. 44
shame 32, 35, 36*t.3.1*, 38
  bypassed 40–1
  definitions 2
  origins 32
  as plot in writing 32–3
  and sociology 35
  and solidarity 41
Sharia law 61
Shaver, P. 37
Shepherd, A. 22
Shropshire, J. 109
Siegrist, J. 120
Silber, N. 22
silent shaming 86
Simmel, G. 54, 55
Simonsen, E. 49–50
Smith, A. 1–2, 65
Smith, I. 189
social assistance 12, 17, 60, 82, 98–9, 101,
     153, 190–1
  and European model 62
  means-tested 60, 115
  South Korea 101, 116, 128–30
  Uganda 175
social capital 66
social cohesion 12, 37, 52
social exclusion 1, 2, 21, 64, 66, 147
social harmony 37
social isolation 130–1
social media 57–8
social mobility 8–9
  normal norms 67, 74, 86, 90
social realism 97–8
social stigma 55–6, 58, 67
societies, without poverty 5
Solinger, D. 151, 174
Source Book for Poverty Reduction Strategies
  (World Bank) 31
South Africa 102
South Asia 28, 29, 79–80
South East Asia 13
South Korea 2, 37, 42, 55, 61, 68, 69, 71, 72–3,
     74, 125, 128–9, 128, 150–1, 155
  capitalism 87
  Confucius 71
  films 69, 74, 86, 87, 88, 96
  respondents 107, 114, 116
Soviet Union 26
Spicker, P. 54
standards of living 19, 22, 30, 183, 185

Stanlis, P. 158
Steffes, S. 45
Stets, J. 35, 37, 42
stigma 49–50, 52, 53, 54, 62
  and benefits 64–5
  and mental illness 50
  and relationships 51
  and shame 179
  term 51–2
Stiles, P. 45
Stjernø, S. 177
Stuber, J. 54
Stuenkel, D. 50, 51
Stuewig, J. 40, 88, 127
Sub-Saharan Africa 26, 28, 137
subjective poverty 18
subsistence farmers 100
suicide 71, 77, 82, 87, 97, 120, 126, 186
sullenness 87
Supplementary Benefit, means-tested 55
Surender, R. 59
Sutherland, J. 69
Svallfors, S. 57

Tangney, J. 33, 38, 39–40, 50, 88, 120, 127
  Home and Guilt 50
'Tao' 6
taxpayer 64
Taylor, D. 120
Taylor-Gooby, P. 57
Teichman, D. 39, 45, 46
Thessalonians II, 3:10 14
thinking 159, 163, 178–9
Thompson, J. 118
Thompson, T. 193
tithes 10
Titmuss, R. 150
Todman, L. 20
Tomlinson, M. 22, 196
Townsend, P. 2, 17, 18–19, 120
Tracy, J. 32, 33
Tressell, R.:
  Ragged Trousered Philanthropists, The 73
Tsai, J. 33, 37, 38, 71
Tudor Poor Law 11–12
  Britain 11–12
Turner, J. 35, 37, 52

Uganda 61, 68, 71, 73–4, 79, 83, 87, 93–4,
     98, 100, 104, 110–11, 125, 129–30,
     138, 143
  accommodation 103
  Black Mamba (Ruganda) 80
  Burdens, The (Ruganda) 81
  children 99, 109, 149–50
  and drinking 126

and parents 110, 123
plays 80
respondents 106, 108, 114, 116, 123, 124, 125, 130
schools 115, 150
subsistence farmers 105
women 111
UK 17, 20, 22, 192
films 69
UK West Midlands 37
UN High Commission on Human Rights (OHCHR) 23, 25
UN World Development Reports 17
unemployment 45, 56, 81, 91, 169–70
benefits 152
humiliation 61–2
United Nations (UN) 23, 24, 29, 188, 194, 196, 197
General Assembly 195
subsistence measure 30
United Nations' Decade for the Eradication of Poverty 24
United Nations Developmment Programme (UNCDP) 19, 22
United States (US) 15, 17, 37, 42, 56, 57, 63
and healthcare 60
poverty standard 17
and welfare benefits 55, 57
Universal Declaration of Human Rights 23, 195
Urdu 70, 71, 73, 75–6, 77, 89, 90
poet 76

Vedic Culture 6–7, 13
Veit-Wilson, J. 17
Versailles Treaty 41
Viard, T. 24
violence 24, 41, 97, 127
domestic 88
Voipio, T. 8, 24

Wallbott, H. 42
Walker, R. 12, 21, 22, 43, 54, 55, 56, 58, 59, 61, 62, 68, 75, 86, 101, 107, 122, 129, 131, 137, 150, 153, 167, 174, 178, 191, 192, 196
Wang, D. 169
Washington consensus 59
Wasswa, J. 164
Waxman, C. 64, 188
welfare 173–4
institutions 81
policies 12
provision 60, 62, 115, 165, 167, 168, 178
reforms 59
spending 59
welfare benefits 53–4, 59, 150, 167
means-tested 54

receipts 56
recipients 81
take-up of 55
well-being 20, 21, 32, 44, 101
Wells, M. 193
Whelan, C. 19, 20
Wiesfeld, G. 34
Wilkinson, R. 43
Williams, B. 45
Willis, P. 37
willpower, lack of 134, 135, **135**, 136, 162, **162**
Wiseman, M. 63
Woden, Q. 25
women 83, 89, 103, 119, 143
Chinese 81
and children 78
forced into prostitution 78
Wong, V. 50, 51
Wong, Y. 33, 37, 38, 71
work 161, 190–1
ethic 174–5, 177, 189
laziness **161**
and money **162**
and society **161**
workplace 112, 114
World 38, 42, 47
World Bank 1, 25, 26, 31, 59, 118
World Values Survey 132–3, 134, 135, 139, 142–3
Wresinski, Father J. 24, 25, 196
Wright, S. 61
Wright, T. 95

Xu, X. 88
Xue, J. 174
Xun, Lu 93

Yahoo 52
YAN., M. 57, 68, 70–1, 75, 85, 100, 127, 137, 165, 169
Yang, S. 152
Yavetz, Z. 9
Yeo, E. 116
York 16

Zakat 10–11, 56, 61, 113, 139, 143, 146, 150, 151, 152
Zetterholm, S. 69
Zhao, S. 153
Zhenyun, Liu 85–6
Yidi jimao [Scattered Feathers] 85–6
Zhong, W. 174
Zhou, S. 55, 151, 152
Zhu, J. 150, 153
Zysow, A. 11

Printed and bound by CPI Group (UK) Ltd, Croydon, CR0 4YY